M000081395

THE JOYS OF PSYCHOPATH-OCRACY

FDA

OIPC
ICPO
INTERPOL
INTERPOL

Alpha Omega Labs'
Cansema®
BLACK TOPICAL SALVE
"CLINICAL USE" SIZE
Use as directed • 102 g.

Alpha Omega Labs

ECUADOR
Quito
Tulcán
Latacunga
Tena
Ambato
Puyo
Riobamba
Babahoyo
Guayaquil
Macas
Azogues
Cuenca
Machala

THE JOYS OF PSYCHOPATH-OCRACY

Why Criminality Is Essential To Effective Modern Government

Our Rebirth In The Wake Of Their Destruction Of Our World

GREG CATON

Herbologics
8345 NW 66th St., #7093
Miami, FL 33166
(305) 851-2305
Email: joys@gregcaton.com

Copyright © 2017 by Greg Caton
All rights reserved. No part of this book may be reproduced or transmitted in any form or by any means, electronic or mechanical, including photocopying, recording, or any information storage and retrieval system, without the written permission of the author, except where permitted by law.

Editor: Michel Blanchard
Editor / Proofreader: Richard Sauder
Proofreader: Julia Chaney
Cover Concept and Design / Illustrations: David Dees (ddees.com)
Interior Design and Layout: Andrea Vera Tandazo

Printed in the U.S.A. by CreateSpace, an Amazon.com company

Library of Congress Cataloging-in-Publication Data

Greg Caton, 1956 –
The Joys of Psychopathocracy: Why Criminal Conspiracies Are Essential to Effective Modern / Our Rebirth in The Wake of Their Destruction of Our World.

1. Political Science 2. Anthroposophy 3. Metaphysics 4. New Earth 5. Ascension

Library of Congress Catalog Card Number: 2017912442
ISBN: 978-0-939955-01-5

Published by: Herbologics -- Miami, FL

Table of Contents

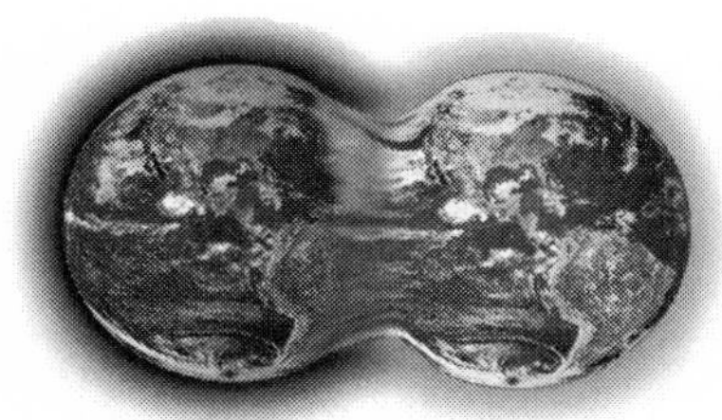

Function Conforms to Original Design

This is a spoon.

There are many things you can do with a spoon.

You can use it to dig small holes.

You can bang it against other spoons or objects to create what you think is music.

You can use it to help fill the radiator of your car with water when you can't find a water hose, a pitcher, a carton, a funnel, or a small glass.

You can use it to annoy your cat.

There are a thousand uses you can find for a spoon.

Yet there is only one function for which it is best suited and for which people use it more than 99% of the time:

To eat food or take medicine.

In other words, you use it to ingest things through your mouth, particularly small quantities of liquid or soft food.

The reason that this is a spoon's best function is because that is the purpose for which it was created. Any other function is artificial and not in keeping with the spoon's original design – or its essential nature.

This is Government.

There are many things you can do with Government.

You can use it to rally people to a cause.

You can use it to tell people how much you care about social justice, civil rights, law and order, the environment, world peace, racism, or democracy.

There are a thousand uses you can find for Government.

Yet there is only one function for which it is best suited and for which its designers use it 99% of the time:

To mask, nurture, cultivate and actuate criminal conspiracies.

In other words, it is used to create the appearance of goodness when, in fact, it acts as a cover for the most evil and hideous human activities imaginable.

The reason that this is a Government's best function is because that is the purpose for which it was created. Any other function is artificial and not in keeping with Government's original design – or its essential nature.

The book you are about to read deals with the true nature of things – not contrived appearances. It provides an easy-to-understand model that transcends in simplicity, power, and irrefutability anything else you have ever seen, or been taught, to explain how your world really works.

It is the most honest and timely book you may ever read.

It ends with a view to escaping the planetary destruction that runaway Government must inevitably bring, a process that is now well underway. We close with something that is as positive and uplifting as the negativity that is giving it birth.

I hope you find it as enlightening and life-changing to read as I did writing it.

The image of the Government building (Capitol Building, Washington, D.C.), was adapted from Nicolas Raymond Photography. This work is licensed under a Creative Commons Attribution 3.0 Unported License.

List of Charts & Illustrations

Acknowledgements

Isaac Newton is credited with the famous statement, "If I have seen further, it is by standing on the shoulders of giants." Likewise, I would never have come to the conclusions that comprise the present work had I not been exposed to the work of many hundreds of other authors, philosophers, and commentators, spread out over a 45 year period of intense personal study. My ideas come from the distillation of information from countless sources, too numerous to list. First and foremost, I am most thankful for a life partner – my wife, Cathryn – without whose support and understanding I could never endured this most arduous sojourn.

I want to thank my editors, Michel Blanchard and Richard Sauder; the esteemed political illustrator, David Dees; and my designer, Andrea Vera Tandazo – all of whom were indispensible in the production of this work.

Introduction

This book was written for those who feel that there is something very wrong, even ominous, with the world around them, and can't explain the plenitude of its absurdities, even to themselves. At the other end of the spectrum, it is written for those who are quite attuned to what is going on around them, but lack a satisfying model that would tie it all together in a comprehensive way and allow them to explain these same absurdities to others. I close this book addressing those at ***either*** end of the spectrum, because no problem of the magnitude that consumes the majority of the present work can be satisfactorily presented without providing an adequate solution.

The primary focus here is the true nature of Government in our modern world . . . but only because in a mansion with a hundred doors, you can only choose to enter through one of them. Once inside, other doors can be viewed from the interior, and then their place, purpose, and connection to the whole are understood. Specifically, though the focus of this work is on Government, once entrance is gained, we too may look around at our civilization in its totality and understand its interior in a way never understood before.

Some may find this approach curious. Governments, like corporations, are not living organisms. They do nothing without the labor of people who are seduced to serve them. And yet, it is these very artificial constructs – I found quite by accident – that allow us to capture a panoramic view of ourselves, our relationship with our neighbors, other life forms and the Earth herself. It is these very constructs which provide the holographic images, the evidence concerning the dark forces that shape our lives . . . the very things about which we should be most rigorously posing vital questions, if we only knew what to ask.

I admit, the manner in which I approach my subject is unusual and oblique. The majority of nonfiction works which address Government corruption attempt to highlight one or more specific areas of concern, abuse or aberration. What follows are self-styled, sometimes novel, sometimes ingenious, but usually, as yet, untested reforms.

The approach of the present work dispenses with this format entirely, for reasons that become readily apparent.

Although Governments, like any other measurable entity, vary in quality . . . vary in the degree to which they will redirect their obsession with monied interests long enough to show a momentary, albeit artificially induced and ultimately self-serving concern for the true needs of their people, on the whole, **modern Government isn't reformable**.

It has evolved in our age into a monster of unequalled, destructive tendency. What is worse is that the larger, more "effective" Governments with the most influence, operate with an air – like carbon monoxide poisoning – saturating their surroundings, killing in their wake whatever doesn't serve their short-term purposes, without alerting the senses before it's too late. Those good and honest souls who now struggle within the over two hundred nation states, trying to make positive changes in the world, consistently find themselves outnumbered by unseen forces that make it nearly impossible to make meaningful course alterations. By this we mean any positive change – in its relationship with its governed, its own internal ecosystems, its neighbors, or the planet we all share.

Additionally, attempting reform is highly dangerous work.

And yet those of you who find all this self-evident are the same ones who will sit in front of your TV and listen to the most preposterous, mind-numbing nonsense from the latest news feed, pretending that what you're seeing is real, honest, or relevant – and not highly scripted programming from an overpaid corp of "presstitutes" (journalists whose style and content reflect an allegiance to monied interests), for the hopelessly gullible and truly uninformed.

Why do you do that? You should know better.

Why do any of us do that? We should all know better.

My feeling is that no one has yet provided an intellectual framework that has the power to dispense with the cognitive dissonance and allow us all to make sense of the world. There have been attempts, but they all have logical flaws.

Until now.

I realize that this is a tall claim, and you have a right to feel it's audacious. But frankly, you should know I would never have written this book if I didn't feel I had stumbled upon a way of explaining it all. I would like to use the term "worldview," but then that makes it sound like these are my opinions, when, in fact, there are few people who read my prepublication manuscript who didn't come back to me and say something like, "This makes so much sense. Why didn't I think of this?"

It's intellectually, emotionally, and spiritually transformative.

Before getting started, I have just a few comments to make about the book's structure and the best way to read it.

Many books can be read liberally and you can skip around, if you wish, without losing the author's essential points. This is not one of those books. Concepts are built sequentially, particularly in the early chapters, so if you begin in the middle, you will, as it were, be lost in the end. Additionally, the copious footnotes are an integral part of this work and will greatly enhance your experience.

Follow the book from beginning to end and you will have the experience I intend to impart. If I fail to give you a truly life-changing experience – one that is uncommon in the world of book reading, it will only be because in your case I failed to present the material adequately, or you simply gave up. There is an element of courage that is required to face up to how truly screwed up our world really is and how distant the prospects appear that we can right what is ostensibly so incorrigible. But there really is hope, and I pray you'll stick with me to the end here to find that out.

In an earlier, unfinished online work, **Meditopia®**, I explained, in quite some detail, the "Alice in Wonderland" circumstances that led to my own epiphany.[1] The present treatise, on the other hand, is not intended to be autobiographical, and yet, if I leave out certain salient points, I will have removed much of

[1] See: www.meditopia.org/chap1.htm

the connective tissue that bridges together its expansive musculature. Therefore, the reading itself is interlaced with personal experiences and conclusions, but only to the extent necessary to fortify the underlying material.

What you are about to read is not a philosophical or spiritual exposé, though its detractors – and this book has the potential to create quite a number of them – will attempt to so characterize it. My foundational premises are not based on personal perspective, though it took very personal events to arrive at the book's conclusions. I have little respect for mere opinion in these matters, even my own. Neither is my work an attempt to create yet another "theory of everything." I quickly realized that the gravity of the concepts themselves was betrayed with a "tongue-in-cheek" presentation. Moreover, you will find nowhere in the pages that follow any attempt to label the concepts and premises as mere theories. The world is awash in ill-conceived theories . . . concerning, well, just about everything.

This much I can say confidently: no one writes a book like this without creating enormous grief for themselves. If anything like what you are about to read had been published by someone else, I would have simply preferred to redirect people to that work.

Additionally, I would like to point out that much initial criticism was directed at the fact that an inordinate number of examples I use in the book concern the U.S. Government. I found this puzzling. I'm an American author, a former holder of a high security clearance in the U.S. intelligence community, and I've lived in the U.S. for the vast majority of my life.

You should expect that I have a better perspective on U.S. Government corruption than any other. If this book were written by a Russian author, I would expect the Russian authorities to figure prominently. Nonetheless, examples would be plentiful no matter where I came from originally.

Lastly, I would encourage you to contact and network with other readers, not only to reinforce what you learn, but to assist in helping with the recommendations that are made in the second half of the book. You can find more information in this regard at: **gregcaton.com**.

I'd like to make a few comments about this book's structure:

The book is divided into two sections: "Book I: The Great Winding," and "Book II: The Great Unwinding." The Great Winding broadly refers to a society's descent into increasingly greater tendencies towards ecological self-destruction, organizations of institutionalized exploitation, "negative reciprocity," which I explain in Chapter One, and what most people would describe as "evil." The Great Unwinding is the process of undoing this descent and returning to a general state of happiness, wholeness, and fulfillment for the vast majority of people.

The stark difference becomes more apparent as we proceed.

Book I:

The Great Winding

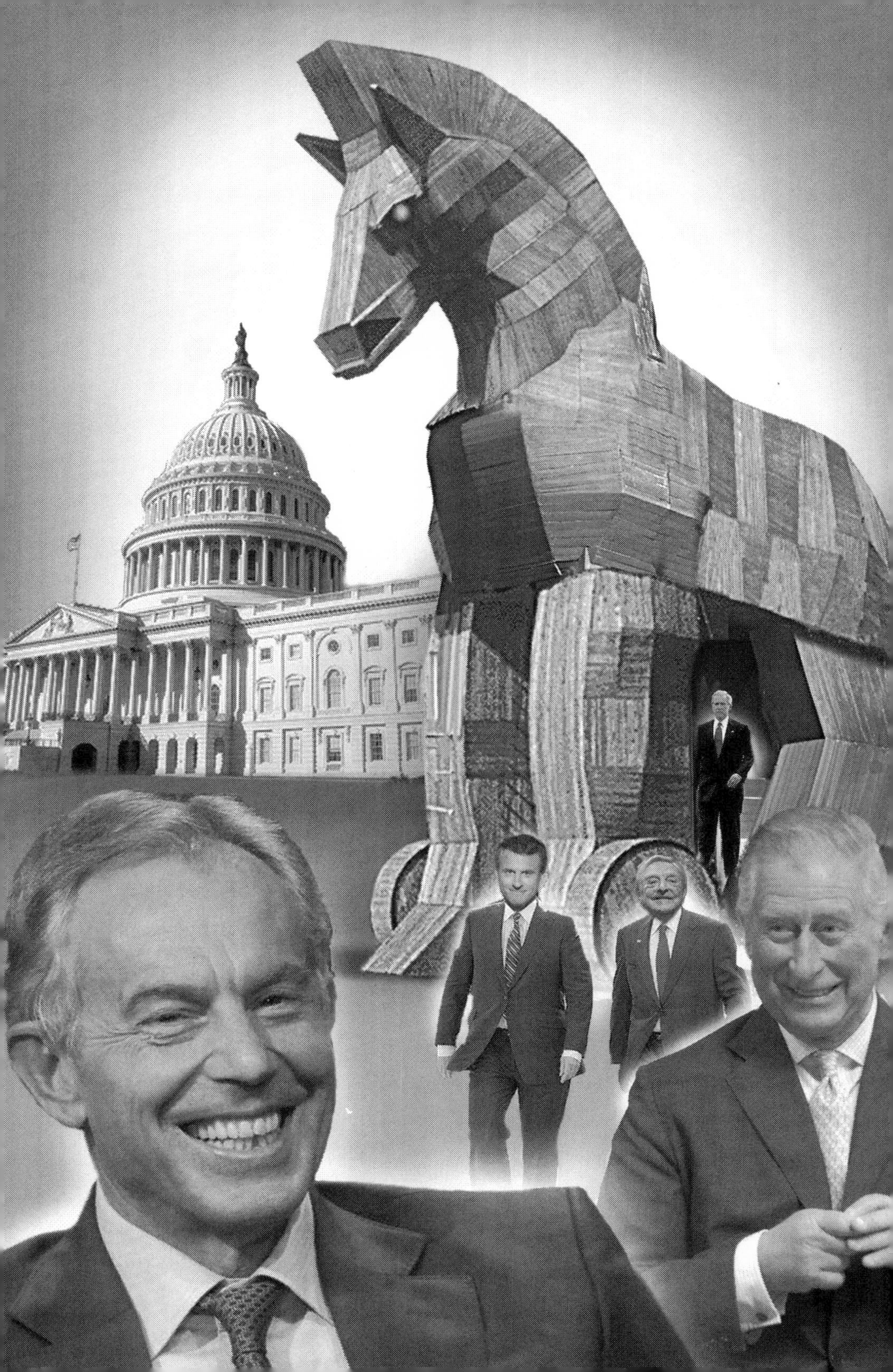

Chapter 1:

Government's Evil Genes: An Obviousness We Can No Longer Ignore

At first, the suggestion that criminal conspiracies lie at the very heart of effective modern state governance – that without them, Government's very existence sits in jeopardy – may appear delusional. To most uninitiated observers, the notion comes across as the meandering thought of a stand-up comic at best, or of the seriously deranged at worst.

I myself might have never entertained the proposition had I not been dragged through the U.S. criminal justice system, during which I was exposed to a near laughably large number of gross violations to U.S. and international law on the part of those purportedly paid to enforce it.[1] My coerced plea agreement was obtained by threatening family members and employees and accompanied a mind-numbing array of crimes by those connected to the prosecutor's office: grand larceny, perjury, insurance fraud, intellectual property theft, kidnapping, bribery, etc. Indeed, there was no crime that the U.S. officials I encountered weren't willing to commit, no act too immoral or unethical, no escapade too brazen, as long as it promoted their agenda as it pertained to my case. The end always justified the means, giving one the impression that if it had taken kidnapping to obtain back payment on, say, a $50 parking ticket, such actions would have been fully justified. That I am able to cite so many other examples throughout this book – all drawn from the last year I was incarcerated in the U.S. – only accentuates this point as being the custom and not the exception.

Given my origins, it may thus appear paradoxical that I come from a national culture which regards its own political in-

[1] The first four chapters of **Meditopia®** -- **www.meditopia.org** – are devoted to these issues, particularly Chapter 3.

stitutions as "Government at its best." And yet there has always been opposition to this narrative. Indeed, the dissent has been well articulated from the very founding of the American Republic to the present.

Monroe, Madison, Franklin, Hamilton, and others would describe the ways that their new American Government could be tyrannical.[2] Early U.S. Senator John Taylor of Caroline offered an alternative vision to avoid being tyrannical.[3] Tocqueville graced us with the observation that the seeds of tyranny had already been planted in the grand American political experiment.[4] More recently, the writings of Howard Zinn, John Blum, William Appleman Williams, Derrick Jensen, John Zerzan, and others would tell us that – surprise! – American Government has been skillfully and stealthily tyrannical all along.[5]

But the current volume isn't merely about tyrannical acts or intentions, or even the inclinations of Government. Nor does it confine itself to its uniquely American expressions. My thesis is directed not solely at what Government can be, or could be, or should be . . . though these are inescapable areas that must be touched upon. My central point contends with the unspoken nature of Government's evil genes – its very constitution in our current age.

Whereas Jefferson would tell you that "Government is a ***necessary*** evil," I would remove the euphemistic framework from this portrait of modern Government and dare to speak more plainly:

Government is *necessarily* evil – and, as it relates to im-

[2] See: Alexander Hamilton, James Madison and John Jay, The Federalist Papers, written in 1788, among other early American publications, which devote considerable space to this topic.

[3] See: John Taylor of Caroline, Tyranny Unmasked,(1821).

[4] See: Alexis de Tocqueville, Democracy in America, (1835).

[5] See: Howard Zinn, Paul Buhle and Mike Konopacki, A People's History of American Empire, (2008). Also see: William Appleman Williams, The Contours of American History, (1988). The author's disdain for American Empire and its tyrannical tendencies is spread throughout his work, though an excellent sampling of its early origins can be found in the section called "The Constitution as a Feudal and Mercantilist Instrument of Government." p. 157-162 of the book. Also see: Derrick Jensen, The Culture of Make-Believe, (2004). Derrick Jensen is best known for his work on the ecologically destructive nature of Western civilization, though he delivers a thought-provoking critique of tyranny as a dominant theme in American history and culture. See also: John Zerzan, Running on Emptiness: The Pathology of Civilization, (2008).

proving the lives of ordinary people, is ***neither necessary nor reformable***.

And when a Government fails to manifest its evil genes, it risks falling prey to one that does. Criminal conspiracies and a general environment of deep-seated corruption are not anomalous in the course of modern Government. They comprise the rule, the "sine qua non" . . . the coin of the realm. Not content to demonstrate the simple principle that "might is right," modern governance has devolved to a point where supremacy, if not modest success, is predicated on being "more evil than Thou." This runs quite contrary to not only the propagandistic formula scripts that guide Hollywood political thrillers, but also to the "benign common narrative" (or what I will hereinafter call BCN for short) of cultures throughout Western civilization. This is elaborated throughout the book.

The BCN is the generally held, loveably skewed, belief system which a people accept as given – about themselves, their collective principles, their culture, their country – their Government. To be clear, my use of "benign" common narrative is different than the sociological term "common narrative" in the sense that what we have all been lead to believe is deliberately sculpted to hide maliciousness.

Curiously, my views on this subject were reinforced by observing, in my own country, the increasingly absurd lengths that U.S. Government supporters would go in order to hide its more outrageous atrocities with the ubiquitous "conspiracy theory" tag.

My investigations and efforts would lead to a nightmare of repeated litigation and my personal imprisonment in the U.S. federal system.

Allow me to explain . . .

An Indisputable Cure For Cancer
(discovered/published in 1858)

In the pantheon of unsubstantiated "conspiracy theories," there are few candidates for the capstone of this pyramid of possible contenders more worthy than that of the "suppressed cancer cure."

The "common narrative" as it pertains to cancer is clear, intractable, and for the better part of the past 150 years, unchanged. The Government-sanctioned treatments for cancer are all invasive, dangerous, and toxic, including radiation, chemotherapy, and radical surgery, and more likely to be your cause of death than the cancer condition for which you accepted that treatment in the first place. Conversely, alternative approaches are tagged by orthodox medicine and the Government authorities who support them as "cancer quackery" – irrespective of the evidence that many such approaches are safer, cheaper, and more efficacious. Moreover, none of the official "remedies" – if I may be so profane as to so reference them – can rightly be called "cures."

They are not cures.

They are "treatments."

A "cancer cure" would jeopardize the multi-billion dollar cancer research industry, not to mention destroy the revenue streams that come from treating the cancer patient over and over and over again "'till death do they part," which we will address later.

Consequently, I was most unenthused initially when, in 1989, I was presented an opportunity to explore a "cancer cure" . . . not a treatment, mind you, a cancer cure, from an associate in Louisiana.

The initial embodiment was a salve that works on skin cancers, regardless of type, better than 99% of the time, while internal versions have been shown to be effective in over 50% of all cases. I have produced videos on YouTube showing people how to make the salve in their kitchen, if only to deflate orthodox medical supporters who would have you believe that I'm just a "cancer quack" or a huckster, only promoting this cancer remedy to make a dollar. (Keep in mind that the conventional, medical industrial cancer complex, far from being philanthropic, is an intensely profit-driven, multibillion dollar industry.)

My proofs are presented online,[6] and my wife's laboratory still operates in South America,[7] where other associates of mine carry on the work.

The basic formula was presented to the world as an effective cancer remedy in 1858 by what was then one of the most orthodox medical establishments in the West: Middlesex Hospital, in London.

As I detail in Meditopia, it was not long after its revelation that medical authorities suppressed the discovery. This action was predictable, given how effective the remedy is, how cheap and simple it is to make, and how deleterious the economic effect would be to the medical field if the common man knew about it, then and now. If you've been dumbed down by your culture's "common narrative", you will find this and most of the revelations in this book . . . well . . . counterintuitive.

For those who believe that the suppression of any cancer cure is overstated, I can personally attest that it is not. From 2003 to 2011, my own personal involvement in alternative cancer research caused not only my personal imprisonment, but one of the strangest stories in the history of the U.S. criminal justice system.[8]

What follows is part of my story.

[6] Again, see www.meditopia.org

[7] An archive of our work resides at www.altcancer.net; the lab itself sells products to the U.S. and Canada at **www.herbhealers.com**; while products sold outside the U.S. and Canada are sold through a separate web outlet, **www.alphaomegalabs.com**. That any web merchant should have to create such a convoluted arrangement – all at the insistence of his FDA attorney – is itself a testament to the absurdity of U.S. Government regulations.

[8] It is beyond the scope of this book to recount all the details about my case, but I do so exhaustively in Chapter 3 of Meditopia. Again, a free read at: www.meditopia.org.

U.S. Criminal Justice: Unspeakable Corruption Where Nothing Is Too Outrageous

In September, 2007, I became aware of a conspiracy involving the U.S. Prosecutor's Office in Lafayette, Louisiana.

At issue was a former employee of mine who embezzled over $20,000 from one of my companies during my first false imprisonment (2003-2006).[9] To cover up her crimes, she went to authorities and falsely claimed that I was violating the terms of my probation (i.e., supervised release).

She even went so far as to brag about her cooperation with U.S. authorities in a sworn deposition taken on October 10, 2007. The reasoning she gave under oath for having fabricated events which never took place was that she felt slighted for having been fired from one of my formerly held businesses, Lumen Foods. Amazingly, she felt it was my fault she had been dismissed by the new owner of the business I had sold. (The real reason is that she became intolerably insubordinate almost immediately after I sold the business.)

My response? Having been granted permission to travel to Ecuador during my probation, I simply decided not to return to the U.S., nor continue my probation reporting requirements. I already knew that "facts" had no place in a U.S. court of law if they conflicted with the objectives of the Prosecutor's Office.

In addition, I met with two of Ecuador's highest ranking officials, Gustavo Larrea, then Ecuador's Minister of Government, together with the Governor of the Province of Guayas (where I was living) to explain my circumstances. Both of them assured me that although there wasn't a legal framework in place to give me political asylum, which I was actively seeking, I should stop worrying because I would not be arbitrarily abducted without the benefit of an extradition hearing. As long as I prevailed in

[9] See Chapter 3, Section 3 of **Meditopia®** (www.meditopia.org/chap3-1.htm).

my extradiction hearing – which they concluded from the facts presented that I would – I had nothing to worry about. They both turned out to be dead wrong, as you'll discover momentarily.

On November 19, 2008, U.S. agents, together with officials from the Ecuadorean Ministry of Immigration and National Police, raided the home of an associate at the time, the late Mr. Neville Solomon. Thinking that Mr. Solomon was actually me, they abducted Neville and his 15 year old son, Michael, and took them to the Ministry of Immigration building in Guayaquil. After more than ninety minutes of interrogation, realizing that Neville ***wasn't*** me and had no useful information he was willing to provide about my whereabouts, they let Neville and his son go.

Neville proceeded to call me on his cell phone as soon as he was free. At the time of the call I was driving through the Andes mountains, hoping to return to my home in Guayaquil before sunset. Neville not only told me about his abduction, but also about an arrest warrant he viewed during the ordeal with my name on it, signed by about a half dozen different U.S. officials, including then Secretary of State Condoleezza Rice. For the next few days, friends hid me at various locations while we attempted to get a better sense of what was happening. I changed residences frequently and switched between different cell phones almost daily, since I had reason to believe that the U.S. was monitoring my phone traffic.

Those were scary days. In one instance, a good friend, (who was being monitored and physically followed), and her fourteen year old daughter viewed Ecuadorean police storming their apartment building at Puerto Azul, on the outskirts of Guayaquil, wearing black shirts with the letters "FBI" emblazoned in big white letters. Great. Now I had to contend with corrupt Ecuadorean police who were, under the guidance of the U.S. State Department and without the knowledge or permission of their own Government, acting as U.S. FBI agents. It was surreal.

My next step was a very secretive drive to Quito, during which I hid in the back of a van for the entire trip.

I spent two days at the Venezuelan Embassy in Quito re-

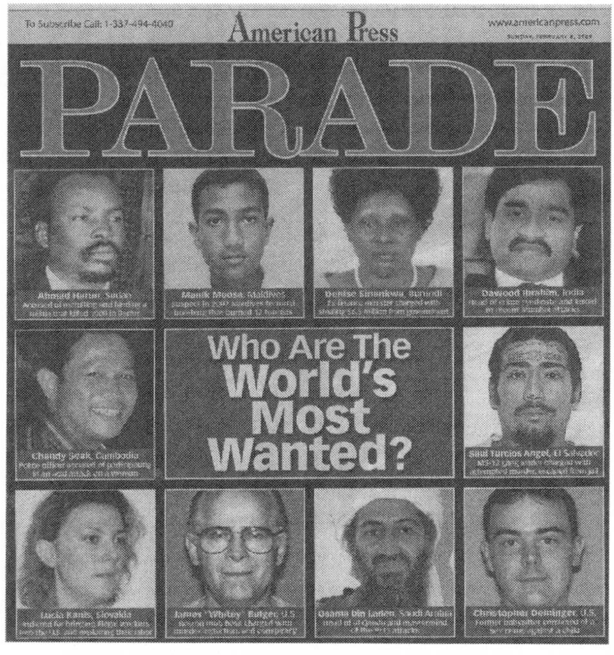
To Subscribe Call: 1-337-494-4040 | American Press | www.americanpress.com

PARADE

Ahmad Harun, Sudan

Manik Moosa, Maldives

Denise Sinankwa, Burundi

Dawood Ibrahim, India

Who Are The World's Most Wanted?

Chandy Seak, Cambodia

Saul Turcios Angel, El Salvador

Lucia Kanis, Slovakia

James "Whitey" Bulger, U.S.

Osama bin Laden, Saudi Arabia

Christopher Deininger, U.S.

Americans on the Run

These four, wanted by U.S. authorities, may be at large in this country or could have fled abroad.

Gregory James Caton, U.S. Convicted of selling fake, harmful cancer drugs and other meds to duped consumers

Metin Atilan, Turkey & U.S. Defense contractor indicted for bribery of U.S. military officials to win lucrative jobs in Iraq

Marlyn Dean Hinders, U.S. Indicted for helping to run an offshore Ponzi scheme that swindled $80 million from investors

Neeraj Gulati, India & U.S. Accused of raping a maid in India; fled the country before the local authorities could arrest him

Taken from Parade Magazine, February 8, 2009

questing political asylum in that country.[10] A considerable degree of effort went into this project, including the assemblage of all my documentation, their translations, and notarized copies, etc. In the end, I never heard so much as a word back from anyone connected with that Government.

Terrified, it was not long after that incident that my wife and I packed off to Cuenca, vowing to stay out of Guayaquil as much as possible. It was a feeble move, but our options were limited and we didn't know what else to do. We had purchased land there and were in the process of building a home.

Looking back now, I was so foolish . . . and naive. I felt that if we lived a quiet life in the mountains, our problems might begin to dissipate.

They didn't. They were only just beginning.

In response to their own incompetence in detaining the wrong person, U.S. officials placed me on the Interpol "Red List," and I was reported in the U.S. media as **one of the world's most wanted criminals, even pictured along with Osama bin Laden!** The preceding picture shows the cover of the February 8, 2009 edition of Parade Magazine wherein, on page six, it stated that I was "convicted of selling fake, harmful cancer drugs and other meds to duped consumers" (see picture). That this simply wasn't true didn't seem to embarrass U.S. Department of Justice officials who are accustomed to feeding the most outrageous lies to the mass media without question. Subsequently, I was illegally kidnapped in Ecuador – the second attempt – in the afternoon of December 2, 2009.

Following an extradition hearing in Guayaquil, Ecuador, several days later – in which I prevailed – I was then "extraordinarily renditioned" back to the U.S. This occurred with the assistance of corrupt Ecuadorean National Police, U.S. State Dept. officials, and an American Airlines pilot who refused to acknowledge the direct order that my Ecuadorean Federal Judge had decreed at the airport tower, that I was to be removed from

[10] Considering the depths to which that country has since descended, I am fortunate that this effort was unsuccessful.

the plane immediately.

What was my offense justifying being labeled one of the world's most wanted criminals? What could I have possibly done to put me in the same league as Osama bin Laden? (Keep in mind that there were never any additional charges filed.) It turned out to be only the probation violation itself. Now, under U.S. law, the "sentencing guidelines" suggest an automatic 3 to 9 month term of imprisonment for this. It was not a new charge. It is rendered almost automatically. My sentencing judge, Tucker Melancon, went ahead and gave me the maximum sentence the law allowed.

He repeatedly queried the prosecutor if he agreed that he was restricted in only giving me two more years of imprisonment – on top of the 33 months in prison and 16 months of probation I had already served. This left the impression that he would have given me ten more years if he could just find a law that would allow him to do so. Given my circumstances, the judge sentenced me to two more years of prison, setting the stage for an international incident.

These, and a host of similarly ridiculous incidents surrounding my case, are the subject of Chapter 3 of the online book, Meditopia.[11]

Nevertheless, whether or not you believe in the existence of an effective cancer cure that has been suppressed by medical authorities and by their Government backers for 150 years, is ultimately beside the point. (Although I encourage you to do the research by browsing the aforementioned websites – all at no cost – to come to a more informed conclusion.) I provide this background merely to reveal the seed thought from which the quest arose to see if this was a deviation, or an expression of a much darker and broader character of Western governmental authority, or effective modern governance at large. In this effort, I was assisted by another author who found similar "anomalies" in the field of business and general organizational management: C. Northcote Parkinson.

[11] Again, see Chapter 3, Section 3 of Meditopia, http://www.meditopia.org/chap3-3.htm

The Presentational Precursor: The Collaries Of Parkinson's Laws

Strange as it may sound, a commentator on observed anomalies of business management, deserves much credit for the style of this book's presentation and its structured "premises."

C. Northcote Parkinson was a British author, made famous for his book, Parkinson's Law: The Pursuit of Progress,[12] originally printed in 1958. Marginalized as a "humorous criticism of the administration of business or Government," most people in business are familiar with its signature principle, "Parkinson's Law," usually stated as "work expands so as to fill the time available for its completion."

In studying Parkinson's monograph, I found little evidence of any attempt to produce a parody or a comical piece. Parkinson took himself seriously; however, he touched upon subjects too sensitive to be taken seriously. So establishment observers have, for nearly 60 years now, written his work off as a comedy, which is an easy way to trash the validity of the author's underlying work. You will find Parkinson mentioned in most dictionaries and encyclopedias. Read for yourself. Rarely is he taken seriously.

But even if I'm wrong in my interpretation, even if you studied Parkinson and came to a different conclusion about his method of delivery, it would not change the validity of his observations. For even Shakespeare was taken to note that "many a truth has been spoken in jest." It's like the medicine dispensed to children that comes in a sugar cube. We have all observed how comedy or fictional storytelling can make a nasty truth more palatable. I realized this when, in 2002, I composed a series of four "Corollaries of Parkinson's Law" to similarly bring forth observations that were not politically correct.[13] These Corollaries used to be online on a page entitled, "Impossible Dream," but

[12] See: C. Northcote Parkinson, Parkinson's Law: The Pursuit of Progress, (2002).

[13] Still readable as originally published at the Alpha Omega Labs archive site, **www.altcancer.net/lysis5.htm.** Although the website was taken down after the FDA destroyed our lab in 2003, it was put back up a couple of years later.

were later deleted in a vain attempt to appease the "truth suppression" camp at the U.S. FDA – which loathes any exercise in freedom of speech which vexes its pharmaceutical company clients. My "Corollaries" ran thusly:

IMPOSSIBLE DREAM

Why The Cancer Industry Is Committed To Not Finding A Cure, And If They Do Run Across One, Suppressing It.

Or: "Why certain fundamental principles of organizational management work to (1) ensure that the cancer research and clinical establishment *never come close* to providing any meaningful cancer cure, and (2) guarantee that each and every dollar donated to cancer research is unwittingly used to suppress *real* effective cancer remedies."

Introduction

Many people who read the materials in our "suppression page,"[14] or read Chapter 4 of Meditopia,[15] seem dumbfounded that so many effective cancer therapies could have been uncovered – only to be suppressed by the very establishment created to find and implement effective therapies.

That widespread suppression does exist and has been going on in the West, at least as it relates to cancer, for well over one hundred years, is a given. All you have to do is read a handful of the books discussed in the suppression page to realize that suppression is the standard operating procedure of the medical industrial complex.

This page doesn't ask what ... it answers why.

'The Impossible Mandate Principles'
New Corollaries of Parkinson's Law

Most students of business management are familiar with at least the first of Parkinson's major laws – that "work expands so as to fill the time allotted for its completion." First published in 1955 and expanded in the widely popular book, Parkinson's Law: The Pursuit of Progress,[16] (first published in 1958), Professor Cyril Northcote Parkinson, a noted British novelist and historian, whose book is mentioned earlier, came up with the principles to explain certain quirks of human behavior and how they relate to the management of organizations.

Given the assertions of his critics that his work was satirical, and in light of the unsettling political realities that a study of his principles would reveal, it is not surprising that he chose to deliver his ideas with a tongue-in-cheek spin.

[14] This links to: www.altcancer.net/lysis.htm
[15] See: www.meditopia.org/chap4.htm
[16] See: C. Northcote Parkinson, Parkinson's Law: The Pursuit of Progress, (2002).

The First Corollary:

"In only the rarest of circumstances can an organization succeed if the fulfillment of a singular assigned mission means an end to the purpose which created it. If not provided with a subsequent mission, the organization will actually impede the goal(s) for which it owes its very existence."

The stated purpose of the American Cancer Society, and hundreds of lesser lights in what would become known as the "War on Cancer," is to **find a cure for cancer**!

Year after year, these organizations collect hundreds of millions of dollars promising that effective treatment for cancer is right around the corner. "We can complete the Mission. We can stamp out cancer in your lifetime. But we need your help!"

It is disastrously naive to think that a highly funded establishment set up to find a cancer cure could ever effectively work to that aim. All organizational structures assume macrobiological characteristics taken from the organisms who comprise them. In the current context, they are human – and like all animals, **each is organically programmed to live, survive, grow, expand, procreate**. And so it is with the organizations humans create. To ask the American Cancer Society or the National Cancer Institute to find a cancer cure is to say, "Now go. Be successful. And once you have achieved your aim, **promptly commit suicide**." For once a real cancer cure or cures are announced, these organizations, which collect hundreds of billions of dollars in the aggregate annually for treatment and research – from Governments, agencies, foundations, corporations, insurance companies, and private individuals – all of them, without exception, will have lost their reason for existence. That is why a cancer cure will never come from their quarter. The very nature of their mandate is a violation of Natural Law. It is a grand act of political expediency and managerial stupidity that has taken what should have been an easy-to-solve medical puzzle and turned it into the single greatest act of man-made carnage in history, a fraud of unspeakable magnitude that has spanned more than a century, and has needlessly caused the premature deaths of tens of millions of people.

Year after year, more and more money is spent on a virtual potpourri of money-seeking cancer foundations, agencies and societies. And, year after year, **cancer incidence grows higher and higher**.[17] What little progress is reported by the Pollyannas of the cancer industry can primarily be attributable to early detection and prevention – relatively low cost, proactive measures which cannot begin to justify the astronomically large sums invested each year in cancer research and treatment.

> "In terms of the big picture, we are continuing to make progress, but we have a very long way to go."
>
> **Michael Thun**
> Head of Epidemiology
> American Cancer Society (Atlanta)[18]

Translation: every year we must show you results. After all, you won't support us if you don't think we're getting something done. On the other hand, we can't be too successful – and we most certainly can't afford to come up with a cure – after all, if we did that, how could we come back to you next year and get more of your money? Get real. Do you have any idea how many people would be out of work if anybody uncovered a real cure for cancer?

[17] See: http://www.medicaldaily.com/cancer-trends-2017-why-are-cancer-rates-increasing-407270

[18] Quote taken from: USA Today, Health & Science section, June 5, 2001.

The Second Corollary:

"Organizations assigned to 'finding a cure' – for anything, regardless of what it is, will always lean towards those treatments which are the most expensive, the most complicated, and least accommodating to self-administration. Only in this way can the organization justify its propensities for greater growth and funding requirements, restrict competition by raising the thresholds of specialized education and knowledge, and filter out potential rivals by setting large capital requirements as a 'sine qua non' for even participating."

To anyone who has had to go through the agony of dealing with a relative who has advanced cancer, the usual questions always arise: Why are the therapeutic options so expensive? Why are the protocols so involved? Isn't there more that we can do from our side to help our loved one? Why aren't there any simpler or less expensive solutions?

The Second Corollary makes all this clear.

In the past, before the emergence of the Medical Industrial Complex, the great diseases of the ages also presented great challenges. Mankind sought cures – and in time cures were found. Easy, cheap, self-administered cures. For pellagra? Niacin. The cure for scurvy? Vitamin C. The cure for rickets? Vitamin D.

Many easy solutions were found because they often came from traditional cultures without commercialized medicine (i.e. from an indigenous culture) and there were no established, highly funded, self-serving organizations around to suppress them. This is, admittedly, a simplification of the historical facts, but the fundamental principle is not easily debated. Money does not aid the search for cures; in fact, on balance it actually acts more as a deterrent.

Our Second Corollary draws from the second of Parkinson's Laws – "expenditures rise to meet income." Every year, the collection plate goes out – to Government, industry, foundations and private individuals. "Give us your money . . . because we're making progress every day and we can't stop now – we're too close!"

Revenues rise, so therefore, expenditures must be created to justify the revenues. This makes the search for medical solutions that are inexpensive, easy, or self-administered so anathema. It is why the entire apparatus of the medical establishment, the food and drug authorities, and the pharmaceutical industries are set up to suppress anything that does not support their endemic need for big, expensive solutions.

To embrace more simplistic approaches is suicidal. That is why and how the medical field, most particularly as it pertains to the cancer industry, has become so corrupt. It wasn't born corrupt. It became corrupt because money and organizations have their own unique dynamic.

Or, to rephrase our First Corollary: "The need to survive and grow is greater than the need for the organization to fulfill its original purpose." This in turn plays upon another of Parkinson's own corollaries: "Officials want to multiply subordinates, not rivals." You cannot justify the need for growth and an increase in subordinates by chasing easy, inexpensive solutions.

The Third Corollary:

"The lack of a 'deadline' will always infect an organization on a mission as obscure as finding a 'cure' with structural elephantiasis. Parkinson's original law also stated, 'Any project assigned without a deadline is likely never to be completed.' The fact that the organization itself, out of survival, will band with like organizations to suppress rivals who would suggest that the mission is completed and the deadline past, only puts this principle on steroids and produces yet greater obstruction to the original mission."

This corollary explains why the cancer industry is so hyper about the words "cancer" and "cure" ever appearing together. "Cure" translates into "end of mission." "End of mission," in turn, translates into "end of the gravy train." Again, success in cancer treatment means death to those assigned to find effective treatment.

The Fourth Corollary:

"If you want to make your organization bigger (and all of them do) then you must make the problem bigger. Big budgets cannot be sustained in the presence of easy solutions. That means that survival demands that you use whatever means are at your disposal to suppress alternatives by rivals that would prove compellingly contrary. You cannot sustain the illusion in the public mind that the problem is bigger than it really is if you aren't willing to squelch those capable of undoing the big lie that forms the cornerstone of your operation. Advancing your cause requires a maximum sustained effort to destroy those capable of providing an end to your grand 'raison d'être' and the many growing, demanding, and expensive projects which it consequently spawns."

Back in 2002, I was visiting friends in Hot Springs, Montana, located on the Flathead Indian Reservation (a name not appreciated by its inhabitants, the Salish and Kootenai Indians). On visiting a Salish chief to talk about indigenous herbs north of the Bitterroot Valley, I heard amazing stories. "My grandmother lived to be 103 years old," he said. "She cured herself of many illnesses throughout her life, primarily through the use of herbs. Back in those days, you didn't have modern medicine. You didn't have all these expensive hospitals, with their expensive drugs, expensive procedures; white men brought all that crazy stuff."

"Every tribe had its own knowledge and its own medicine men. They knew the healing ability of the plants on the land, how and when to pick them, what parts to use, when and how to use them. It was all simple and natural. We had the Kootenai to the North and the Blackfoot to the East."

"We are losing all that knowledge now. White men have polluted our youth with the idea that our ways of the Earth are backwards. This lack of respect extends even to our language. There are only 50 people remaining on the Earth who can still speak the Salish tongue. I know – because I teach a small class for those in our tribe who still want to learn."

"Recently we lost our (shaman) . . . she was an old woman when she died, and although she looked for a young protégé to continue with her work, she never found one. She took great knowledge with her . . . many things I am sure no one still alive knows."

Whatever this knowledge was that was taken from the Earth, it was, no doubt, a victim of the Fourth Corollary . . .

Now what you've read above is the "Impossible Dream¨essay I posted in 2002. Still, I wanted to make sure that my readers understood **why** the cancer industry – itself just a small part of the Medical Industrial Complex – was so incorrigibly corrupt, so I created a web page sidebar with an amazingly simple story, and I labeled it, "Mother Goose Metaphors," because only newborns can't comprehend these things. It reads like this:

John Dribble was a project manager at the Kah-Kah Cola Bottling Company. His job was to create newer and better versions of his company's best-selling soft drinks –and he wasn't content with mere feeble attempts to improve the company's flagship products.

To John, making the best Kah-Kah ever, was top priority.

One day, John had a thought: what if he could make Kah-Kah so filling, so satisfying and so thirst-quenching, that the customer could go for a year or more without experiencing a need for another soft drink.

"Imagine," John thought to himself, "we'll have the only soft drink in the world that gives so much value to the customer, so much fulfillment . . . why would anyone buy any other soft drink? Everybody will buy Kah-Kah!"

So John went to work using his department's extensive financial resources, hiring the best minds in biochemistry, food & beverage science and product development. Although the company officials who were working above him knew John was committed to making a better product – they had no idea how serious he was about making the best product. One year turned into two years . . . two years turned into three.

Finally, just about the time he had exhausted all available favors from friends and colleagues at Kah-Kah, he did it. John found a way to make Kah-Kah into the ultimate beverage experience. It was complete and fulfilling in every way.

To test his new prototype, John began giving his product away to other employees within the company. Members of his staff and employees in the engineering department were the first to try the product. And then it spread. Soon, employees all over the company were asking for John's new version of Kah-Kah, bringing it home to their friends and family.

John was so pleased that so many people fell in love with **his** version of Kah-Kah – but then, something even stranger happened. Suddenly, without warning, people at his company stopped asking for the product.

John asked his secretary, Cherry, "What do you think is happening?"

"I don't know," Cherry replied: "The Kah-Kah you gave me was the best I ever tasted. It was **wonderful** – only it was so good and so fulfilling, I haven't wanted any Kah-Kah since!"

It was then that John realized that he had created the ultimate soft drink.

The next morning John reported to work at his usual time – 8 a.m. – grabbed his usual cup of coffee, and headed for his office.

Much to his surprise, when he got to his office, John was greeted by the President of Kah-Kah Cola, Mr. Isaac Tapdanz, who was sitting at John's desk.

"Good morning, John."

"Why, Mr. Tapdanz...!"

"Save it, John," the chief executive said, interrupting, "we have an emergency Board Meeting in 10 minutes, and you're the guest of honor!"

John was stunned. He didn't know what to say, but he followed Mr. Tapdanz into the next building and up the elevator to the boardroom on the 38th Floor.

"Gentlemen!" Mr. Tapdanz boomed as he announced John's arrival, "This is our very own Mr. John Dribble - the man we've all been hearing so much about!"

Following a few moments of acknowledgements and handshakes, the Board sat down at every available seat, leaving only John standing at the edge of the Board's long oak table.

"John," Mr. Tapdanz said, breaking the ice, "This is our Chairman, Murray Pembers. You know him, of course, but you two have never met. He also represents the majority shareholders in our company and is the great-great grandson of our founder. He would like to have a few words with you."

"Mr. Dribble – are you the one responsible for this new product, the one everyone seems to be talking about?"

"Yes, sir," John replied proudly.

"Do you have any idea what you've done!" the Chairman exploded.

"But, Mr. Pembers, I thought this was my job. I'm **supposed** to work to make the product better, to make drinking Kah-Kah as fulfilling as possible."

"Your job is to do no such thing," Pembers interjected. "This business is built on repeat sales. It is built, like all consumer-product companies, on the primary goal of making consumers **dependent** on what we sell – to maximize revenues for the benefit of our stakeholders. To the extent that it gives them what they want, fine. To the extent that it deters the number of people who use our products **or** the amount of sales we can exact per customer, you can forget it."

Turning to Mr. Tapdanz, Pembers added, "How could you let such an imbecile get to such a position of importance in our organization?"

"I can explain . . ." John Dribble insisted.

"Never mind," Pembers interrupted, after which he gave John Dribble specific instructions and asked him to leave the boardroom.

"Is this everything?" Mr. Tapdanz inquired an hour later, convening with John in his office.

"Yes, sir – all my notebooks, all the lab reports, formularies, five remaining cases of prototype – that's it – everything," John Dribble noted dutifully.

"John, I want you know that you've done an incredible job. You're the best product development man I know in the beverage industry. You've done more with less and accomplished greater things in less time than any previous technician in your field. I know this project was dear to your heart, and I know you would have liked to see the very best version of Kah-Kah succeed in our business."

"Yes, sir . . . I would," John reaffirmed, standing attentively.

"Maybe in the future – when people are ready for it. Perhaps when competitive forces require us to create a comparable product."

"Yes, sir. I understand perfectly," John added, turning to walk towards the office door.

"Oh . . . and John."

"Mr. Tapdanz?"

"Please see my secretary on your way down the hall. She has your personal belongings and a check waiting . . . you're fired!"

So ended my first foray into using "Parkinson's Law" type corollaries and metaphors to try and reconstruct the modern world in a way that made sense – in this case, concerning the insane, pathological tendencies that infected the cancer industry.

Its relevance in the current volume should be self-evident, because **the forces that guide the successes of big business and big Government are much the same**. Even aside from the more serious atrocities alluded to in the "Impossible Dream" piece, there is an underlying common sense from which the impartial observer cannot escape. For, as it is, most people who know how the cancer business works and do not benefit from it, will come to the same conclusion: we're talking about letting people die in order to make more money. That's really the bottom line. Nonetheless, to understand why this kind of behavior is inevitable, we must analyze why large organizational structures are so deceitful to begin with, why their actions are in complete opposition to what they preach. Many years earlier, this was my starting point . . . and as we begin our study, it will be yours, too.

Premise On The Critical Importance Of A "Benign Common Narrative"

The creation of a "benign common narrative" (BCN) is critical to modern governance, no less than the deceptive methods of other successful parasites: bacteria, viruses, yeasts, and other microbes, who can only feed off their hosts by disarming the latter's immune system as it pertains to their presence and/or effect.

More than ten years prior to my introduction to the world of suppressed cancer remedies, I had worked as a cryptologic technician for the U.S. Navy. This job required a Top Secret clearance level, as well as additional compartmentalized security clearances.

Few people in the military intelligence community fully grasp the implications of their work, where the things a Government tells its people are dramatically different from what's really going on.

I know that I was unaware.

It wasn't until I realized the implications of my work with Alpha Omega Labs[19] in the mid 1990's that I was able to reflect back on my military service in a new light. Whereas lying to the public seemed innocuous and natural enough, supported under that monolithic rubric of "national security," how did it compare to effectively seeing millions – **millions** – of Americans murdered for private profit through the use of high profit, low efficacy cancer treatments when low profit, highly effective remedies had already been discovered and suppressed?

If the U.S. and other Western Governments, all sitting at the pinnacle of power among the world's hierarchy of prevailing national authorities, were complicit in this – acts so heinous that if committed by an individual we would regard that person as psychopathic – is there any act too dark, too evil, too malicious to its own people or to others, that a powerful Government of our time would not engage if it felt that a substantial amount of money or power were at stake?

I couldn't think of one.

This is a conclusion I reached only after searching the underbelly of modern Government's many false fronts, systems of self-serving propaganda, and manipulation of its constituents with the use of "common narrative," or more specifically "benign common narrative" (BCN). For the crucial question I had to ask after determining the extent of the cover-ups in the field of medicine – because it wasn't long until I discovered that suppressed cures could be found for countless ailments (again, painfully and abundantly evidenced within the contents of Meditopia), was this: is the phenomenon isolated or systemic? If you superficially cut yourself, the problem is localized. If you are

[19] Alpha Omega Labs refers to an herbal company that my wife Cathryn and I created in the early 90's. When it became apparent that the Internet would evolve into the worldwide medium for commerce, we launched Alpha Omega Labs as Altcancer.com in September, 1995. This site now stands as a historical repository for our work of over 27 years. Today we continue to operate two small herbal shops online: Herbhealers.com for customer in the U.S. and Canada; and AlphaOmegaLabs.com for customers in all other countries.

suffering from malaria, a competent physician can take a blood sample from anywhere . . . an arm, leg, your neck . . . and diagnose the same problem. The affliction is systemic and affects the whole body.

And that's the central issue here.

The problem with psychopathocracy is that it's systemic. In our time it is ubiquitous, on every level of the body politic, planet-wide.

Unfortunately, like many mental pathologies, the condition is progressive, and from a planetary perspective it appears to be fatal . . . more broadly so than alluded to above. We are quickly approaching a potpourri of potential doomsday scenarios, initiated or aggravated by our planet's most successful governmental systems, the likes of which have already initiated an extinction process more severe then that of the Permian-Triassic die-off over 250 million years ago. In fact, we are already well into this man-made "Holocene Extinction Event," which we will discuss later.

We have it in our power to destroy all physical life on this planet and render it no more fertile than the surface of our moon. As you proceed through Book I, you'll learn why there is an elite group in charge of our earthly affairs who would rather see that happen than to sacrifice even a modicum of their psychopathic hold on power.

Our dire plight and its serious consequences are something we simply can no longer avoid.

There are, no doubt, benefits to psychopathocracy . . . for a few . . . for a time. But do the "joys of psychopathocracy" for the privileged outweigh the burden on everyone else – all the other humans, animals, the plants, and all other earthly life forms? Hoping that the question itself is rhetorical, we will later address the endgame – something I call "The Great Unwinding."

For no pathology of this worldwide magnitude can survive forever . . .

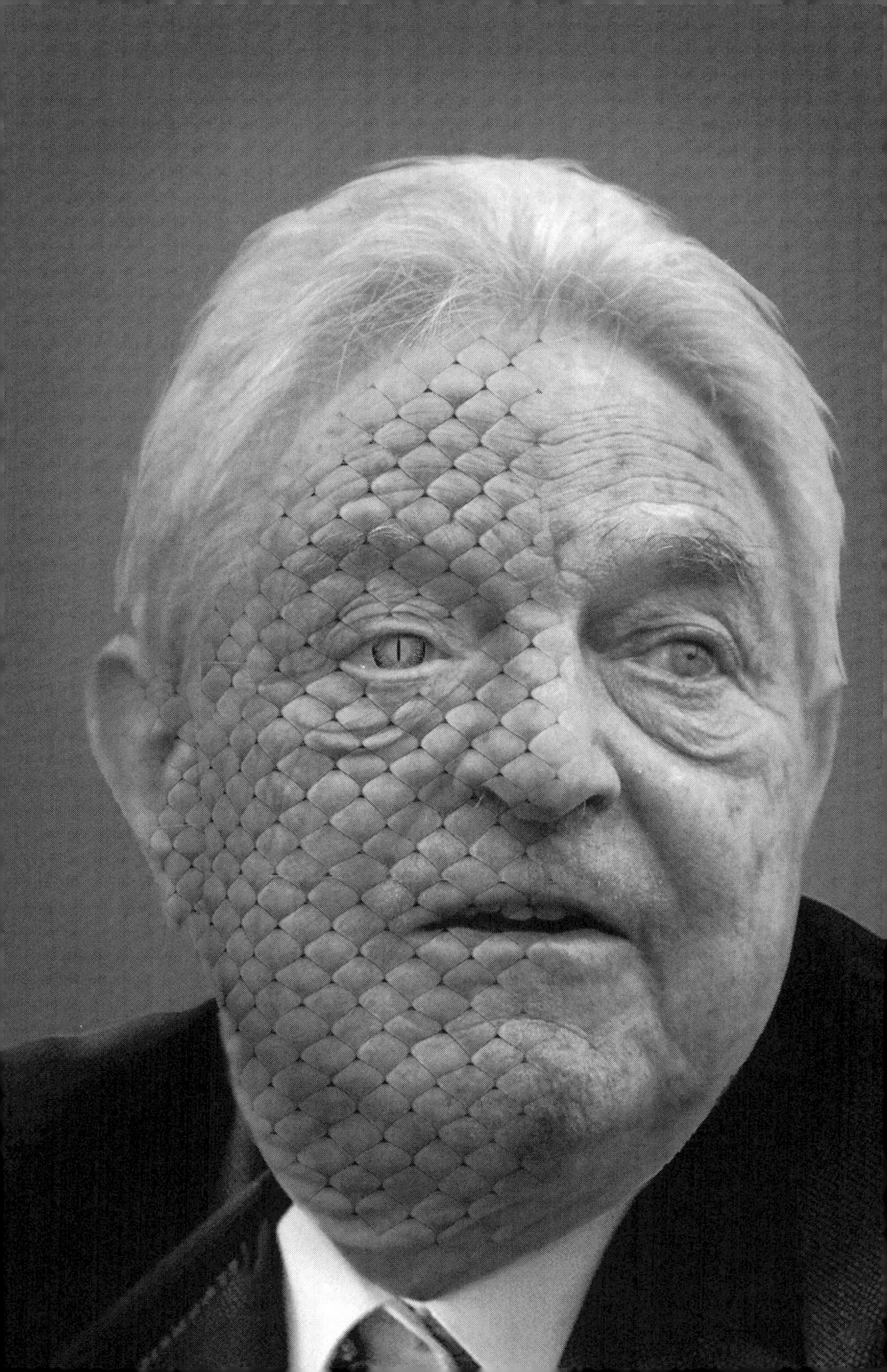

Chapter 2:

Understanding "Negaprocity" Masquerading As Benevolence: The Fundamental Roots Of "Doublespeak"

The root of all governance in human affairs begins with the family. Intuitively, we understand the relationship that exists between a mother and her child: the unconditional love that parents express for their offspring. We see this nurturing as a predominating influence even throughout the animal kingdom, with relationships created where no thought of return, no expectation of reciprocity on the individual's expenditure of time or available resources exists.

Throughout indigenous communities all over the world, the same phenomenon has been observed, wherein love and mutual concern govern the actions and motives of tribal peoples. As one moves away from the core family, where giving without expectation is commonplace, one sees a movement out of the domain of unconditional love towards less generous conditions of exchange. "Generalized reciprocity," where "generosity" and "freely giving" are still prominent but where some return on the part of the recipient is still weakly anticipated, guides daily life between families and within the village. For this reason, it is also called "weak reciprocity."[1]

As one leaves the warmth, security, and kinship of village life, we find that this exchange takes on a more distinct character that charts the first appearance of "economic life" among primitive peoples: "balanced reciprocity" at the tribal level. This is where direct exchange, trade, barter – I'll give you two of my "x's" if you'll give me three of your "y's" – resides. We are no longer sheltered in the loving embrace of "non-market economics." Now we're talking business. Here there is a peaceable,

[1] See: Marshall Sahlins, Stone Age Economics, (1972), p. 194.

acknowledged exchange of goods or services where both parties are agreeing to part with items of commensurate worth.

Up to this point, our discussion on reciprocity has been centered on concepts that are little more than hornbook cultural anthropology. American anthropologist Marshall Sahlins popularized these concepts, and in the drawing below, illustrated that reciprocity declines as one increases "sectoral distance."

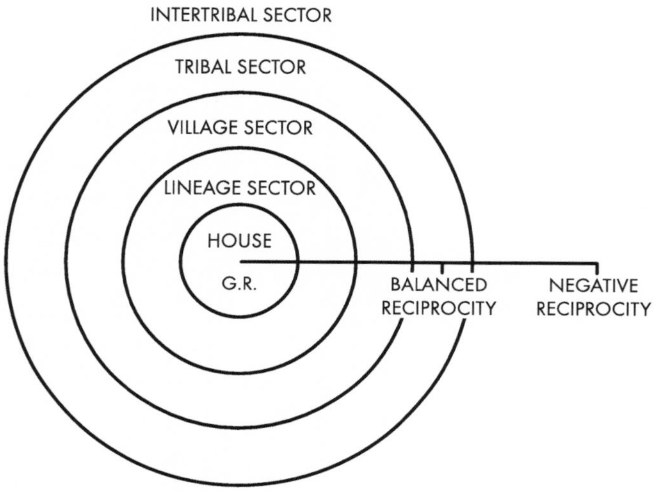

As a general rule, one doesn't see "hard bargaining" – or the efforts of one party attempting to take advantage of the other bargaining party – until we leave the tribal sector. This intuitively makes sense. Most people are less likely to risk bad feelings by taking advantage of someone they have to live around than they are someone that they see very seldom, if ever again, at the close of a transaction.

This domain is referred to as **"negative reciprocity,"** because the optimal goal is not fair exchange, but trading so as to achieve the upper hand. Since we'll be using this concept extensively throughout the rest of the book, let's just shorthand the term and call it **"negaprocity."**[2]

The area inside the outer ring before we get to negaprocity we will call Sahlins' "Reciprocity Zone" – the area outside it,

[2] Extending the term, we'll use "negaciprocal" in the adjectival..

the "Negaprocity Zone." (Later in this chapter, I will delineate this area more thoroughly with my own chart.)

What I'm attempting to do in this chapter is qualify the "negative reciprocity" territory to the degree that anthropologists have delineated "positive reciprocity." Now if we understand the correlation that field anthropologists have found using this model, specifically that "reciprocity inclines toward balance and chicane in proportion to sectoral distance," we may be tempted – or at least I was – to bookend the process before filling in the center. For example, if we begin by describing the social center where "reciprocity" is at its most positive, in the nuclear family, it really isn't reciprocity at all. It's family love. **But where does the other extreme take us?** I found it most curious that anthropologists don't seem as interested in mapping the negative territory as they are the positive. For it takes little imagination to realize that there are gradations in negaprocity that can be as well defined as those in reciprocity. It takes even less imagination to realize that extreme negaprocity will take you well into institutionalized, psychopathic criminality. Let's discuss an everyday example to get a sense of the range of negaciprocal possibility.

Think about leaving a store and returning to the parking lot to get your car. Out of nowhere a thief assaults you, takes your wallet, and leaves you penniless. This is clear negaprocity: a transaction occurred – a theft, but a transaction, nonetheless – and the thief is the sole beneficiary. Your trauma only adds to the element of negaprocity: the thief may feel better, but you feel much worse. Now, would you place that on the same level of negaprocity as the tribal trader who simply drives a hard bargain, perhaps is even deceptive in his presentation of the goods he is "selling," and leaves the transaction where the deceived party only "thinks" that the exchange was fair? It isn't the same, is it?

Now let's go back to the parking lot. The thief takes your wallet. He still benefits and you're cheated. But now, he considers the consequences of your ability to pick him out of a police lineup. From the thief's point of view, that's not good business, for him at least. So he pulls out a gun, drills you with four .38 rounds to the chest, kills you, and then leaves. This is much worse . . . for you. It wasn't a favorable exchange for you in the first place: you lost everything in your wallet and got nothing in return. But this is incomparably less preferable.

You're now a victim of even worse negaprocity. The thief may still feel better; he has your money. But you don't feel anything. You're dead.

For the sake of comparison, let's consider another, less extreme scenario of robbery in the parking lot. We'll assume that as you go to insert your car key into the driver-side door, your assailant stands before you with a knife. He demands that you hand over your wallet. You comply with his wishes and watch while he takes the money out of your wallet, throws the wallet back in your direction, with all your credit and bank cards and identification he chose not to steal. If we're attempting to qualify degrees of negaprocity, you would have to admit, this wasn't as bad as losing your entire wallet. And it wouldn't even compare to losing your life.

From these simple examples, it becomes apparent that in examining negaprocity, the full measure of the transaction can't be weighed only in terms of the winner's net gain. Rather, it can only be properly viewed by what the winner gains, what the loser loses, and the relation between the two – all against the backdrop of the perpetrator, or "active" party's intentions. In taking your life, the thief gained next to nothing: perhaps some added assurance that his act wouldn't be discovered by authorities, but your loss is much, much worse.

For the purposes of our study, we will then define the outer limits of negaprocity as "extreme negaprocity." The example we discussed, where the loser in the transaction loses his life, would clearly be a more advanced negaciprocal act, approaching "extreme negaprocity." (When Governments do this to an entire group of people, we call that **genocide**, and I guess you could say that's worse, but we'll get to that.)

So as not to get lost in hair-splitting, we will loosely define "extreme negaprocity" as the most advanced exploitative states that the average person can imagine, representing the most criminal acts by humans against not only other human beings, but against their environment. This is not an area that naysayers are going to easily cloud with arguments of moral relativism. Ordinary people who are not suffering from one or more severe psychological disorders – the kind that now infect the majority of politicians in the world's most influential Governments (for reasons I will make clear shortly) – can all agree with these broad brush strokes. No normal person thinks that murdering innocent people, for instance, or torture, rape, pedophilia, forced child labor, and similar acts of barbarous exploitation, are anything short of criminal. Only criminal minds can view them as innocuous and make excuses for perpetrating them. In an upcoming Negaprocity Chart – an extension of Sahlins' diagram, really – we will delineate negaciprocal states in terms of degrees or intensity of criminality against the "victim(s)": the greater the criminality, the greater the degree of negaprocity.

Those readers who are better versed in world history will, no doubt, sense the direction in which I'm heading. Truly, the greatest atrocities in history – from the extermination and subjugation of native peoples by the U.S. Government, to Stalin's purges, to Mao's Chinese Cultural Revolution, to Pol Pot's ethnic cleansing, etc. – are all good examples of modern Government's propensity for extreme negaprocity. It must not have been difficult for German sociologist Max Weber, to come to the conclusion that a claimed "monopoly on murder" was one of Government's defining characteristics. And yet, I watch consistently as citizens in my country of birth are bombarded with the most ridiculous self-serving (for the Government, that is) lies and deceitful ploys, and citizens are none the wiser.

I remember, while imprisoned in Beaumont, Texas[3] watching other inmates betting on the outcome of professional wrestling matches. Now it goes without saying that professional wrestling matches are scripted, theatrical presentations. The players are not athletes. They're actors. And yet to watch inmates carry on in their excitement over a given match, one would get the

[3] See: https://www.bop.gov/locations/institutions/bml/

distinct impression that in order to really "enjoy the show," you had to temporarily suspend your sense of reality.

"Suspending one's sense of reality" isn't necessarily harmful in and of itself. We all engage in it when we watch Hollywood movies. Our desire to "pretend" is so central to human nature that we expect to see pretending as a healthy sign of child development. So many of the games we design for children, and the vast majority of adult video games you see on the market, cannot be enjoyed unless you employ this creative device.

The inherent problem in understanding Government is that most people look upon the deceitful activities of their Government and behave as if they're watching professional wrestling. Most Governments, for their part, appease human nature, knowing that the citizenry want to believe that their country is righteous and good, that the Government is not, by its very nature, parasitic. People want to believe that their Government, their country, their world, is loveable.

As I stated there, and I believe it bears repeating, Freud incisively underscored this imperative human need when he wrote: "What happens (thusly) when the world (around us) becomes unlovable and our work impossible? If love is not just a psychic discharge but a way of being in the world, then that way of being demands that the world present itself to us as worthy of our love . . . If love is not just a feeling but the force that makes the world go around," as Freud speculated, "then loving the world and being able to love the world because the world is lovable are two sides of the same coin. We make the world meaningful with our love, and the world makes our lives meaningful by being lovable. When one partner fails, both do. The meaning of life depends on our ability to remain in a love affair with the world. Like any long-term love affair, this means that the world must love us back, even if this only means remaining worthy of our love."[4]

When our world is not loveable, or more to the present point, when Government is not loveable, how quickly do most people pretend – like a fan of professional wrestling – that

[4] See: C. Fred Alford, Whistleblowers: Broken Lives and Organizational Power, (2001), p. 52.

they're watching the "real thing"? Or that Government is not, as American actor and former politician, Jesse Ventura, so aptly puts it, "just show business"?

It wasn't until I began studying "game theory" in researching Meditopia, that I realized why Governments, particularly larger ones, have a nearly unavoidable tendency to be evil and underhanded, first towards others, and then, in time, towards their own people. I discuss "game theory" extensively elsewhere,[5] so I won't elaborate on its fundamentals here. Suffice it to say, that the conclusion of game theorists that reciprocity is key to winning is nowhere supported in the historical record when it comes to the study of politics. Game theory largely depends on the presumption that both "players" are equally well-informed and know what the other is doing. But our everyday observations tell us that Governments operate with a considerable degree of secrecy. They know what we're doing and appear to show great interest in having lots of information about us. Do we know anywhere near as much about the inner workings of our Government as our Government does about us? Could we ever hope to have the resources to know as much about our Government as our Government knows about us? That Governments operate with negaprocity while pretending to be benevolent is obvious to even the casual observer who isn't viewing the situation in professional wrestling mode. But why? Is this characteristic alterable, or does it just come with the territory?

One discipline that provides the tools to give us a meaningful answer is thermodynamics.

Premise on The Thermodynamics Of Governance

All Governments – with few exceptions – are essentially parasitic to the masses they rule. Because of the resources they must secure to support their infrastructure and ongoing operations, they will always take more from the general public than

[5] See: Meditopia – the discussion on "Prisoner's Dilemma" at: http://www.meditopia.org/chap5.htm

they give back in return. The more successful the Government, the more pronounced this characteristic. And because of their entropic nature – where the net direction of resources makes Governments thermodynamically centripetal, not centrifugal – they will always tend to align with Elite, monied, or resource-rich constituents that serve to covertly enslave financially the majority who are not so resource-rich.[6]

Simply put, thermodynamics is the applied study of heat and related forms of energy and how they behave within various closed systems. Intuitively, we can sense that Government, too, is a thermodynamic system, operating within a world that is, itself, a closed system. By closed system we mean a planet that has finite resources in the same way that Governments operate with relatively finite resources. The currency that provides it with its working energy isn't heat, however, it's money. Money translates into the power to do things in the same way that we think of heat as providing work potential within classical thermodynamic systems. Governments which have access to more money and more energy have a distinct advantage over other Governments which possess less.

Since thermodynamics, entropy, and "thermodynamic potential" are important concepts as we continue our study, let's take a moment to describe them more fully, because they aren't as scary as they sound. As Jeremy Rifkin noted, "Thermodynamics sounds like a complicated concept. In actuality, it is both the simplest and at the same time the most impressive scientific conception we know of. Both laws of thermodynamics can be stated in one tiny sentence: 'The total energy content of the universe is constant and the total entropy is continually increas-

[6] See: Joseph A. Tainter, The Collapse of Complex Societies, (1990), p. 91. "Human societies and political organizations, like all living systems, are maintained by a continuous flow of energy. From the simplest familial unit to the most complex regional hierarchy, the institutions and patterned interactions that comprise a human society are dependent on energy. At the same time, the mechanisms by which human groups acquire and distribute basic resources are conditioned by, and integrated within, sociopolitical institutions. Energy flow and sociopolitical organization are opposite sides of an equation. Neither can exist, in a human group, without the other, nor can either undergo substantial change without altering both the opposite member and the balance of the equation. Energy flow and sociopolitical organizations must evolve in harmony."

ing.'""[7]

Einstein called this "the premier law of all science"; Sir Arthur Eddington deemed it "the supreme metaphysical law of the entire universe." Rifkin continues: "The Entropy Law is the second law of thermodynamics. The first law states that all matter and energy in the universe is constant, that it cannot be created or destroyed." Or, put another way: "Nothing is created, nothing is destroyed, everything is transformed."

"Only its form can change but never its essence. The second law, The Entropy Law, states that matter and energy can only be changed in one direction, that is, from usable to unusable, or from available to unavailable, or from ordered to disordered. In essence, the second law says that everything in the entire universe began with structure and value and is irrevocably moving in the direction of random chaos and waste. Entropy is the measure of the extent to which available energy in any subsystem of the universe is transformed into an unavailable form. According to the Entropy Law, whenever a semblance of order is created anywhere on Earth or in the universe, it is done at the expense of causing an even greater disorder in the surrounding environment." [8]

Since we aren't concerned with classical physics here, for our purposes and to simplify our analysis, we'll think of entropy as the tendency and process of a system – any system – to go from order to chaos, intelligent structure to random disintegration, function to dysfunction, a state of living to a state of death, etc., without the infusion of additional useable energy to support and maintain that system's functions.

We see signs of entropy everywhere in our daily lives, even though we don't think about it. If you don't put any "energy" into cleaning your room, what happens? Well, with time, it gets messier and more disorganized. If you do nothing to maintain your car, if you put no energy into maintaining it, it breaks

[7] See: Jeremy Rifkin, Entropy: A New World View, (1981), p. 33. Rifkin's "tiny sentence" is taken from: Isaac Asimov, "In the game of energy and thermodynamics, you can't even break even," Smithsonian, August, (1970), p. 9. Note that there are four "laws of thermodynamics," but most references focus on the first and second.

[8] Jeremy Rifkin, ibid,. p. 6

down. It ages and falls into disrepair. It takes energy to maintain order. It takes energy to ensure that the constructs of civilization continue to function and don't break down and fall into disuse.

Any society, regardless of the underlying culture, has to deal with entropy. It does this by investing energy into maintaining order: maintaining infrastructure – roads, buildings, bridges, schools, hospitals, etc. You don't have to study the nature of Governments for very long before you realize that as creatures of negaprocity, Governments actually "accelerate entropy," or operate at a "higher entropy state" than if the governed society were left to its own devices and operated at a "lower entropy state" with shorter sectoral distances.

Let's go back to the "dirty room" metaphor for a moment. If you don't clean your room, it will get messy on its own. You don't have to "work" at making it messy. But what if your big brother comes into your room and decides he's going to deliberately mess things up for his own pleasure and personal entertainment? By investing energy into making things more disorderly instead of orderly, he is essentially "accelerating entropy." You aren't trying to mess up your room. Fact is, it gets messy on its own. You're operating at a "lower rate of entropy." But your big brother has sped up the process by operating at a "higher entropy state." He has sped up the timeline between orderliness and disorderliness.

This is precisely what Governments have done from the beginning of their existence. They aren't simply entropic by nature; they actually accelerate the phenomenon. This occurs because there is a correlation between entropy and negaprocity, almost by definition. Negaprocity and entropy go hand in hand, because whereas reciprocity cultivates the need to take into account the needs of family, neighbors, fellow tribesmen, the environment, etc., which translates into an investment of energy into sustaining orderliness, negaprocity recognizes no such needs. Whereas reciprocity says, "How can we cooperate and create more love, beauty, and harmony in our surroundings," negaprocity says, "Fuck that. What's in it for me?"

A by-product of accelerating entropy is a Government's

ability to redirect the energy sources around it to suit its purposes and objectives. The more that a Government is able to commandeer or sequester the resources to which it has access, the more "thermodynamic potential" that it has. It is important to note that I use this term differently than do classical physicists.[9] Thermodynamic potential is the energy and/or resources which an entity has at its disposal to commit to its objectives, which are, more often than not, devoted to accelerating entropy. The more thermodynamic potential a Government has, the more successful it will be, all other factors being equal.

Governments are creatures of Extreme Negaprocity almost by morphological definition. They are so far removed from our hearts, our homes, our mothers, our kin . . . so far are they removed from our lives, so great is their "sectoral distance," that we should expect Governments to view us no differently than a cattle rancher views his herd before sending it to the slaughterhouse. But why isn't this obvious to the average person?

After studying cancer for nearly 20 years and uncovering what I believe to be the single, greatest criminal act in history (i.e., the deliberate suppression of effective cancer cures), I believe I know the perfect example. Cancers and Governments are astonishingly similar: they both feed off their hosts in insidious ways. They are both parasitic, as people can live just fine without Government – and, in fact, did so quite happily for eons before the current age – while Governments, like vampires, will die without a host of people from which to feed. They both manage to fool their hosts by pretending to be friendly, so they aren't attacked. They are both fatal if left unchecked. They are both very threatened by the host knowing how they really operate. They both invest considerable energy into cloaking their real intentions. They both possess morphogenetic properties to protect themselves, and in their latter stages – think Oswald Spengler's "Caesarism"[10] – their final ill-intentions towards their own people are too often detected after it's too late.

[9] See: https://simple.wikipedia.org/wiki/Thermodynamic_potential.

[10] See: https://www.counter-currents.com/2016/05/oswald-spengler-and-the-controversy-of-caesarism/

Despite the obvious parallels, something is left unanswered that requires further explanation. It may seem obvious to the reader why Governments – these creatures who are so distanced from those they pretend to serve – are naturally negaciprocal. What isn't so clear to the average person is why they go to such extreme contrary lengths to appear benevolent.

To really uncover how and why Governments behave as they do, you really have to enter into a psychopathic frame of mind – the same frame of mind as those at the highest level of advanced Western power. Think of it this way: if you were a murdering rapist, what is the first order of business after you have commenced with your ungodly act? Isn't it keeping the girl quiet . . . quiet while you're raping her . . . quiet while your slitting her throat . . . quiet while you figure out how to dispose of the body and delay any detection by authorities? It isn't comfortable contemplating such things, but if you're going to enter into a serious study of how effective, modern Governments operate, you have no choice. You cannot begin to study a psychopath unless you can understand how psychopaths think. And, in the lexicon of political expressions concerning the governance of peoples, keeping people happy at a visibly superficial level is tantamount to keeping the rape victim silent.

In no way is the comparison a stretch.

War is Peace, Freedom Is Slavery, And Ignorance Is Strength

These inherent contradictions – made manifest in the policies of modern Governments, regardless of whether they are ostensibly monarchic, capitalistic, communist, socialist, fascist, and every flavor and combination in between – became the mantras outlining the boundaries of governmental nonsense in George Orwell's work that came to be known as "Doublespeak." All Governments exhibit elements of Doublespeak in varying degrees, but few people understand why, believing that if an errant Government could simply be reformed, this tendency could either be held in check or extinguished entirely. **Few**

people realize that Governments that skillfully rule through the exercise of Doublespeak are at a distinct advantage over Governments that don't.

It is my contention that Doublespeak exists as a by-product of Government's natural state as a creature of negaprocity. Moreover, a Government that can get its people to accept these contradictions, accept its "professional wrestling spectacles" in a suspended state of unjustified belief, held captive by our natural desire to see our world as worthy of our love, has distinct advantages and enjoys greater privileges.

This is because increased use of Doublespeak provides Governments with greater thermodynamic potential. Through the institutionalization of these self-serving contradictions, Governments strengthen their negaprocity with the element of perpetuity. It should be obvious that the pickpocket who can lift your wallet once has nothing over the pickpocket who reaches into your pocket every day of the year.

Let's go back to the parking lot.

Applying Doublespeak to that situation, we might summarize the "transaction" as "Thievery is Generosity." You don't have to be a particularly bright person to see that people who are able to take from you at will, while providing comparatively little or nothing in return, have a distinct advantage over those who are not.

The problem is that I cannot get away with stealing from you repeatedly unless I can get you to respond as if the act itself is reciprocal.

By way of a recent example, the U.S. Government has authorized the bailout of large Wall Street institutions to the tune of trillions of dollars since 2008, thus burdening the entire rest of the U.S. citizenry by hyper-diluting the common currency, piling up the public debt, and impoverishing untold generations of future Americans. The official rationale is that if the U.S. Government had not provided these bailouts, the economy would have ended up in far worse shape than it already is. What nonsense. Never mind that in a true capitalist society, which, the last time I checked, the U.S. still claims to be, having launched an untold number of military conflicts that were purported to support this value, there are no "too big to fail" companies. You let ailing companies die of their own accord; the bankrupt pieces are picked up by investors and managers who will hopefully do a better job, and customers remain unaffected by the change in management and ownership.

Returning to the parking lot, it's like the thief concluding your "transaction" by telling you that if he hadn't taken your money, you wouldn't be able to appreciate the value of security. It's for your own good. You should be thanking him. You'd be ungrateful if you didn't. What psychopathic rapist doesn't see the optimal outcome as the victim being made to believe that "it was for your own good," thanking the rapist for a job well done? As absurd as this sounds, you have billions of people all over the world who spend their entire lives doing just that. We might go so far as to say that the rapist – Government – who can achieve this aim is more effective than the rapist who ends up with a vengeful victim (i.e., an electorate turned revolutionary), and certainly more effective than the rapist who gets caught and ends up having to pay for his crimes (i.e., bring out the guillotine).

Doublespeak always exists within a broader context. It can only exist where a governed people – a people brought into the kind of financial servitude that is part and parcel of institutionalized negaprocity – are made to voluntarily accept their own chains of servitude.

Having examined, therefore, how modern, effective Governments operate with a considerable degree of inherent contradiction, having seen how benevolent-looking negaprocity increases Government opportunities for those who are able to control it, the role of thermodynamic potential, and the need for the perpetrators of negaprocity to mask their intentions as one increases sectoral distance, what are we left with? More specifically, going back to Sahlins' diagram of anthropological "sectors" and their relationship with reciprocity, what should our new territory look like? How would we describe and define the sectoral areas of the negaciprocal region?

I would propose that our territory would look something like the chart that follows. (You will, by the way, want to mark this page, because you'll be referring back frequently to this chart for the remainder of this chapter.)

If we were to categorize or create gradations of "negaprocity," their visual representations might look something like the sectors in the following chart. The "Negaprocity Zone" (as opposed to Sahlins' "Reciprocity Zone") is first broken down into the Inner Band and the Extreme Negaprocity of the "Outer Band." Following a discussion of each Band, the sectors themselves are defined and their attributes discussed.

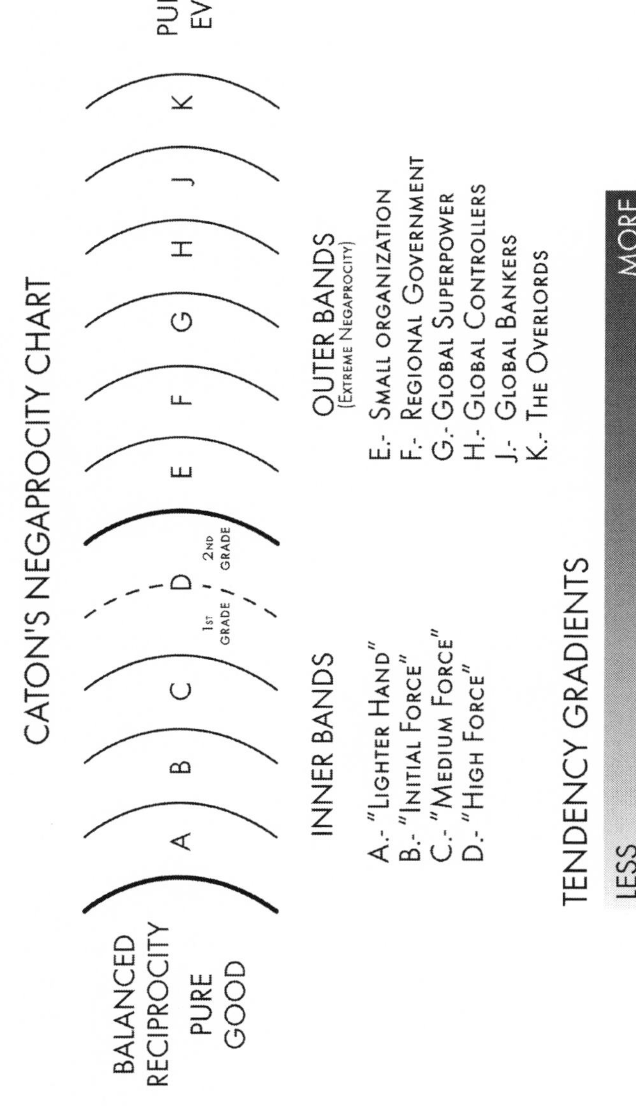

Control/Power Potential
Thermodynamic Potential
"Victim Resistance" Suppression Necessity
Secrecy Requirements
Chaos/Entropy Potential

The Inner Bands

The first four sectors of negaprocity are grouped together in what I call the "Inner Bands." As you would expect, the farther away from Sahlins' levels of "balanced reciprocity" you go, the more negaciprocal conditions become. Moreover, the "Inner Bands" normally involve a low level of organization and very little institutionalization. One might say that the "Inner Bands" principally describe what negaciprocally inclined people ***do***.

The area of "Extreme Negaprocity" that follows defines what these people ***are***: negaprocity is so incorporated into the lives of its perpetrators, "active agents," and the institutions that support their activities – so integral is it to their way of operating – that if you took away its negaciprocal ways, the institutions would become either unrecognizable or would cease to exist.

Those on the receiving end of "active agent" activity on the "Inner Bands" – for whom I use the terms "passive agents" or "victims" interchangeably – tend to be individuals or smaller groups. "Passive agents" within "Extreme Negaprocity" territory tend to be larger groups or constituents. Smaller governing agencies or Governments can exhibit behavior that is typical of activity on the "Inner Bands," but larger, modern, effective Governments find their domain almost exclusively in more negaciprocal territory.

Their very existence requires it.

Sector A

"Lighter Hand" or "Soft" Negaprocity: here negaprocity is used to obtain advantage in transacting, primarily in business affairs. (Outside of global banking, the vast majority of business transactions are either "balanced reciprocity" or "Lighter Hand.") The demeanor of the "active agent" is outwardly friendly, and there are no overt expressions of ill will. Additionally, there is no violence. Any "victim resistance" invoked is usually minimal. Relations between parties – "active" and "victim" –

are generally considered by both parties to be relatively equal. In place of propaganda and related tools of deception, "victim resistance" is usually evoked by sleight of hand or low level trickery. This would incorporate low level fraud. Examples: the used car salesman who sells you a lemon. You could have said no, but you trusted him. You could have said, "Forget it, I don't think your car is worth the price," but you relied on his inaccurate information. Some might say it's your fault because you should have been more careful. You may have been tricked, but you voluntarily made a choice and nobody forced you to do it. You never felt threatened. Gradations within "Lighter Hand" are primarily based on the disparity in value between what the "active agent" gained and the "victim" received. In its early stages, "Lighter Hand" is only a shade away from "generalized reciprocity." Example: let's say you are approached by a rough looking man on the street who tells you he needs a couple of dollars to buy a sandwich. If you feel sorry for him and unthreatened, there is no conveyed threat, and you give the money purely out of generosity, that's "generalized reciprocity." You probably feel you've generated good will, and your good deed or beneficial karma will come back to you. However, if the man's a drunk, pesters you for the money, and you end up giving it to him just to get rid of an annoyance, that's "Lighter Hand."

Sector B

"Initial Force" Negaprocity: still, as in "Lighter Hand," the purpose is usually to obtain advantage in transacting – but more often governmental than business. Here, the potential use of force is implied – conveyed as such by the "active agent" and perceived as such by the "victim." The "implied force" can be physical or non-physical. If physical, the threat is not lethal. This is the first stage of negaprocity where the "victim" feels threatened. Among the indigenous people, this tactic might be used by a belligerent tribe with superior weapons or numbers. All Governments employ "Initial Force," though their institutionalization of it puts them in a much "higher" sector – and we'll get to that in a moment. "Initial Force," for example, is endemic to almost all state revenue collection agencies in the world. Propaganda usage is minimal, if any at all. This form of negaprocity is normally not sustained, and that's because either the "victim" finds a way to disengage from the relationship or circumvent interaction, or the "active agent" takes the relationship to a higher functioning level of negaprocity. There is, however, greater "victim resistance" here, because of the implied potential use of force. Example: the school yard bully who asks you, "Can I have your lunch money?" The question is rhetorical. He can be dangerous. But you weren't threatened in specific terms.

Sector C

"Medium Force" Negaprocity: here, force is more than implied. There is a "quid pro quo" in the transacting – basically, "We either do things my way, or I'll kick your ass." Transactions are often singular events and not of a sustained nature. Example: the school yard bully who tells you, "Give me your lunch money, or I'll give you a black eye." Nonetheless, any threat of violence is non-lethal and exists only as a leverage for negaciprocal transacting. Violence does not yet exist as a source of pleasure for its own sake. Additionally, "Medium Force" may not involve physicality. Many types of blackmail are "Medium Force." Example: a married man goes to a bar and meets an attractive "barfly." They have an affair, and after a short time, the woman threatens to tell his wife if he doesn't pay her. Yup, she's a "Medium Forcer." (I experienced this level of negaprocity throughout my criminal case, beginning with the U.S. Prosecutor's threat that if I didn't agree to his Plea Agreement, which was outrageously bogus, he would imprison my wife and think of charges later, not to mention what he could do to my seven year old son. I took the threats seriously and hid my son in Texas for several months from U.S. authorities. My complaints about the coercive threats to my family and employees, as I detail in Meditopia, are in my court transcripts . . . and made no difference whatsoever to the judge.) "Medium Force" is also the first stage along the path to increased negaprocity that most people would regard as clearly criminal.

Sector D

"High Force" Negaprocity: this is "Medium Force" taken to the next logical level. This is the school yard bully who grows up to be a thug and gets proficient with a gun. His previous threats of, "Give me your lunch money or I'll give you a black eye," have now graduated to, "Give me all your money," which he says while waving that gun. The threat of violence that could include lethality is clear and unmistakable, always on the part of the "active agent" and almost always on the part of the victim. "High Force" would also include torture, rape, and any premeditated acts that involve serious harm or murder to the "victim." The completion of the act of violence takes "high force" to its most serious level. A planned murder that doesn't go as planned doesn't make it "Medium Force." Within the body of criminal law in almost any country, the majority of serious crimes – except for drug crimes, spying and treason, which exist because they involve competing with Government – are acts of "High Force" negaprocity. Within "High Force," I provide delineation between "first grade" and "second grade." The former involves acts of lethal violence to achieve monetary or other resource-given aims. However, "second grade" involves committing violence out of sheer sadistic pleasure – with or without a resource motive. "Second grade – high force" usually involves the possibility of generating thermodynamic potential, i.e. through inflicted fear in a community, etc., that remains unrealized.

Extreme Negaprocity (Outer Bands)

"Extreme negaprocity" is a collective term for the "Outer Bands" of negaciprocal activity. Before defining its sectors and discussing their attributes, let's examine several factors that make Extreme Negaprocity unique.

(1) **The Institutionalization of Negaciprocal Activity.** This involves the creation of cultural constructs, rules, regulations, laws, and narratives that make what normal people consider criminal in the Inner Bands socially acceptable in the Outer. Different organizational structures are able to establish a foothold in the Outer Bands. Organized crime syndicates accomplish this to a limited degree: their sphere of influence is predominantly inside their organization, and to a lesser extent, within the communities in which larger, governmental authorities exert weaker inhibiting countermeasures against their activities. But, truly, the Outer Bands lend themselves primarily to national Government – it is the domain of States – because few other social organizations can secure the kind of thermodynamic potential required to employ and enforce measures against "victim resistance," affect common narratives that a majority of the governed will accept as benign, even beneficent, and achieve the kind of hegemony that can resist pesky competitors. In fact, to any well-established State that is able to quell the dissent of its own people, the only real remaining threats are other Governments – and, of course, certain "acts of God" which Mother Nature will occasionally dispense, and could potentially unseat a Government.

(2) **The Enforcement of Social Stratification and Consolidation of Approved Criminality.** Modern Government is born out of, sustains, and nurtures the polarization of society – at a level and to an extreme that is unheard of among indigenous peoples. People are segregated into those who have influence over Government (i.e., an Elite in the minority) and those who do not (i.e., the governed in the majority) . . . those who have knowledge of the true, inner workings of Government and those who do not . . . those who need protection for their sizeable accumulation of property and those who do not . . . those who, with rare exception, may violate laws without fear of undesirable consequences to achieve their aims and those who may not

. . . those who understand the deliberate contradictions of BCN/ Doublespeak and benefit from it, and the masses who are taught not to know any better. Regardless of BCN rhetoric, effective, modern Governments cannot work to eradicate the boundaries that sustain social injustices and inequities, because those same Governments are its enforcers. If a Government, any Government, works to eradicate a social injustice, it is only acting as a "steam pressure relief valve," an indicator that its internally generated propaganda and the force of the BCN isn't working, or is in need of reinforcement. Governmental apologists work endlessly to convince the Public that they can serve two masters – in fact, this is a fundamental building block of the BCN. Modern Government – as we may know, understand, and experience it after the "professional wrestling mode" button has been put on pause – wouldn't exist without its perpetual support for class stratification.

I readily admit that this simplified explanation takes a world brimming with millions of shades of color and attempts – for the purposes of explanation – to reduce it to black and white. There is no question that among the "have nots" and the "haves" and – to borrow from former U.S. President G.W. Bush – the "have mores," there is further stratification into various hierarchical groupings. However, this initial bifurcation has been delineated by countless previous authors, philosophers, and historians to an unquestionably homogenous degree. You may own a large pastry shop that sells a hundred different confections and fifty different flavors of ice cream, but any one of the pastries is still pastry and any flavor of ice cream is still ice cream.

Social stratification is not weakened by even the best, well-intentioned of Governments. It is strengthened by it. This simple observation provides the backdrop for the instructive, allegorical work of George Orwell. For example, it is singularly the most powerful "take away" imparted by his most famous book, <u>Animal Farm</u>.

(3) **The Emergence of Propaganda and Disinformation.** Upon leaving Sahlins' balanced reciprocity sectors, "victim resistance" arises with the "Initial Force" sector. In the absence of effective countermeasures, it will continue to rise as we increase our "sectoral distance" from reciprocity. In the Outer Bands, effective "resistance" cannot be tolerated. This provides us with an insight into why the mass media of any country tends to side with the prevailing Government's version of events – regardless of how absurd. Government requires a subservient media more than any given people will assert their "right to know the truth". In fact, the BCN is designed to turn off people's desire to question Government. In any struggle to gain the allegiance of the media, it is almost always the prevailing Government that wins over the needs of its own people. This helps explain why mass media in the most outer regions of Extreme Negaprocity – and this has become glaringly obvious in the U.S. – has become laughably irrelevant to the needs of ordinary people. This explains why, with each passing year, their coverage of current events has become ever more superficial, jingoistic, propagandistic and outright fabricated, in many cases.

(4) **Dramatically Increased Thermodynamic Requirements.** Perpetrators in the Inner Bands rarely put significant energy into masking their activities, primarily because they don't have the resources to do so. If they had the resources to do so, they could graduate to Extreme Negaprocity and start their own Government. In Extreme Negaprocity, thermodynamic potential is maximized, but so are energy requirements. It is here that we may confront the "chicken or the egg" riddle: do Governments, residing in Extreme Negaprocity territory, produce big thermodynamic potentials because they have big energy requirements? Or do they have big energy requirements because of what they have to do to produce increased thermal potential? The answer is easier and more obvious than the riddle: both. In the world of negaprocity, modern Governments are the big game hunters; however, their blood sport comes with a price. To stay in business, they have to eat what they kill. We have now touched upon another of Parkinson's truisms: "In modern organizations, expenses tend to rise to meet revenues."

(5) **Evil as A Way of Life.** We began our journey with the purity and innocence of family love – giving freely, joyfully, and affectionately with no thought of return. That purity and love diminishes as we increase sectoral distance from the center of Sahlins' chart. Therefore, it should come as no surprise that corruption, deception, cruelty, and all manner of psychopathic perversion – the attributes and conditions of thought and action that ordinary people would ascribe to evil – will be found flowering with Extreme Negaprocity. Researchers of Government conspiracies are often shocked when they first discover that many of the secret societies and other institutions of high privilege that work behind the scenes to exert their influence inside the world's most powerful Governments are saturated in Luciferian symbolism, blood rituals, animal sacrifices, oaths to serving the dark side of life, etc. In fact, it is often difficult to tell the difference between the "sacraments" of secret societies and those of Satanic worshippers. The difficulty arises from the fact that fundamentally there is no difference. Evil and maximized thermodynamic potential go hand-in-hand. This principle is the basis for the common expression: "Good guys finish last." The cruelest oxymoron ever uttered is "Benign Empire."

(6) **Extreme Negaprocity Tends to Breed More of the Same.** Within the Outer Bands, the more sectoral distance you have, the more you get of everything which negaprocity brings: more thermodynamic potential, greater need to quell potential "victim resistance" and more inherent contradictions produced by the diametrical opposition of the BCN and reality (i.e. Doublespeak). This tendency is what brings the most successful Governments – Empires – to their unplanned deaths: consumed by their ever ascending greed and self-centeredness, nothing is ever enough. Perpetuity is a critical goal and the defining characteristic of well-executed Extreme Negaprocity; and, in fact, some of the most nefarious political institutions in history have lasted for the better part of a thousand years or more – think Roman Empire. Ultimately, however, all Empires are unsustainable. They fall . . . and then survivors are left to begin the race to renew Extreme Negaprocity on a grand scale all over again.

(7) **Additional Energy Inputs Usually Add More Negaprocity in the Outer Bands – Rarely Less.** Sucking the blood out of non-Elites is not the only way that Governments can increase thermodynamic potential. Cutting deeper into the bounty of Nature also has the same effect. Over the past three centuries, for instance, modern civilization has changed its primary energy source from vegetation (i.e. wood) to coal, to petroleum . . . and, until recently, nuclear energy was a strong, rising contender. With each graduation, modern Governments have used that increased potential to foster the severity of their negaprocity – not only towards their fellow man, but towards the world's ecologies and Nature. In the latter case, it is being done with awe-inspiring ferocity, negligence, cruelty, and disregard for future consequence. In Sahlins' study, you often saw tribal chiefs go out of their way to **increase** reciprocity to their people whenever a surplus arose. This is uncommon in the Outer Bands, and when it does occur it is almost always to suppress "victim resistance" – never out of collective kind-heartedness or true charity.

(8) **Institutions in the Outer Bands, With Few Exceptions, Will Always Be Beholden to Banking.** In the modern world, the single, most powerful medium of thermodynamic potential is money. The original, founding patriarch of the Rothschild banking dynasty illustrated this best when he said, "Give me control of a nation's money and I care not who makes its laws."[11] Let's do a quick thought experiment. Which feels like a greater source of thermodynamic potential to you, the systems of taxation levied against the governed – always collectible in the common currency of prevailing Government? Or is it the private banking cartel in charge that prints that money for the cost of ink and paper (or now with a few computer keystrokes) and has been able to use its subservient, sycophant politicians to

[11] Although the earliest attribution of this is said by many to be by Gertrude M. Coogan, Money Creators, (1935). It would be accurate to say that there is nothing in the policies and actions of the House of Rothschild that do not reflect the employment of this principle.

accept that "free money" as its own debt? Who is the Government going to listen to first? You? Or the source of the money?

Let's do another thought experiment. Let's say that you and I are among a group of twenty friends living in a small village. We all have gardens, chickens, and perhaps a cow or two. We are all self-sufficient. When we want different things from each other, we simply barter on mutually agreeable terms. Now let us say that I find a grove of oak trees on my property. They are unique. In fact, no one else has oak trees on their property like mine. One day I propose that the singularly unique acorns that come from these oak trees be used in place of bartering. In fact, I am going to propose to you that when you want to obtain something, you have to use "Caton's acorns" as your currency. I propose creating "laws" that make it "illegal" to use anything other than my acorns to effect your transactions. My laws contain draconian penalties for coming up with anything that could compete with my acorns as an accepted medium of exchange. Most amazingly, I am able to get everyone else to agree to my scheme.

I have just invented money.

When any of the rest of you want something, you must work for it and give up resources to obtain my acorns. When I want something, I just go into my backyard and pick up some acorns – as many as I want. You have to work for your "money," but I don't. I create money from nothing. If you want to "borrow" some of my acorns – which cost me nothing – charging you interest isn't enough. You must hand me title to your possessions as "collateral security" for the privilege of borrowing my nothing.

I realize that this arrangement is so grossly unfair that sooner or later you may wake up to the manner in which I have brilliantly enslaved you. So I get together with "oak masters" in other villages who have been similarly able to enslave **their** people. We create "Governments" to codify the power we have obtained and enforce provisions to keep our scheme in place.

Now, to whom are those Governments going to be beholden? You . . . who were gullible enough to allow yourselves to be so enslaved, giving up your time and your resources for our "acorn nothings," or . . . will those Governments be beholden to us "oak masters" who have proven our ability to lead by the fact that we were able to get people to agree to our scheme? Keep in mind that we can generate as many acorns as we want. The sky's the limit. You cannot.

With our unlimited supply of acorns we can make and break Governments at will. We can use our acorns to buy unlimited weapons and other tools of enforcement . . . and we can find an endless number of people who will go into battle and do whatever we want just to get more acorns. Compared to what we can do . . . what can you do?

Now do you see why moneymakers and Governments have interests that are so aligned? First and foremost, they are both in the Extreme Negaprocity business.

Returning to current affairs, my thought experiment helps make this aspect of negaprocity understandable. With the multi-trillion dollar bailouts of the Bush and Obama Administrations in the U.S., this principle has been hugely self-evident for the whole world to see. If the line separating Government from banking appears to be so paper thin as to be nearly non-existent, it shouldn't. If you have now used your common sense to get the connection, don't browbeat yourself over your frustration in understanding this principle. With this new perception, you are now well ahead of 95% of the non-Elite governed living anywhere in the world today.

You now see the "professional wrestling mode" exhibited in 95% of governed peoples when they lament how the Government is spending its money. A common theme in Government reform movements is getting the Government in question to "spend the people's money more wisely," or "stop wasting taxpayer dollars," etc.

Get over that nonsense.

It isn't your money. It never was and it never will be.

If it was your money, you, too, would be able to manufacture your own "nothings," get people to accept them in exchange for their labor and resources, lend them out and secure claim to real assets, charge people interest on your nothings, and take away people's assets when they found themselves unable to meet your terms. Then and only then could you call it your money.

Non-owners of the money who temporarily possess more of it – whether it be in the form of hard cash or bank account balance – certainly have a wider range of options than people who do not. But it still isn't their money. . . and Governments routinely remind people of this fact through systems of income and inheritance taxation for which the Elite exercise all manner of circumvention.

When Governments shovel billions or trillions of dollars out the back door for their special projects, lining their pockets in the process, they aren't wasting your money. It's their money. When they dilute the currency – which is nothing more than premeditated, low-tech thievery – they aren't taking away your money. It's their money, and they have a right to waste it any way they see fit. You gave them that right when you agreed to accept their nothings as something of value in the first place.

(9) **Extreme Negaprocity is Inherently Anti-Nature.** As discussed elsewhere in this book in more detail, Extreme Negaprocity always lends itself to the defilement of Nature. It is not enough that Governments use intermediary devices and institutions to maximize their thermodynamic activity, or dumb down their citizens. They also extract resources at the highest possible profit, subverting the very processes of Nature.[12] Above all else, ecosystems involve untold layers of reciprocity. Their life and vitality are held together in an enormous web of complex exchange and recycling, involving the unwitting cooperation of hundreds of thousands of species. There is nothing about the workings of Mother Nature that helps advance the cause of Extreme Negaprocity. The good news is that in the ultimate battle

[12] John Locke makes a suberb argument that the act preceeding Government – the "social covenant" wherein people agree to enter into the state of civil society – is itself the abrogation of one's "state of nature." See: J. Budziszewski, Written on the Heart: The Case for Natural Law, (2009), p. 99.

between Government and Mother Nature, negative reciprocity ultimately loses.

(10) **Criminal Conspiracies are Native to Extreme Negaprocity.** You should expect me to say this. It's a rewording of this book's subtitle. But what is a criminal conspiracy and how does it relate to Extreme Negaprocity? Firstly, a criminal conspiracy involves doing things that in the Inner Bands are clearly recognized by ordinary people as criminal – murder, rape, torture, grand theft, etc. – the very things that Governments do routinely. Secondly, conspiracy denotes secrecy and cooperation between perpetrators in such a way that their activities are kept secret from other parties. How on earth can you operate in the realm of Extreme Negaprocity if you aren't committing criminal conspiracies? You can't. It is for this reason that the BCN – at least in the "higher sectors" of the Outer Bands – is so adamant in pushing the "conspiracy theorist" tag on anyone who questions the Government's criminal activities.

(11) **Core versus Periphery Model Germinates.** Not content to parasitically feed off its own people, advanced States in the Outer Band co-opt smaller Governments in Sector E so that the smaller Government ends up giving up valuable resources in exchange for personal enrichment. The short version: "Dear President Traitor: if you will just give us the resource concessions we want, we will be happy to secretly put $20 million in your Swiss bank account. Don't worry about assistance. We'll give you all the help you need to sabotage the interests of your own people." You get the idea. In fact, under the Monroe Doctrine, this approach has been used by the U.S. Government to get ambition-hungry politicians in Latin America to assist in the financial enslavement of their own peoples for nearly 200 years.

By nurturing the "core" (the governed at home) at the expense of the "periphery" (non-citizens in other countries and their lower sector Governments), these bigger, more "effective," more "modern" Governments at a higher sector level can appear to be more reciprocal than they ever would without organized exploitation outside their borders.

This model is hugely important to imperialistic Governments because it allows them to "bring home more bacon" as a "victim resistance" countermeasure. The U.S. has droves of senior citizens, who, because they get social security, Medicare, Medicaid, and a handful of other Government handouts, think that their Government must be just swell. In their self-centeredness, it occurs to few of them what enormous sacrifice the citizens in other countries have to make so that they can have their brief period of luxury. And brief it is, because "entitlement programs," a feature of the U.S. landscape for less than 80 years – the lifespan of just one person – are already bankrupt, measured using accrual accounting.[13] Like all Ponzi schemes, the U.S. entitlement system is collapsing under the weight of its unsustainable tenets. The Core versus Periphery Model is like a cocaine habit. It works quite well when things are in full swing, but things can get messy when the party's over.

Now, having examined some of the characteristics of the Outer Bands, let's define the sectors themselves.

Sector E – Small Organization

This is a smaller organization or national Government that is primarily concerned with its own internal affairs. It can sequester just enough thermodynamic potential and positive effects from its immunosuppressive BCN (i.e. reduced "victim resistance") to keep itself in power and partner effectively with its Elite. At this level, there are no imperial ambitions, no dreams of world conquest, no efforts to influence elections in foreign countries. If there is anything to be found in Government that is positive or life-supporting, it must be found at this level, because it only gets worse from here on.

Now I realize that some people will object to this placement, because the implication of the Chart is that even the "best of Governments," that is to say, Governments who are sincere in

[13] See: https://www.caseyresearch.com/us-government-bankrupt/ and also: https://www.cato.org/publications/policy-analysis/bankrupt-entitlements-federal-budget

taking good care of their citizens – we might say "Governments that truly **want** to be reciprocal with their people" – are worse than "High Force." The unspoken implication is that there is no such thing as "good Government," or that there are no good people working in Government.

Neither assumption is correct, because there must be a distinction between Governments as institutions and the people who work to sustain their functions and fulfill their goals.

First, Governments are distinct entities apart from the politicians who hold office within them. They have properties and privileges which individual people do not possess. For example, presidents of the world's most powerful Governments can commit unbelievably heinous acts under the cover of a "justified war." (We've all heard the expression, "All is fair in love and war.") Yet if a president commits even a single act of murder outside the jurisdiction of his office, he could be held accountable – if only because the cost of inaction, if publicized to enough people in the world community where the original Government does not control the media – would be a threat to the BCN. Such an act would be taking place within the Inner Bands, where such a politician would not find the same level of protection.

Second, any given Government, by definition, has the right – exercised more often than not – to partake in acts that meet or exceed in negaciprocal character those that are routinely found in "High Force." Just because any given Government's inherent "criminal rights" are held at bay for an extended time doesn't take it out of the Outer Bands. If I'm a serial killer, and on a certain day I go out, rape, and murder three women, and then for the next year I behave like a little angel, I am no less a killer. If I attempted to make the claim that I was only 1/365 bad – and 364/365 good – so I should be regarded as far more good than bad, you wouldn't buy that ridiculous argument, now would you? Of course not. Just because I put a moratorium on exercising my dark character doesn't change what I am.

Governments are inherently evil, because they cannot perform the functions that put them into business in the first place unless they **are evil**. Those brave souls who wish to make their

Governments reciprocal – essentially dropping them into the category of "Lighter Hand" – will find themselves prey to one or more other Governments in the Outer Bands who will use their superior thermodynamic potential to co-opt them for their own purposes.

No Government can serve both its own people and an Elite who stands willing, able, and sufficiently resourceful to harvest its thermodynamic potential. In this "tug-of-war" the people usually lose because ordinary people cannot see through the BCN long enough to recognize that Governments are inherently negaciprocal – in the extreme.

Sector F – Regional Government

This is a Government that has secured the achievements of Sector E and can now assume a strong leadership role *regionally*. It may employ more moderate methods of sucking thermodynamic potential off its neighbors, but these activities must be handled delicately, otherwise it risks confrontation with the world hegemons in Sector G. Sector F is where the "core vs. periphery model" of increasing thermodynamic potential first makes its appearance.

Sector G – Global Superpower

This is the euphemism for those rare Governments that can rise to the level of "global superpower." Most Americans are quite proud of the U.S. as the sole, current global superpower – not realizing the enormous toll such an entity exacts on the rest of the world.

Sector H – Global Controllers

These are shell organizations that are global in scope and hold the same, superordinate view of individual Governments that those individual Governments, in turn, hold of their own citizens. These are the true "puppet masters," and the people who run these institutions – which include entities like the IMF (International Monetary Fund), Trilateral Commission, Council on Foreign Relations, and the Bilderbergers – view the entire world as their personal fiefdom. Their function is to make the entities in Sectors E through G do their bidding. The reason they sit farther out in the Outer Bands is that the activities of the entities in Sector H make all Governments more negaciprocal than they would be if left to their own devices. This is particularly true of entities residing in Sectors F and G. Whereas most Governments operate within a specific geographic area, Sector H entities operate as multinationals.

Speaking of multinationals, most large multinational corporations are either Sector G or Sector H players. They earn this privileged placement on our chart because they openly support the criminal activities of Governments and their associated multinational partners in these sectors. They partner with Governments, providing them with financial support – token offerings of our all important "acorn nothings." In exchange, they benefit from favors, contracts, kickbacks, political hits, suppression of competition, freedom from prosecution or mitigation thereof, in connection with their own illegal activities. The enactment of laws supporting their agenda, favorable tax treatment, special loopholes, special considerations related to trade and tariffs, preferable public relations treatment, better media coverage, etc., all serve this purpose. Never forget that the financial backer who pays a hitman is no less guilty of a murder than the person pulling the trigger.

One of the things we see as we proceed from the Inner Bands through the Outer Bands, is increasing levels of secrecy and deviation from the BCN. This is not an accident. True power thrives under the same conditions as mushrooms: they need darkness and live on dung – though in the latter case it is primarily from the detritus that is of their own making. True power abhors transparency and thrives in secrecy, thus making it conspiratorial by its very nature. True power knows no "term limits," as the accumulation of power takes time – measured not in years or generations, but centuries. True power does not subject itself to elections or consent of the governed, but uses Governments as its intermediaries to accomplish its aims. By using Governments as insulation, entire nations may fall and the real power that had been pulling the strings for the entirety of their existence, operating behind drawn curtains, remains untouched. There are entire metaphysical doctrines that are devoted to the dark arts of acquiring and maintaining power.

I use the word "shell" to describe these institutions, because it is the people behind these "front organizations" that call the shots, such that the organizations themselves can be dissolved and replaced by something newer, while still committing itself to the same purpose. The aforementioned multinational organizations have all been created within the past 60 years. Their most influential members belong to families that have been in power for centuries. If you've ever wondered why "bloodlines" are such a recurring theme in the extant literature on those at the highest level of secret societies, now you know why.

Not everyone who participates in the organizations in Sector H is privileged. Many card carrying members of these organizations are highly placed people in the media, business, political and intellectual communities. They serve as window dressing to make Sector H organizations appear more inclusive and egalitarian, but by no means do they call the shots.

Sector J – Global Bankers

There was the temptation to include Global Bankers in Sector H; however, this group possesses a level of power, profit, and privilege that is distinctly higher than that of the "Global Controllers." Those belonging to this sector are exceedingly small: select members of the Rothschilds, the Rockefellers and other similar banking families, many of which can trace their family's involvement in this sector back to at least the 1600s.

We have all heard the Biblical expression, "Money is the root of all evil." Few people really realize how true this expression really is.

Sector K – The Overlords

Also called "The Overlords." In several of his books from the 1990s, British political writer, David Icke, wrote extensively on "reptilian bloodlines" that operate at the pinnacle of the world hierarchical power structure. (He quotes Princess Diana, who, before her assassination, was alleged to have made the comment that "the Queen (Elizabeth) is not human." With the utmost gravitas, Icke has emphasized that the comment was not metaphorical.)[14]

I realize that the whole notion that there could be extraterrestrial mongrels running around, controlling *Homo sapiens* – and through us all other life on this planet – with the same ease and insouciance that cattle ranchers tend to their grass munchers is . . . well . . . a bit of a stretch for some. I must admit that I myself have never, to the best of my knowledge, met a "shape-shifting reptilian," though there are a handful of YouTube video presentations on the subject that I've found more than somewhat compelling. So hold that thought.

And consider the following . . .

Throughout all of recorded history, when conquistadors have wanted to subjugate a people, did they not do so through its apparent leadership? Do not wars end because an armistice is signed with just one or a handful of the representatives of a defeated people? Were not the lands of the American Indians handed over to the U.S. Government because of deals that were crafted with their chiefs? And so, again, a small thought experiment: if there were a race of beings out there who had the potential of treating and managing us in the same manner that we treat our cattle, through whom would they be working? A broad spectrum of society (not supported by the historical record), or as few people as possible at the very summit of a hierarchical power pyramid that they themselves have created and maintained? Would they be operating in the open, so everyone knew what they were doing, or would they be putting a considerable

[14] See: David Icke, The Biggest Secret, (2001), p. 32.

degree of effort into remaining as ***secretive*** as possible?

I would feel so much better believing that Icke's proposition is either creative fiction or just lunacy – except that I am then left with an intractable intellectual splinter in my brain, an itch that won't go away, one that begs the question: "If Icke is wrong, then why does everything in the world behave as if he's right?" Or, going one step farther: "If Icke is wrong, why can't I come up with a better explanation or model, taking into account the hundreds of thousands of pieces of information I've amassed that would explain why the world is so perennially screwed up, getting more screwed up every day, with no end to the insanity in sight?"

So that we can move on – because I'll return to this subject later – let us forget Icke for a moment and assume that Sector J is just a theoretical concept. Even Albert Einstein, by his own admission, and today's most authoritative physicists, could not and cannot comprehend a force as ever-present as gravity. Still, it doesn't prevent them from working around their ignorance and telling us what they understand about our physical universe. So for now we'll do likewise.

I believe everyone could agree on this: if there were such a thing as inter-dimensional beings, demonic entities, or extraterrestrials who wished to use this planet to extract energy or resources, this is the sector in which they would be operating: above that of the human global controllers and the global bankers.

It is important to emphasize at this point that the negaciprocal "sectors" within Caton's Negaprocity Chart are no more strict and unyielding than they are in Sahlins' Reciprocity Zone. Like any model, there are exceptions. As in the case with most illustrative tools, the most valuable thing to be derived from my chart is an understanding of the underlying principles and how they fundamentally command human behavior, more times than not, subverting intentions and creating end results which are undesirable, self-reinforcing, and often irreversible.

Tendency Gradients

At the bottom of my Negaprocity Chart, you will notice a "Tendency Gradient" bar that indicates the growth of certain characteristics as one proceeds to the right, away from the Reciprocity Zone. The "Tendency Gradient" bar characteristics are explained in greater detail below.

Control/Power Potential

There are different kinds of power. There is the power to bring about good in the world, reciprocity – which incorporates charity, empathy, and love – and then there is the power to control people and co-opt their resources which is, by definition, negaciprocal. By any measure that normal people use to compare "good" versus "evil" – irrespective of religious or cultural background – the road from reciprocity to negaprocity is a road that takes one from good to evil.

The greater the negaprocity, the greater the power to control, the greater the evil.

Thermodynamic Potential

As we've discussed elsewhere, increased thermodynamic potential results from increased negaprocity.

"Victim Resistance" Suppression Necessity

As negaprocity increases, accompanied by accumulated thermodynamic potential, so does resistance from the receiving end of the negaciprocal actions. If we find ourselves the victim of "Lighter Hand," we may be tempted to write it off to bad luck or our own gullibility. However, if we're still alive, we are not apt to take kindly to being victimized by "High Force."

The active agents of Extreme Negaprocity understand this better than anyone. This is why the High Hand of the world's most effective, modern Governments are knee-deep in every conceivable program and activity imaginable to control the minds of the governed – through media propaganda, the maintenance of the BCN, carefully controlled educational systems, fluoridated water, salt and toothpaste,[15] debilitating food additives, harmful pharmaceutical drugs, etc. The goal of negaprocity, particularly in the Outer Bands, is to maximize the gains of thermodynamic potential while minimizing the cost of suppressing victim resistance. Such suppression is truly effective only when those victimized have been made to accept their lot. (In the next section, we will touch upon the "intermediaries" that are used as agents to quell victim resistance.)

Suffice it for now to say that the more that "active agents" victimize their targeted group, the more likely it is that victims are to object to their victimization. This very simple fact is the basis for suppressing victim resistance.

Secrecy Requirements

In order to function optimally, every sector in the Negaprocity Zone requires some degree of secrecy, but the need for secrecy increases with sectoral distance. Parallel to this is the paucity of common knowledge about the activities within a sector as we increase sectoral distance. Everyone is aware of most of the particulars concerning what governs conditions in the Inner Bands. The vast majority of people are clueless as to the inner workings in the Outer Bands, and this ignorance becomes more pronounced with yet more distance, until you get to Sector K, where mankind, as a species, is almost totally ignorant.

[15] See the following regarding fluoride: https://www.globalhealingcenter.com/natural-health/how-safe-is-fluoride/; http://www.mbschachter.com/dangers_of_fluoride_and_fluorida.htm; https://www.naturalnews.com/033919_fluoride_infant_health.html
Also see, in relation to "halogen displacement": http://www.altcancer.net/lugols.htm

Chaos/Entropy Potential

Every ecological system on this planet survives through the "give and take" – the reciprocity – of countless life forms and self-nourishing systems. Life itself is an act of defiance against The Law of Entropy. We are creatures of "negative entropy," creating order and structure in a closed system where, left to its own devices, the system breeds disorder and chaos.

Life requires energy to maintain its order, structure, and self-perpetuating processes. Negaprocity is a thief that takes the energy and life force out of its environment, thereby accelerating chaos and destroying its environment. This helps explain why our planet is in such horrific shape today . . . and why we are having our Holocene Extinction Event.[16]

The more negaprocity, the more entropy, the more chaos.

There is no such thing as "order out of chaos" – a 33rd degree Masonic motto – in the world of negaprocity. To declare that there is, is just more Doublespeak. Negaprocity only generates "chaos out of order."

A good example of this can be found in so many of the man-made deserts we have today around the world. The Sahara Desert, for example, used to be a verdant jungle teeming with life. It remained this way through millions of years of advanced humanoid life. Today it is a botanical black hole, a dead zone that stands as evidence of man's negaciprocal activities going back thousands of years ago.[17] When man finished sucking the life out of North Africa, he just moved on to greener pastures. What we will do when we have allowed the Overlords to help us turn the rest of our planet into a Sahara?

Where will we go then?

[16] See: Elizabeth Kolbert, The Sixth Extinction: An Unnatural History, (2015).

[17] See: Steve Taylor, The Fall, (2005), p. 3-4.; and Chapter 2 "The Pre-Fall Era", p. 29-49.

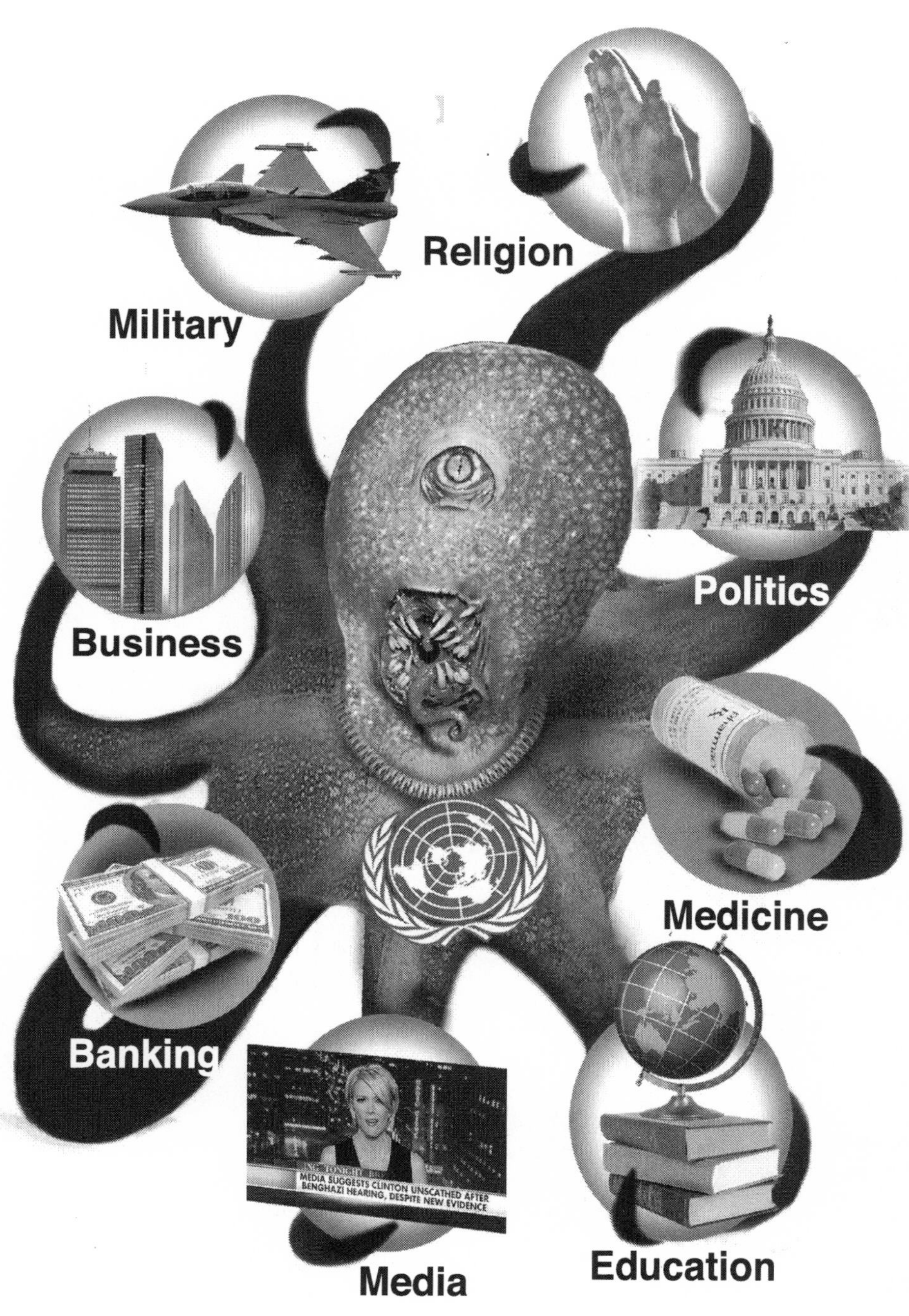
Religion
Military
Business
Politics
Medicine
Banking
MEDIA SUGGESTS CLINTON UNSCATHED AFTER
BENGHAZI HEARING, DESPITE NEW EVIDENCE
Media
Education

Chapter 3

It Is the Nature Of Governments, As Creatures Of Extreme Negaprocity, To Create And Nurture Systems Of "Intermediaryism"[1] That Extend And Preserve Their Negaciprocal Activities

When Jerry Mander wrote The Four Arguments for the Elimination of Television in 1975, his first argument was that television was creating an "intermediary" world where people were divorced from their own experience of reality.[2] Having been near the pinnacle of the television advertising business for years, he could see, first-hand, how television allowed vested interests to create realities that distorted, subverted, and misdirected not only people's own personal interests, but how it disconnected them from any meaningful interaction with the natural world around them. He was able to see how television was being used to program people in insidious ways.

Television, however, is only one artifact of intermediary subversion that saturates the landscape of modern life. The arguments that Mander made could well be applied to a host of technological gadgets and devices. If Thoreau's assessment of modern technology has any validity, that we have become "tools of our tools," its role can only attain true meaning with an understanding of the intent of the tools' designers and those who can subsequently control their uses. All tools are created with purpose – the obvious, the not so obvious, that which is inherently unchangeable, and that which can be co-opted to serve an unseen agenda.[3]

[1] Although not in the dictionary, I use "intermediarysm" to describe systems of intermediary entities.

[2] See Jerry Mander, Four Arguments for the Elimination of Television, (1978); p. 53-112.

[3] See Neil Postman, Technopoly: The Surrender of Culture to Technology, (1993). The entirety of Chapter 1, "The Judgment of Thamus," deals with precisely this point.

Since Government itself is a parasitic intermediary in the lives of its people, (we have only to look at how well the Internet has operated with little to no governmental intervention to see what is possible when you put an end to all the bloodsucking), it only makes sense that the tools it creates or supports would uphold its own nature and further its own aims.

Likewise, it only makes sense that Government would work to suppress, eradicate, or subversively co-opt the tools which people create that are contrary to its aims, reduce its thermodynamic potential, or do not lend themselves to co-optation. Co-optation is indispensable to any modern, effective Government, for power can only be secure on the grand, political chessboard when the hand that moves the white pieces and the hand that moves the black pieces, is the same hand.

Uncertainty is anathema to power, and you can never eliminate uncertainty unless you control both sides to any given conflict. To operate without this understanding and to govern without the exercise of its philosophy is to operate as a truly lesser power. This is really quite obvious to those students of history who have taken the time to study how often the world's banking Elite have funded both sides of major military confrontations. If you're sitting at the higher echelons of the world's banking establishment and you have the power to produce money from nothing, while turning politicians into traitors to the very people they "serve" by getting them to accept that money as their own debt – and there's another truism that escapes most people's attention or comprehension – it would really be quite foolish not to fund "both sides," as discussed in the earlier chessboard metaphor. Please.

Let's be consistent here: "Treason is Patriotism."

Aside from the elements of intermediaryism that reside in the field of obstetrics and pediatrics – which I'll set aside for now because we'll get to organized medicine later – the first and most significant interaction that most people have with intermediaryism is in the area of modern education. The benign common narrative as it pertains to education in Western civilization is that it provides the building blocks for the individual's intellectual growth, integration into society, and personal advancement.

On the surface of things, modern education appears to provide all those things. Were modern education solely devoted to these aims, we would have little to discuss here, but it isn't. You get a sense of education as a tool with both a seen and an unseen purpose if you've ever encountered the vitriolic attitude that is directed towards homeschooling by major Governments[4]. Interestingly, those homeschooling students who are encouraged to diligently adhere to an approved regimen consistently do better than their counterparts in either the public or private school sector in survey after survey. Moreover, the resistance to homeschooling can hardly be attributed to economics because parents who opt to take this educational course of action bear significant costs that thereby relieve the State. So why such resistance? Well, there are a number of reasons, really, and every one of them are integrally linked to Government's commitment to intermediaryism.

First and foremost – and I make this point throughout Meditopia[5] – it is a Government's primary objective, and this is true of any Government, to make its people believe that it needs them. Government is a huge cost – and given enough time, an insurmountable burden to its people. If you can't sustain the illusion that you are indispensible, history has shown us repeatedly that common people will often find a way to communicate that you're not a very clever parasite. Such sentiments have acted as the cornerstone for popular uprisings throughout the modern era. People can survive just fine without Government. My indigenous friends in the Ecuadorean Amazon live very happily, work

[4] See: https://billmuehlenberg.com/2010/12/03/the-secular-state%E2%80%99s-homeschooling-crackdown/. Additionally, those seeking a more panoramic view of how formal education has degraded into pathetic, mind-numbing indoctrination should review the following, written by John Taylor Gatto: Weapons of Mass Instruction: A Schoolteacher's Journey Through the Dark World of Compulsory Schooling, (2010); see also: Katharine Washburn and John Thorton, Dumbing Down: Essays on the Strip Mining of American Culture, (1997), and my personal favorite, which although, once again, the focus is on developments in the U.S., notes educational developments that are occurring globally: Charlotte Thomson Iserbyt, The Deliberate Dumbing Down of America, (2011).

[5] Again, see www.meditopia.org

no more than two to three hours per day (a fact of indigenous life that Marshall Sahlins superbly documented), and live with only the most modest reminders that a national Government or authoritarian entity is even in existence.

Premise On The Role Of Government In Education

Because the BCN is a critical component of the sustained propaganda that disarms the political immune system of the masses, all successful Governments must, by necessity, intervene in the educational system of the society over which they rule, and strive to marginalize critical, independent thinking. Because personal success in life rarely grows out of a culture of strict conformity, most Government-backed educational endeavors must work at odds with their own stated objectives.

The initial step into intermediaryism begins with Government as an artificial insertion into Man's relationship with Nature. He can live without the former. He cannot live without the latter. Because little thought is required to bring this reality into focus, Governments work overtime to prove that their many self-serving activities are most needful. We're back to the rapist who would really, really be happy if you'd just acknowledge that his violation of you is for your own good, if you'd only be gullible enough to acknowledge it. Wouldn't it be wonderful if your rapist could educate you from an early age to accept a version of reality that is as rife with as many artificial constructs as is necessary to elevate his interests over your own? What could possibly be more important to any parasitic organism than to make the host believe that his activities were innocuous, needful, and mutually beneficial? Is it reasonable to expect that a Government could ever do this without controlling the educational process of the children over whom it governs? How could you ever produce an optimal outcome and cloak your real intentions unless you made the process as uniform and homogenous as possible? How could you ever make artificial consensus a substitute for direct knowledge unless you could firmly control education?

The answers to these questions are self-evident, and it appears that few people ever take the time to consider the reality or its implications. One thing that is clear, however, is that the effort doesn't work as well if people are able to "opt out," which is why homeschoolers, particularly in the U.S., are made to look like oddballs, and their parents, dysfunctional social misfits.

The "Bearing vs. Heading" Premise On Sustaining Legitimacy In Government

Because the BCN must stand in opposition to the Government's true intentions, objectives, and, in fact, its very reason for being, Governments must always – above all other commitments – expend energy to sustain their "legitimacy."

The second reason Governments resist independence in the educational process is that mass participation confers its own degree of **legitimacy**.[6] After all, you couldn't possibly get the vast majority of people in any given country to agree to accept a common narrative as their own if it weren't chockful of painfully contradictory Doublespeak, now could you? If your goal is to suppress independence of thought, which is a necessity, and to foster conformity of belief, could you ever hope to achieve this aim if you couldn't make ***any*** clarity of thought that resists that common narrative appear like a social aberration? Of course not.

The third reason is that a Government that cannot artificially insert itself into the relationship between parents and their own children risks being viewed as impotent. Part of being legitimate, as a Government, is the ability to make ordinary people

[6] See: Joseph Tainter, The Collapse of Complex Societies, (1990). "Legitimacy is a recurrent factor in the modern study of the nature of complex societies, and is pertinent to understanding their collapse." Throughout Tainter's study, the need of the State to appear "legitimate" is a recurrent theme.

believe it deserves to be in charge. Mass education, irrespective of any of its other supposed attributes, is a demonstration of both power and mass acceptance of a Government's legitimacy. Replacing the "guild system" of the Middle Ages – where apprentices learned from aging journeymen how to perfect their craft – was not an improvement to education, it was an improvement to the art of Government control.

Fourthly, Government-approved mass education lends itself to the creation of a professional corps of teachers and administrators who are themselves kept in line with the common narrative, with sanctions, threats, loss of tenure, etc., available as remedial tools for those who can't quite seem to stay in line. Movements like homeschooling threaten their legitimacy, because most parents would never reject Government-approved education unless they felt it was inadequate, substandard, replaceable, unnecessary, or a combination of these – none of which help affirm legitimacy.

Fifthly, independence in education is, in and of itself, a rejection of intermediaryism as a practice and a concept. If you can't trust your Government to be competent in the education of small children, what else can you not trust it to do effectively? This is yet another threat to legitimacy.

Before we leave education to consider other examples of Government's inherent commitment to intermediaryism, I feel an example of the disastrous effects of an undeserved embrace of the benign common narrative is in order, because without it, some readers will feel that I have too harshly – and without justification – tarnished the "accomplishments" of modern, Western education.

In the first chapter, I mentioned my odyssey in uncovering the suppression of a cancer cure discovered in 1858 that I myself used to cure thousands of people of cancer over a twenty year period. (It is the subject of chapters one and two of Meditopia.)

Throughout the entirety of my formal education from the very beginnings, and all through college, I lived with a common narrative that chemotherapy, radiation, and radical surgery were the most proven therapies in the treatment of cancer – blinded to the reality that collectively they are among the greatest killers in the Western world. (Strangely, I had a beloved paternal great-grandmother who died of cancer at 76, as did her ten other siblings – every one of them – and yet I have encountered peoples in the Amazon who have no word in their language for cancer because so few, if anybody at all, ever get it . . . in any of its many familiar forms in the West.)

So adamant are Western Governments in their commitment to this shameful lie that is heavily reinforced by educational systems worldwide and Elite lackeys in the mainstream as it relates to "conventional cancer treatment," that they will do anything to prevent ordinary people from being any wiser. As I demonstrate in Chapter 4 of Meditopia,[7] it really is astonishing how many truly effective cancer cures there are, if you take a few years of your life to investigate them. In my own case – as I detailed in this book's Introduction – I was kidnapped by U.S. officials in Ecuador in 2009 following a successful outcome in my extradition hearing that the U.S. Government didn't like. It was their second such illegal kidnapping attempt which, this time, was successful, but only after I was placed on the Interpol "Red List" in early 2009 as one of the world's most wanted fugitives and labeled as a "cancer quack." Never mind that nothing in my previous paperwork with the U.S. Government or in any that followed said anything about being a "cancer quack."

Never mind that I stated clearly on the record that the only reason I signed a "plea agreement" was to protect my wife, my son, and my employees.[8] Amazingly, nothing appeared to irri-

[7] See: http://meditopia.org/chap4.htm

[8] See **www.meditopia.org/chap3-1.htm**; cites the official plea hearing transcript, p. 5, L. 22-25. When asked by the U.S. Federal Judge in my criminal case to "explain (to me) in your own words what it is that you're here to do today," rather than confess that I was there to sign a plea agreement because I had done something wrong, I replied, "I'm here to enter pleas to protect my wife and my employees and others." I simply refused to go through the plea agreement process without stating on the record in clear and unmistakeable language that I was being coerced into admitting things that were false. I even went so far as to tell the judge (on the record) that: "If this [plea agreement] document said I must serve five years in prison **because I improperly emptied a kitty litter box**, I would be forced to sign that. I don't really have a choice in the matter . . . What this [plea agreement] says [is], it doesn't matter whether it's true or not, I have to sign it." Under Footnotes: http://www.altcancer.net/ashwin/ashw0908.htm. For reasons that this book makes abundantly clear, the judge had no problem with this. For as any U.S. Federal Judge who will set aside their "God complex" long enough to display any

tate my sentencing judge more during my hearings in 2010 than the hundreds of letters of support which had been sent to him justifying the legitimacy of my work.[9]

Contrary to the U.S. version of my case, I never ran "from the law" . . . only from the law*less*.

Returning to the mendacity at hand, just how would you quantify the success of today's most powerful Governments in getting people to believe that highly expensive forms of cancer therapy that have ridiculously low rates of success when compared to inexpensive, proven, natural alternatives are better for you? I'd say they're pretty darn successful. In fact, going back to our rapist metaphor, I would say that they have achieved the equivalent of getting women everywhere to say, "I know now that rape is good for me. I can't thank you enough for choosing me to be your victim. And what's more, you can charge me and my health insurance company whatever you want . . . $50,000 . . . $100,000, because I trust you to do the right thing. Women everywhere should know how good it feels to be raped and have to pay their life's savings to experience the privilege of being chosen." More Doublespeak: Education is stupidity. Iatrogenic murder is responsible health care.

I understand that I ruffle a lot of feathers in the orthodox medical community when I bring up this subject, but, honestly, I can't think of a better example to show how stupid people can be made to be, how disastrous it is to trust Government and not think for yourself, and how easily your own interest can be subordinated to corporate pickpockets who could never get away with as much as they do without Government intervention. It's been turning my stomach for nearly a quarter century.

If ordinary people would believe their murderous lies when it comes to Government-approved cancer therapy, is there anything too ludicrous that ordinary people cannot be made to accept who are gullible enough to believe that Governments have their interest at heart and are not acting with Extreme Negaprocity?

modicum of candor will admit, they're in the coercion business.

[9] See: http://www.meditopia.org/s/03-17-10-Caton.pdf – p. 6

What is at stake in this example is your very life. You will end up in a state of considerable pain and debilitation if you make the wrong therapeutic choice, and quite often the loss of your life's savings. If you can be made to voluntarily agree that all of this is in your best interest, if your Government can turn your brain into such a pathetic state of wobbling jello, if it can get you to agree to something that mind-numbingly ridiculous, what can't it get you to do? Can you begin to understand how Government officials behave one way in front of the camera, but behind the scenes loathe you for your very gullibility which they themselves have cultivated while they laugh all the way to the bank?

I have to wonder, even as I write this, if the consequences I'm going to face for writing this book are even worth it. In fact, while I was working on Meditopia in 2006 I happened to have a private phone conversation with author Rodney Stich, author of Defrauding America,[10] and after describing the work I was doing, the conversation proceeded something like this:

"Why would you want to author something like that?" he asked.

"Excuse me? . . . I don't know what you mean," I responded, somewhat taken aback.

"I've heard what you have to say and I understand what you're trying to do, but listen to me, because I'm in my 80s and I've been doing this a lot longer than you have. (Rodney has authored over a dozen books on U.S. Government corruption since his first exposé, Unfriendly Skies).[11] If you write about the corruption in the orthodox medical field using the kind of information you've described – and, hell, who doesn't already know that medicine is all about the money? – you're going to create a hellstorm for you and your family . . . and whose life are you going to really change?"

"Well, you have to make an effort somehow," I shot back as I struggled for a sensible reply. "Look, **you** did!"

"Listen, Greg . . . Listen to someone who's been fighting

[10] See: Rodney Stich, Defrauding America, (1994).

[11] See: Rodney Stich, Unfriendly Skies : Saga of Corruption, (1990).

this battle since the 70s. The people who would be inclined to read your book already know what's going on and are just looking to reconfirm things they already know. But those who really need the information, the people you really want to reach and really need to know what you have to say, they're not going to read your book or listen to your message. I wish I could give you positive encouragement. There's a risk/reward formula when you get tangled up in this whistleblower business, and from what I'm hearing, you've already gotten a taste for how weighty the risk side is. Don't do this. That's the best advice I can give you. It really is. Just don't do it."

This wasn't advice I was expecting to hear. Rodney's books, especially Defrauding America, have been widely quoted by other authors, and from the sheer volume of his work (which takes up over a linear foot on a shelf in my own library), I would have expected an entirely different kind of feedback.

I interject this story here because I'm trying to convey the gravity of what's being discussed. Alan Watts used to say that "every concept has its degrees of intensity." I would have added that certain concepts cover a much broader range of intensity than others. We live in a time when it's dangerous to speak Truth of any real consequence. I'll give you two examples – brief, contemporary, and typical – that come to mind before continuing with our discussion of intermediaryism, and both of them involve authors who used to work for the CIA.

The first is Chalmers Johnson, who closed out his book, Nemesis: The Last Days of the American Republic (2006), by reminding his readers how dangerous it was for him to be writing on such sensitive subjects.[12] The other is a story told by Derrick Jensen in A Language Older Than Words. At the end of a lecture about various nefarious activities he observed while a CIA station chief, John Stockman was approached by Jensen, who asked him bluntly, "Why aren't you dead yet?" To which

[12] Chalmers Johnson's closing paragraph in Nemesis: The Last Days of the American Republic, (2008), reads, in part, thusly: "Ozaki tried to warn his own Government about its misguided ventures. For his troubles he was hanged as a traitor by the Japanese Government . . . I hope not to meet a similar fate . . ."

Stockman replied, "Because they're still winning."[13]

Apologists for this unholy alliance between modern Government and modern education will be quick to bring out the talking points as to its many supposed accomplishments: higher literacy rates, its role in advancing a technological society, its superior performance when compared to homeschooling, where a well-developed curriculum is not adhered to, in which case the practice degrades into its own form of truancy, etc.

Moreover, I should add that my position does not embrace the notion that modern education doesn't have any value. It is simply an inferior one, based on deliberate ill intent. Any system or practice must always be judged on the basis of its designer's intent. As a close friend of mine in Montana loves to say: "Never forget that rat poison is 98% 'good food' . . . it's the 2% that'll kill ya." It doesn't matter that 98% of what's in rat poison won't hurt you or the rats. That's just the carrier that's necessary to get the job done. The real intent behind why the rat poison is produced in the first place can be found in the 2% – not the 98% "good food." This concept is not foreign to those who have studied the science of political propaganda as it is now practiced throughout Governments in the Western world. In that political discipline it is well understood that their 95% "good food" is essential to make the source believable, so that the 5% "payload" can be delivered to the audience and made palatable and acceptable.

I came to appreciate the real effects of that 2% when reading Elements of General History: Ancient and Modern, written by a Professor Alexander Frazier in 1837.[14] This comprehensive history text was written for twelve-year olds, before the rise of modern education, before the establishment of a professional teaching corps, before the U.S. Federal Government had acquired the wherewithal to be the intermediary leviathan in educational matters that it is today. Back in those days, children were usually sent to "little red schoolhouses" where it was not uncommon to have children aged 5 to 14, all sitting in the same

[13] See: Derrick Jensen, A Language Older Than Words, (2004).

[14] See: Alexander Fraser Tytler, Elements of General History: Ancient and Modern, (1837).

room. It wasn't a superior educational setting, but the intent was on learning, and we can see the result of that intent when studying the textbooks of the day. You can gauge the extent of the "dumbing down" just by comparing textbooks of early 1800s with those students use today.

Yes, producing simpletons is superior education.
For Government.
Knowledge is ignorance.

Similarly, I began collecting old newspapers, some going back to the 1600s, when I was in my 20s. A friend of mine, Walter Day,[15] had a business where he purchased tons of discarded newspapers from libraries that were throwing them out and converting large portions of their older periodicals to microfiche. He had so many newspapers in the early 1980s that he created a sideline where if you gave him the birthday of a loved one, he would send you a copy of a newspaper that was published on the same day and year.

Older newspapers in the U.S., particularly those printed before the Civil War, are notable for their paucity of halftones and drawings. It isn't that lithographers of that era didn't know how to produce them, it was just considered a waste of valuable space. The English language of the common man, unpolluted by modern education, was far richer, the expression of abstract concepts far deeper, and the sentence structures of the day more demanding – from today's "dumbed down" perspective. As Max Mueller, the famous nineteenth century linguist has noted, the relationship between language and intellect is much like a "hand and glove" fit.[16] You will not see devolution of the one without finding it reflected in the other. On that basis alone, I have been amazed, even within the span of my own life, how much the use of the English language has deteriorated into ever deeper levels

[15] A man of diverse entrepreneurial talents, Walter Day's biography, like my own, can be viewed on Wikipedia. In both cases, the text hardly reflects, with any degree of accuracy, the lives or accomplishments of the subject.

[16] See: G.J. Caton, Lumen: Food for a New Age, (1988), p. 139-141.

of kindergarten simplicity.[17]

Frazier's textbook is a good example. It reads with a complexity of thought, a literary richness, such that undergraduate college students in the U.S. today would have a difficult time comprehending the text. Today's kids have been so "dumbed down" that most college students are not able to readily grasp the concepts that their grade school counterparts – children half their age – could intellectually digest just 200 years prior.

Educational delinquency is educational progress. More Doublespeak. And who do you think benefits from this?

In discussing education, we now have a template for covering other facets of intermediaryism and we now have some tools to enrich our exploration. Since Chapter 1 introduced orthodox modern medicine as the entry point for my own "enlightenment," let's take what we learned from our discussion of modern education and apply it to today's global system of Western medicine.

Premise On The Role Of Government In Medicine

Those systems of health care or practiced medicine which receive the imprimatur of Government will gravitate to the same operating conditions that sustain the Government. Thus, the defining character of orthodox medicine must be psychopathic if it is to sustain its orthodox status – otherwise, it stands to be replaced by an alternative system which is yet more negaciprocal. Since human bodies are artifacts of Nature, not technology, and the most beneficial treatment methods and modalities are those that work in accord with Nature – not artificial, more profitable, man-made systems that subvert Nature – the prevailing ortho-

[17] My U.S. federal prison experience, wherein a large percentage of my fellow inmates were educated and professional white-collar workers, was quite telling. Even among the well educated, proper use of English grammar, syntax, and spelling was greatly diminished. The command of English by prison officials was no better. At the prison facility for Federal inmates in Breaux Bridge, Louisiana, I had to identify the property in my possession as I left. At the top of the list was the following phrase, printed by the sheriff in charge, wherein he described my legal documents thusly: "ligel pappirs."

dox medical model can never escape the propensity to oppose healing approaches that ***actually work****.*

I have been an eyewitness to the heart-wrenching and often fatal effects of iatrogenesis (i.e. death by doctoring) my entire life.

Both my mother and a first cousin were killed off by relatively brief exposure to the painkiller Oxycontin, taken over a mere span of several weeks.

I had just one uncle, Jack, and he died as a result of massive, expensive surgical invention on what should have been an easy to treat cancer.

Another couple to whom I'm related had an experience that's pertinent here. The husband had esophageal cancer and his wife had brain cancer. Both of them cured themselves of their advanced cancers over ten years ago using the kind of alternative cancer remedies that I have been talking about for decades. Their son, however, was not so lucky. He is a walking, breathing vegetable. Today he is twenty-five years old, and he can't talk, isn't potty trained, and will never function at a level of human development that is attained by normal three year olds. He wasn't born that way. Instead, he – along with hundreds of thousands of other children who took mercury-laced RPM vaccinations in the early 1990s – was made that way . . . made that way by a pharmaceutical company that is protected from litigation by paid-off U.S. politicians . . . made that way by a system which must, by its very nature, plant the seeds of disease with ever more audacity and viciousness if it is ever to fulfill its higher thermodynamic potential . . . made that way by a Government that will not and cannot co-exist with its governed without manifesting its negaciprocal tendencies in everything it does. In all fairness, this young man has a level of severe autism that is worse than most, but he belongs to the same group of children who are victims of the same vaccination epidemic, a condition so recently manifest that it wasn't even discovered until 1943.[18]

My paternal grandfather, Jesse, died in 1999 when he was

[18] See: Neil Z. Miller, Vaccines: Are They Really Safe & Effective?, (2015).

90. He was in good health and could easily have lived another ten years if his doctor hadn't put him on heart medication that caused massive kidney damage. He died not long after being put on dialysis. He was married three times in his life, outliving his first two wives: Angelique (my biological grandmother), and Florence, both of whom died at relatively early ages from faulty doctoring.

I have to hand it to these Mengelian monsters in the Medical Industrial Complex. They've nearly killed off or incapacitated my entire family – charging us a fortune for that privilege. And yet, my family is by no means exceptional.

Today, there are hundreds of exposé books on the market which lament the parallels between orthodox medicine and organized crime. The difference between any of those books and this book is that I'm not here to argue for reform. This book isn't about reform – because the inconvenient truth is that the system is not reformable. Effective health care that cures people of their ailments, without toxic side effects, without extortionary pricing models, without huge profits to pay off politicians and bureaucrats who are willing, for a price, to suppress and criminalize effective competition, can never compete with a system that is adept at Extreme Negaprocity.

With all the documentation I can present concerning my own U.S. criminal case, I can prove that I am just one example – but a salient one – that mirrors how people are treated who expose the ruling Elite's tortured lies.

As I make clear in Chapter 4 of Meditopia, health care doesn't cost anything among indigenous peoples. It's covered within layers of "general reciprocity" that exist within the village life sector. In our market economy, reserves of thermodynamic potential are created within the medical community through its own system of "value added" services.

Now in manufacturing, you create more profit from the manipulating of various commodities and low-value inputs by making more complicated products that are further removed from their natural state. I mention this here because it's important to understand that even the steps an entrepreneur goes through to inject value-added features into his product is a form of intermediaryism. And this in itself tells us why the forces of modernity, enforced through the mechanisms of modern Government, are so viciously "anti-Nature." Mother Nature simply doesn't provide the artificial platforms from which artificial profits can be secured and maintained. Whereas Nature employs countless systems of interspecies reciprocity to feed the innumerable ecosystems that make for a healthy planet, it is only in the realms of Extreme Negaprocity that maximum profits can be found and held.

This is why we have vaccinations that are debilitating by design. This is why we have cancer procedures that cause more harm than the cancer itself. This is why I have had innumerable discussions with doctors who privately revealed to me that they were using my products to treat their own family, but that they dare not use these same products on their own patients, for fear of losing their license to practice medicine.

In the early 2000s I began to receive vehement correspondence from orthodox physicians, objecting to my strong language when discussing the nature of medical orthodoxy.

Not all physicians take this position, and, in fact, one of the best books on this subject, Doctors Are More Harmful Than Germs, is written by a medical doctor, Harvey Bigelsen.[19]

However, these doctors saw my commentaries as an attack on their profession. They took it personally, and although I did my best to explain the difference between the inner dynamics of medicine and the intentions of individual providers, I realized that I had yet to find a metaphor that would more perfectly explain my position.

I found that metaphor in one of the pillars of business administration, because – first and foremost – medicine is a business. I knew I would never find an orthodox apologist who would attempt to argue that point. What follows below is an article I wrote in August, 2009, for "The Ashwin," a periodic,

[19] See: Harvey Bigelsen M.D., Doctors Are More Harmful Than Germs, (2011). The author of this book discusses the fact that moderm medicine has not cured one single chronic disease and that surgery is grossly overprescribed.

online newsletter for Alpha Omega Labs. This happened just a couple of months before I was kidnapped in Ecuador. The purpose of this article was to help even the uninitiated understand why modern medicine is not reformable. It has to do with a simple observation concerning the light bulb, planned obsolescence, and what it tells us about that most twisted of intermediaryisms, Modern Medicine.

I present the article below in full, beginning with the previous graphic header and two quotes, followed by the core of the article:[20]

> "The people who run these corporations
> know exactly what they're doing
> They know they're killing people . . .
> They know they're lying,
> And they know they're making a lot of money in the process."

Derrick Jensen

" . . . when you see that money is flowing to those who deal, not in goods, but in favors – when you see that men get richer by graft and pull than by work, and your laws don't protect you against them, but protect them against you – when you see corruption being rewarded and honesty becoming a self-sacrifice – **you may know that your society is doomed.**"

Ayn Rand

[20] See: http://www.altcancer.net/ashwin/ashw0809.htm

Understanding Just Why It Was Never Possible For Orthodox Medicine To Heal More People Than It Maimed, Poisoned & Killed. To Grasp Modern History Is To Realize That Ours Is The "Great Age Of Iatrogenesis"

In every modern country I have visited, the simple "light bulb" is alternatively a metaphor for "new idea," or inventive thought or that next great discovery. The very axiom – "light going off" – incorporates this concept. Therefore, I can't help but find it ironic that this same archetype of modern technology should have served as the basis for my own illumination about what modern medicine was and is really about.

To wit . . . some time in the mid-80s, I happened to read an article in the Reader's Digest about a fire hall in Livermore, California, where a light bulb had been in continuous use since 1901 – for practically the entire existence of the fire station itself. That hand-blown, carbon-filament light bulb, made by Shelby Electric Company, still illuminates that Northern California fire station to this day.

Apparently the ability to manufacture a very cheap light bulb that will last for more than a century isn't much of a technical challenge. They mastered that back in the 1800s – well before Thorstein Veblen coined the term "obsolescence" in 1899 and the Great Seers of Modern Business Practice determined that it was insane to manufacture products that lasted. Any fool could see that it was far more profitable to make things that broke down, or otherwise needed to be replaced with something "newer," "better," "more fashionable," etc., on a very regular basis.

By turning modern society onto the concept of "disposability" and making words like "thrift" and "economy" pejoratives, everyone benefited. Supply lines were evened out, economies of scale were improved, the illusion of unending technological advance as a substitute for the virtue of permanence could more readily be embedded. Moreover, consumers could rest comfortably – knowing that this constant supply of replacement goods was benevolently preventing them from "falling behind the times" – turning consumerism into a brilliant form of financial servitude, but most importantly, manufacturers would move more goods and make more money, not to mention the fact that a new industry could be created that would, in time, become one of the largest and most profitable industries of all time: waste disposal – the landfilling of planet Earth, mostly with toxic garbage.

This ubiquitous new component of modernity did not leave health care untransformed. New diseases came into play that either had never existed before, or were transformed into epidemiological giants, compared to their former selves. The greatest of these was "cancer" – a collective term for approximately 200 different cellular neoplastic developments. And consistent with our civilization's new business model, the term "treatment" was strongly encouraged over the more objectionable, less profitable term "cure." Those forms of treatment that weren't good for business – the medical equivalents of Shelby's 100+ year light bulb – would have to be done away with.

And what could be done with pesky individuals who stumbled upon effective "cures" and didn't play along with the new business model? Well . . . that's easy. There would always be prisons, penitentiaries, torture centers, the convenient practice of "suiciding," kidnapping from far off places like . . . (thinking, thinking, thinking, thinking . . . Guayaquil, Ecuador?) . . . or just outright elimination. (After all, the economy must come first! The needs of the few outweigh the needs of the many . . or the wildlife . . . or the life-support mechanisms of Earth herself!)

None of those thoughts are original. Few people are not aware that "obsolescence" is a major hard-wired component of daily life – though most people may not know that it is so ingrained in the business community that it is virtually a separate discipline within **marketing** – with separate divisions carefully categorized: "technological, psychological, progressive, dynamic," all subsets of "planned obsolescence," which is itself a subset of the most enduring principle of our age, that acquiring money and power is the ultimate end to all means and the most worthy of all pursuits.

How this "prime directive" of modern life translates into modern health care, the dominant species of the ecosystem being allopathic (orthodox) conventional medicine, can be seen everywhere. And yet, average people are oblivious to it, like the hordes of professional wrestling fans who just can't get their cerebral matter around the fact that the matches are rigged and none of the wrestlers are really competing athletes – they're **actors**.

Likewise, you have to **pretend** that modern health care is about "helping" the patient to not be bowled over by the obvious. And it isn't as if there aren't enough breakaway doctors – who have, somehow, regained their conscience and moral footing – to help lead the way. (I bring several prominent figures to the forefront in Chapter 1, 2 and 4 of Meditopia.) Modern medicine is about Empire, and the business of modern medicine is all about "medical obsolescence" – **except that what's designed to wear out and break down prematurely isn't the product itself.**

It's you!

What's good for business is to create more problems that need to be fixed

We see this everywhere in politics (problem–reaction–solution), in the military, and in every facet of product consumerism. Show me someone who will argue that the field of medicine is immune to this horrific cancer that has already infected every other aspect of our culture, and I'll show you a full-fledged medical propagandist. (These "vomit brokers" of the orthodox medical community have a tough sell for those who have their eyes open – namely, that the medical community is an oasis immune to a scourge that infests every other aspect of our culture, contrary not just to common sense, but to all available evidence indicting orthodox medicine for what can readily be called "The

Great Medical Holocaust" – in play since the mid-1800s right up to the present day – as I make clear in Meditopia.)

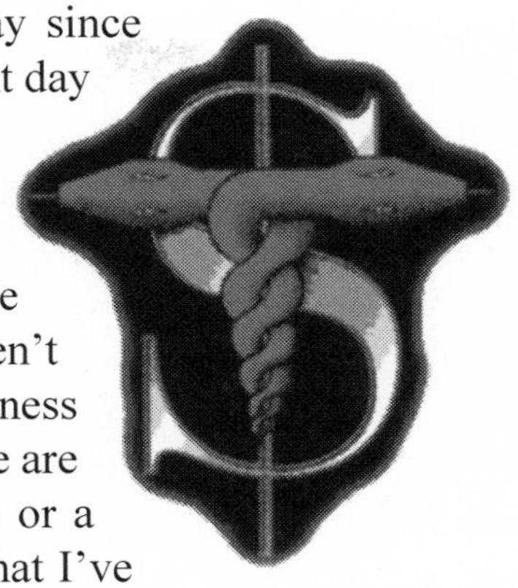

Conversely, what is **not** good for business is your continued health and well-being. Who in the hell can make any money if you aren't getting sick? What kind of business plan is that? People who think these are just the mental musings of a cynic or a conspiracy theorist haven't seen what I've seen. They haven't witnessed one effective therapy after another become the target of the FDA and the other enforcers of modern medicine – not because they weren't safe and effective, but because they threatened pharmaceutical industry profits. If you want more proof, just read Chapter 4 of Meditopia, or my earlier essay, Impossible Dream (2002).[21] (Why else would the FDA support counterfeiters of our products, some of whom we have confirmed are producers of adulterated/mislabeled versions?)[22]

Yes – at its core, modern medicine is imperialistic. It's about taking what isn't yours – be it the livelihood of an indigenous people or the life of a patient whose misplaced trust in a corrupt health care system will cost him or her their life. Were Will and Ariel Durant alive today, they might well choose to name the twelth volume of their ambitious Story of Civilization, The Great Age of Iatrogenesis – though I doubt they'd earn another Pulitzer for the effort.

Until people can connect the dots and realize that the long fingers of "planned obsolescence" are reaching further and further into the sacred spaces of their personal lives, until people begin to understand that a culture that holds so little regard for the planet – which supports us all – will have even less regard for **them**, there can be no reform. (End of article.)

[21] See: http://www.altcancer.net/lysis5.htm

[22] See: http://meditopia.org/old/chap7_2004.htm

Greg Caton --- Founder
Alpha Omega Labs
Guayaquil, ECUADOR

So ended my "Ashwin" piece, which – brief and to the point – describes inconsistencies with which people are made to live. Nonetheless, with just a little more thought, it becomes apparent that the "pillars" of Modern Medicine and the mythology that keep people believing in it could never be held in place were it not for another insidious form of governmental intermediaryism: the media.

Premise On The Role Of Government In Relation To The Media

Managing public perception so that the BCN is upheld is one of Government's primary functions. But since the true motives of Government are inherently concealed and protected by the BCN, one who understands the inherent nature of Government in our time quickly realizes that not only does Government depend on ***lying*** *to its constituency to stay in power, but that its survival depends on its competency in being able to* ***lie*** *– unflinchingly, consistently, confidently, unendingly, and convincingly.*

Its fortunes lay in its ability to do this ***well****.*

Conversely, its existence is threatened when its powers of deception wane.

There can be no greater tragedy for a modern Government than for it to have lost its ability to lie well. Only the well-designed and well-sewn garments of deception protect Government from a critical mass of its constituents being able to view its naked truths and the nefarious motivations that guide its inner workings. This can only be accomplished by control of the media.

It has long been established that it is the nature of mass media to be subverted by authority in order to con their general audience – viewed as the unwashed masses by the Elite, people who cannot figure out on their own that the evening news or the morning paper (pick your favorite channel or publication, it doesn't matter), is just another installment of "smackdown time" à la professional wrestling style.[23]

Most people know intuitively that the rendering of current affairs by their mass media outlet is slanted, but, somehow, people have a difficult time maintaining this state of awareness, and like an ADHD patient, find themselves relapsing. They will find themselves "agreeing" with this or that politician on TV – forgetting that the vast majority of Government initiatives are just elements of misdirection in the larger propaganda picture. Or, going back to our earlier metaphor, the professional wrestling match turns out to be too engrossing, too engaging – and so people begin rooting for their favorite wrestling champ, forgetting that the whole thing is staged.

Once again, nothing brought this fact home to me as thoroughly as the suppression of "cancer cures." It has been 28 years since "escharotics preparations" were first introduced to me, but – still – despite my involvement in the successful treatment of thousands of cancer cases, I have a difficult time really grasping the full importance of Government's all-powerful hold on the

[23] This is not a singular errant or extreme position. See: Into the Buzzsaw: Leading Journalists Expose the Myth of a Free Press, edited by Kristina Borjesson, (2004). The psychopathic dimension of media bias and subservience to the "psychopathic control grid" is further explored in Thomas Sheridan's Puzzling People: The Labyrinth of the Psychopath, (2011) p. 160. Lastly, I think that it is interesting that German journalist, Dr. Udo Ulfkotte, decided to "out" the mainstream media in 2014 for its then latest deceptions. "I've been a journalist for about 25 years, and I was educated to lie, to betray, and not to tell the truth to the public . . . but seeing right now within the last months how the German and American media tries to bring war to the people of Europe, to bring war to Russia – this is a point of no return and I'm going to stand up and say it is not right what I have done in the past, to manipulate people, to make propaganda against Russia, and it is not right what my colleagues do and have done in the past because they are bribed to betray the people, not only in Germany, but all over Europe." Dr. Ulfkotte made a passionate explanation of his position on Russia Today, viewable on YouTube, see: https://www.youtube.com/watch?v=sGqi-k213eE
Dr. Ulfkotte was subsequently assassinated in January, 2017. The method of assassination was most probably the infamous "Venus shooter," which can induce heart attacks from a distance using a powerful electromagnetic pulse.
See: https://www.youtube.com/watch?v=SUmOjQg68wU

psyche. That a simple formula with three easy-to-obtain ingredients could be so easily withheld as an effective cancer remedy – it's just unbelievable. As Freud put it, so great is our desire to find our world loveable, to find our Government believable, our culture reciprocal. And so disappointing is it to discover that not only is our world not at all as it should be, but that Government uses the lever of this basic human need – to find love in the world – to exploit us even more.

The exploitation of man's need for love is leveraged further – aided by the media's abandonment of its expressed mandate to faithfully inform the public – through the misuse of the Hegelian dialectic. The practice is so common in the U.S. that it has been shorthanded with the expression "Wag the Dog" – after a Hollywood movie by the same name. This "problem-reaction-solution" model is well articulated elsewhere, but for the unaware, here's the short version: the Government engineers a problem, acts surprised, as if it has been caught off-guard with a crisis of its own making, and then behaves like a knight in shining armor – ready to save the day – with a solution of its own design that was fully planned before the initial problem was ever executed. The practice is quite prevalent as a prelude to military confrontation – with the deliberate sinking by U.S. agents of the U.S.S. Maine in Havana, the engineered sinking of the Lusitania, the Gulf of Tonkin incident, the withheld intelligence on the Japanese attack on Pearl Harbor, and more recently, the inside job that made the 9/11 attacks possible.

Most people have an easier time accepting that this practice is commonplace when it involves somebody else's Government. No one, for instance, in the U.S. has a problem believing that Adolf Hitler and the Nazi party burned down their own Reichstag in 1933. It's an accepted historical fact. But fewer Americans are willing to confront the ludicrous U.S. official position that the most deadly "terrorist act" to ever take place in America was carried out by a team of ragtag Arabs – failing student pilots with a penchant for strip bars, wielding nothing more than box cutter knives.

On first impulse, it is easy to see that this practice obtains its popularity in Government play books everywhere because it makes Government look more legitimate. After all, isn't it easier to come up with a solution to something if you designed the problem in the first place?

What makes "Wag the Dog" so irresistible on an even deeper level is that it's a cost effective way of buying legitimacy. Government buys its entry into the lives of its citizens by staking a position as a keeper of the peace and a solver of problems. If you're in the business of solving problems – and you're a creature of negaprocity, committed to maximizing your "take-to-give" ratio – doesn't it make sense to create hellish problems for your own people? Isn't it much cheaper to craft a solution to a problem that you have created and can control than it is to deal with a problem of indeterminable cost, for which you have no control and no specific solution? Obviously, the problems you create cannot be small problems. They risk not being noticed. "Wag the Dog" only works if the problems you create are horrific enough to cause the citizenry to cry out for their Government to come to their rescue.

This is why it's so insane to expect that truly effective, modern Governments could ever be expected to be purveyors of peace.[24] What an absurd idea. Think of the many governmental blessings that perpetual war brings: it not only reinforces the need for Government (because who else is prepared to manage the ill will and carnage that only modern Governments can create?); it provides a military supply constituency – in the U.S., the infamous "Military Industrial Complex" – which will always support the Government in its search for more blood-soaked ventures as a means of financial sustenance; it misdirects the public from the many social ills that Governments create which they can never solve – simply because negaprocity is not compatible with solving real social problems and making people happy; and lastly and to the point, since this section is about

[24] This is the point of perpetual emphasis in Gore Vidal's Perpetual War for Perpetual Peace: How We Got to Be So Hated, (2002). One priceless example is found on p. 158 with Truman's initiation of the Cold War through "scaring the American People" in order to secure his "militarized economy."

the media, it makes the media (which takes all its cues from the Government) appear less of a traitor than it already is by serving monied interests over the general welfare of the people.

As in the case with cancer therapies, it is heartbreakingly obtuse to think that Government could ever get out of the business of killing and financially enslaving people for money, because without this negaciprocal commitment, Government cannot stay in business. Sure, there are a few "good Governments" in this world – good in the sense that they attempt to conform to the common narrative of truly benevolent, well-intentioned Government. But do you see yet why that isn't effective Government, why it can never achieve its thermodynamic potential, why it cannot long stand against the power of a modern Government that is fully committed to the Dark Side? Don't feel foolish if it's taken this long to understand how the world works. In fact, some of the most brilliant people in history have missed the boat altogether, so if you're still scratching your head, I suppose you're not in bad company.

I'm thinking now about Nikola Tesla – touted by some as the most brilliant inventor and scientist in modern science – more brilliant and inventive than Thomas Edison or Albert Einstein. In his day, Tesla was believed by many colleagues to be a "mad scientist," giving credence to the expression that to be one step ahead of the public makes you a genius, and to be two steps ahead, a madman. It has only been in the aftermath of his death in 1943 that his scientific contributions have gained wider recognition.

Most people who know of him associate Tesla with the invention and commercialization of alternating current and his development of the electric motor. However, of equal importance was his development of the wireless transmission of power, for which he gave public demonstrations as early as 1893. Tesla was not ignorant in the ways of commerce. He filed numerous patents, ran several different companies, and entered into complex commercial contracts that made use of his discoveries. But his downfall came from a profound lack of understanding concerning the single most important concept imparted by this book:

that Government, as well as those members of the Elite who benefit from its machinations at the expense of the general public, is inherently evil.

In 1900 Tesla entered into an arrangement with $150,000 of J.P. Morgan's money to build a multi-wavelength broadcasting station in Colorado which came to be known as Wardenclyffe, "a landmark as magnificent in concept and execution as America's Golden Age of electrical engineering ever produced."[25]

Out of Tesla's experimental work came several patents, chief among them U.S. Patent No. 1,119,732, "Apparatus for Transmitting Electrical Energy," the development of which would have revolutionized the distribution of electrical power as we know it.[26] For even then, Tesla had achieved technical advances in electrical power generation and transmission which tower over those in general use over a century later.

Unlike today's reigning model, Tesla's vision of electrical provision was the installation and maintenance of small power units sufficient to power homes and factories alike. The cost would involve incurring small monthly fees – much as VOIP (Voice Over Internet Protocol) providers today charge a small monthly fee for unlimited long distance telephone.[27]

Such a development was not to be had. For his part, Morgan had already invested sizeable sums into a previously developed model that would be far more lucrative for electrical energy provisions – a model which burdens power consumers to this very day.[28]

Morgan's response to the discovery that Tesla's heart lay in providing electricity to the masses for a fraction of what a more lucrative strategy promised – then and now – was both swift and predictable. He ceased all further funding and created an environment that made it virtually impossible for Tesla to obtain adequate funding from any other source.

Despite his formidable acumen in some of nature's deepest

[25] See: Margaret Cheney, Tesla: Man Out of Time, (2001), p. 159.
[26] Ibid., p. 165
[27] See: Gerry Vassilatos, Lost Science, (2000), p.135.
[28] See: Margaret Cheney, Ibid.

secrets, Tesla still failed to recognize the inherent negaciprocal nature of the institutions with which he was working. He wanted to help humanity. He felt that technology could be used to better the world. He should have died a billionaire for his numerous accomplishments, but, instead, he died penniless – actually, he was heavily in debt – in a New York hotel room. The history books say he died of a heart attack, but more astute minds have concluded he was the victim of creative assassination.

Using science and technology to better the world?

How regrettably naive.

Tesla could have enjoyed a greatly enriched career had he only known that he was working within a psychopathic control grid,[29] "all science is merely a means to an end. The means is knowledge. The end is control."[30]

If you don't know the many ways in which the media (TV, radio, newspapers, magazines, major book publishers, Internet, cinema, etc.) have worked to suppress a wider knowledge of these facts, it is only because to do so would not have served the interests of the mass media's true master: the prevailing Government to which they must answer, the one empowered to close them down at will, the one which is so closely tied to big-monied interests. The media should serve as an intermediary force between their readers, viewers, listeners, users and the facts. Instead, they serve as an intermediary force to a power structure that is in direct conflict with the interests of ordinary people.

Speaking of "science" – that monumental edifice of truth and respectability – it is amazing the number of people who cannot see the many ways in which Governments and their Elite backers use "science" to distort and pervert the most obvious, provable facts in Nature to their negaciprocal ends. More than one observer has commented on the relationship between "science" and religion . . . that science is, really, a religion.

I have yet to read a satisfying treatise on why ***scientism*** is

[29] See: Thomas Sheridan's Puzzling People: The Labyrinth of the Psychopath, (2011). This single volume, discussed in greater depth later in this book, contains too many references to the psychopathic control grid to focus on any single citation.

[30] See: Phillip Darrell Collins and Paul David Collins, The Ascendancy of the Scientific Dictatorship: An Examination of Epistemic Autocracy From the 19th to the 21st Century, (2006).

as much a faith-based system as the doctrine taught by Greek mythologists two thousand years ago. Both have served as tools of intermediaryism in their time.

You knew this was coming. We've already covered education – the conventional programs used to impart knowledge. It wouldn't make much sense to subvert the conveyance of knowledge if you didn't have the power and forethought to subvert knowledge itself.

Let's examine why.

Premise On The Role Of Government In Scientism

Any system of "knowing" must conform to the more elemental rules of prevailing authority itself. Extreme Negaprocity cannot proceed unimpeded unless those things which a people believe to be true can be integrated into the culture's benign common narrative. If you cannot control what a people think, you cannot control what they do. If you cannot control what people do, you are not in total control of your people and you are therefore an inferior power.

The rules that the Government imposes are not passive. They are active agents in the world. In contrast, true knowledge and ways in which people acquire it and gain acceptance of it are inherently passive. Knowledge, if it is to be pure, innocent and true, must, by its nature, remain untainted by exterior motivation. It cannot be a tool of an exterior controlling agent; because, to be true, it must stand on its own merit.

Under the rules of governance that dominate our age, this simply isn't possible.

I spoke about my "religious conversion" – and I'm using that term here broadly . . . **very** broadly – when, as discussed in Chapter 1, I realized to what absurd lengths my Government and orthodox medicine were going to suppress provably effective cancer cures. Out of this observation have come a million other earth-shattering realizations.

Gautama Buddha acquired enlightenment after meditating for 39 days under the Bodhi tree. I acquired mine after meditating for five years inside the U.S. federal prison system. (If you're a Buddhist and you found that offensive – be patient and have faith. It gets worse.)

While in prison in 2004, I happened to come across the work of Michael Cremo, probably best known for his work, Forbidden Archeology: The Hidden History of the Human Race.[31] Over the past few years, so many archeological findings have been unearthed which defy the very pillars of archeology as it is taught at universities around the world, that one has to wonder why the orthodox establishment of this discipline fights so tenaciously against newcomers like Cremo. British author and researcher Graham Hancock, has experienced the same disconnect in his own work, leading him to suggest that "the reigning model of human history, carefully built-up by scholars over the past two centuries, is sadly and completely wrong . . . [It is something which we cannot] put right with minor tinkering and adjustments. What is needed is for the existing model to be thrown out the window and for us to start again with open minds and with no absolutely no preconceptions."

Were you to substitute "human history" with "orthodox medicine," Graham's exhortation sounds like something I'd say. It's enough to cause a thinking man to wonder if there isn't any discipline which has not likewise been so corrupted that we don't need to start over without the overreaching intermediaryism of prevailing authority.[32]

Indeed, I found the combative obstinance that Cremo and his colleagues have provoked from the establishment to be quite familiar. This is aggravated by the fact that they provide clear, convincing, and contrary evidence that certain long-held tenets are embarrassingly outdated. Now on the surface of things, the science of archeology and medicine would appear to have lit-

[31] See: Michael Cremo and Richard L. Thompson, Forbidden Archeology: The Hidden History of the Human Race, (1998).

[32] This analysis is part of chapter 5 of Meditopia. See: http://meditopia.org/chap5.htm

tle in common aside from their obvious anthropological ties. But we're not talking about the surface of things. We're talking about the unvarnished nature of things. What does any discipline look and sound like without the interference of people who are programmed to stick their intermediary interests – tied as they are to money, power, and control – into the mix?

To find the answers I had to look deeper into the very tenets of scientism itself – the underlying foundation by which any of the physical sciences acquire acceptance in our time. Strangely, I found unusually coherent answers buried, quite without intention, in the famous work of Thomas Kuhn, The Structure of Scientific Revolutions.[33] It is beyond the scope of this work to do an in-depth study of Kuhn's observations, but an examination of some of his more salient points is sufficient for our current purposes.

Throughout my work in the alternative health care field, I have found – as I detail extensively in Meditopia – one false tenet after another. The only common element which I was ever able to find which linked the major therapeutic approaches used by orthodox medicine was profit. Efficacy takes a severely subordinated position to money-making. The common narrative in our world culture tells us that the approaches of modern medicine are based on "medical science," which brings to mind impartial tests for efficacy and toxicity, double-blind studies, peer reviews, etc. Since modern medicine – just one branch of "scientism" – has turned out to be so contrary to its own common narrative, just like Government is, a grounded understanding as to why that is would seem to merit our exploration.

Kuhn begins his work by establishing "scientific community" as the starting point for establishing science as a receptacle of beliefs that can be regarded in society as credible. This, of course, makes sense. If your goal is to control culture with a BCN (again, benign common narrative), it would make sense that controlling specialized knowledge would demand that it possess its own subset of principles within the common narrative. Since all power structures are hierarchical, it then follows

[33] See: Thomas Kuhn, The Structure of Scientific Revolutions, (1962).

that this common narrative be enforced by different communities, each governing a different fragmented piece of knowledge or discipline.

According to Kuhn, each scientific community is endowed with a certain set of "received beliefs," which form the basis of the "educational initiation that prepares and licenses the student for professional practice." The education of the aspiring student is "rigorous and rigid" to ensure that the "received beliefs" exert a "deep hold" on the student's mind.

Exactly where these "received beliefs" come from and the influences that were brought to bear in arriving in their current form rarely elicits sustained inquiry. It came from those in charge. This is where science begins – as an act of faith, unburdened by one's own direct perception or knowledge of the world. The very starting point for science on the part of both the common man and the student aspiring to become part of a scientific community is: "this is what I believe to be true because those in authority say so."

Kuhn then goes on to note that "normal science" means "research firmly based upon one or more past scientific achievements, achievements that some particular scientific community acknowledges for a time as supplying the foundation for its further practice."

With the greatest of conviction, "scientists" of any discipline hold with the gravitas and zeal of the most extreme religious fundamentalists that they "know what the world is like," and they go to great lengths to defend this assumption. Moreover, the scientific community works to suppress "fundamental novelties" because they are necessarily subversive of its basic commitments. It advances its cause through research,"a strenuous and devoted attempt to force nature into the conceptual boxes supplied by professional education."

A shift in thinking occurs only when an anomaly "subverts the existing tradition of scientific practice." It is precisely such a shift that Kuhn characterizes as "scientific revolution" – "the tradition-shattering complements to the tradition-bound activity of normal science."

Science isn't moved by compelling facts or observation, and this is most painfully obvious in the temples of modern medical science. It is moved by events which threaten its prestige and the confidence that those outside the field have in its authority. The rules of sustaining legitimacy are no different in the scientific community than they are in Government. Any new assumption – paradigm/theory – requires a reevaluation of prior assumptions and the reevaluation of prior facts, and is always resisted, sometimes quite vehemently, by the established community.

Few people stop to think of the implications of a system where those who reconfirm the prevailing paradigm get more credit, praise, financial reward, etc., than those who uncover its flaws. Few people realize how hugely inhibitory this is to any impartial pursuit of Knowledge or Truth.

Fast forwarding to the emerging "paradigm" that does manage to alter the position of the scientific community, it is interesting how the textbooks, journals . . . indeed, its very common narrative, are then altered so as to obscure its past. As one academic notes, "the historical reconstruction of previous paradigms and theorists in scientific textbooks makes the history of science look linear or cumulative, a tendency that even affects scientists looking back at their own research. Thus even scientific textbooks present the inaccurate view that science has reached its present state by a series of individual discoveries and inventions that, when gathered together, constitute the modern body of technical knowledge – the addition of bricks to a building."[34]

Curiously absent from Kuhn's work is any serious examination of politics and money, and the influence they bring to the entire process of scientific revolution. It has been my experience that money influences which proposed paradigms become seriously examined in the first place. One example that I detailed in Meditopia is the effort of Linus Pauling to show how hypoascorbemia (deficiency in Vitamin C), and not cholesterol, was the leading contributing factor to heart disease. At the time of his discovery, around 1990 – towards the end of his life – he

[34] See: https://www.uky.edu/~eushe2/Pajares/Kuhn.html

was able to get two prominent journals to publish his results. After the pharmaceutical companies – flush with cash from their cholesterol-reducing drugs – caught wind of Pauling's research, they proceeded to shut him down completely. In other words, even if you are a Nobel Prize winning laureate in your field, you have no power to influence your science if it conflicts with influential monied interests.[35]

What should this tell us about the truthfulness of science? Knowing that Governments support the orthodox positions of any given science, what should this tell us about the truthfulness of Government?

True knowledge comes from understanding Nature as a whole, in all its interconnectedness, and not through the isolation and fragmentation of its discernible parts – a pursuit to which science is wholly devoted. Dr. Gerald Dermer tells the story of an investigator who wanted to know what scientists took the atomic theory to be. So the investigator "asked a distinguished physicist and an eminent chemist whether a single atom of helium was or was not a molecule. Both answered without hesitation, but their answers were not the same. For the chemist, the atom of helium was a molecule because it behaved like one with respect to the kinetic theory of gases. For the physicist, on the other hand, the helium atom was not a molecule, viewing it through his own research, training and practice."[36]

I repeated this story in Meditopia because it illustrates how knowledge is corrupted by scientism's commitment to fragmentation, but it bears repeating in our examination of scientism here . . . so does the following example, also from Gerald Dermer's work, <u>The Immortal Cell: Why Cancer Research Fails</u>.

Gerald Dermer was a pathologist who was struck by the fact that live cancer cells behave totally differently from the cell lines that cancer researchers use in their work. He was puzzled that cancer researchers could use their current methods for the

[35] I expand on this line of thought in the fourth chapter of Meditopia, beginning at: http://www.meditopia.org/chap4.htm.

[36] See: Dr Gerald B. Dermer, <u>The Immortal Cell: Why Cancer Research Fails</u>, (1994).

next 2000 years and still never come up with a cancer cure – guaranteed. (He's missing the whole point now, isn't he?) He described this discrepancy as a "vast and deadly gap between the reality of cancer, which strikes human beings, and the theory of cancer, which thousands of researchers are using in their [supposed] search for a cure." He notes that "although some of my colleagues are aware of this gap, few are willing to risk their careers by discussing it openly. In the absence of public debate, cancer scientists around the country are free to propagate the myth of a productive 'war on cancer.' No one wants to admit that this so-called war has been a worthless investment of taxpayers' money and scientists' time. But as more and more money is spent, with fewer and fewer meaningful results, increasing numbers of patients and their families, taxpayers, and politicians want to know the reasons why . . . it is an account of a scientific and medical scandal of the highest order."[37]

What Dermer failed to realize is that this is scientism unmasked. Fake orthodox cancer diagnosis, treatment and research is currently grossing about $500 billion a year, elevated to hegemonic status by the mafia tactics of the world's leading Governments in their suppression of much safer, more effective, less costly therapeutic approaches. What is more likely to replace the current paradigm that holds it in place? One that is modeled after approaches that are cheap, highly effective and non-toxic? Or one that can replace, in pure profit potential to prevailing authorities, the one that is already in place with even more luxuriant renumeration?

We see this same phenomenon in the very thing that is the basis of good health: agriculture.

Premise On The Role Of Government In Agriculture

After water and air, food is man's most essential requirement. Because of its centrality to human existence, Government

[37] See: Dermer, Ibid.

exerts its heaviest burdens and great abuses on the agricultural sector. Since negaprocity is Government's chief characteristic, it thus follows that agriculture mirrors Government's modus operandi to reflect a destructive, parasitic relationship with its environment.

Left to its own devices, Nature fills the land with innumerable species of plants, insects, nematodes, microbes, amphibians, and small animals. From these, man is able to fulfill all his physical needs, perfectly and without deficiency, so that in most indigenous communities, less than three hours a day are devoted to what most people would call "work."

Several thousand years ago – I doubt anyone knows exactly when – perhaps 10,000 years ago, most certainly within the past 6,000 years, certain groups of men came to the conclusion that this abundance simply wasn't enough. And so began the practice of agriculture, leaning towards domesticated grains (wheat, corn, barley, rye, etc.) and pulses (lentils, peas, etc.) to the exclusion of all other species of plant food. The end result was that people began to harbor far more disease, and, contrary to the common narrative, live far shorter lives than before.[38] The interesting thing about agricultural foods – then and now – is that they are primarily "ruderals." That is, they are short-lived annuals that thrive even in disturbed soil and put considerable energy into reproduction (i.e. seed).[39]

Men discovered that they could extract more food, energy and tradable goods, if they focused on these plants, cultivated them, and tore up the environment to make more space for their expansion. The problem is that replanting every season tears up the ground and disrupts delicate soil ecosystems.

Some people have noted that the emergence of Government came at about the time as agriculture. This makes perfectly good sense.

[38] See: Steve Taylor, The Fall, (2005).

[39] An excellent discussion of the difference in "basic plant strategy" between ruderals and other vegetation in the succession process can be found in Dave Jacke's Edible Forest Gardens, Volume I: Ecological Vision, Theory for Temperate Climate Permaculture, (2005), p. 126 -127.

Both Governments and ruderal plants are highly parasitic.

Both Governments and agriculture are negaciprocal.

Ruderals produce the biggest seeds and the highest yields, but they return little to their environment. It is the perennials that "build extensive root networks and healthy soil, conserve water, and recycle nutrients." In a healthy, natural ecosystem, diverse species live together to create a regenerative environment, of which ruderals are only the initiators in a long process, known in horticulture as "succession." Agriculture destroys the succession process and focuses on only one stage of its activity, all in the name of maximizing return. In the process, it drains aquifers, poisons land and sea, and erodes once fertile plains into wastelands. As plant geneticist, Wes Jackson, has noted, "It's a system that modern agriculture can't sustain . . . but without a new green revolution, we'll destroy our soil trying." We've done a pretty good job of destroying the Earth's topsoil already.

Wes Jackson's recommended solution is to reboot agriculture by domesticating perennial crops, so that growing food becomes more life-supporting and less parasitic. His recommendation would also lead to healthier diets. This is a step in the right direction, but I believe there's a better one: recreating what Nature bestowed in the first place by cultivating "edible forest gardens."[40]

I doubt either of these approaches would ever be endorsed by any major Government, and the reason is glaringly obvious. You will remember that the opening premise of this chapter is that intermediaryism is used to extend Government's negaciprocal activities.

In that same vein, throughout modern history, Governments have continually used agriculture as an intermediary force to support their aims and advance their ambitions. The problem with the sustainable advice of people like Wes Jackson and Dave Jacke is that it rests upon the very reciprocal foundations of Nature which are antithetical to the thermodynamic demands

[40] See: https://www.wired.com/2011/02/ff_madscientist_profiles/5/
"Inside the Mad Science of 7 Renegade Researchers," Wired Magazine, (March, 2011). On reference to edible forest gardens: ibid.

of modern Government. It is for this reason that their sensible counsel will never be taken seriously.

Speaking of the demands of modern Government, if we applied this intermediary principle to modern Government as it pertains to its laws and edicts, what would it look like?

Premise On The Role Of Government In Law

Government's most direct influence on a governed people is in the creation and enforcement of law. The common narrative of all Government is that law exists to uphold social order – a function which is largely non-existent and unnecessary among indigenous peoples. Moreover, the BCN of all law is that it is impartial and that it exists for the benefit of all citizens. The reality is that law – first and foremost – exists to create a barrier between an Elite criminal class in the minority and a large base of victims who are then the governed who must bear its costs. Thus laws allow an Elite to expand their negaciprocal activities with impunity at a relatively low cost. In this way, thermodynamic potential is maximized and victim resistance is minimized.

Governments and law go hand in hand. It is inconceivable to imagine one without the other. Americans who have not been completely dumbed down by the U.S. Government's use of propaganda to control the mainstream media have seen this firsthand through the unending concentration of criminal activities surrounding the recent wars in Serbia, Somalia, Iraq, Afghanistan, Libya, Pakistan, Yemen, Syria, etc. From the drug war in Nicaragua under Reagan, to the bombings in Sudan under Clinton, to the ever expanding military adventures under Obama, who some still question as a Nobel Peace Prize winner, the real function of law has become increasingly obvious. In fact, it is fair to say that the actions of the U.S. Government over the past quarter century most glaringly demonstrate that laws simply don't apply to the Elite. The very actions and motivations that would bring a death sentence in U.S. criminal court are the very things that the U.S. Government does as a normal part of its daily activity, the abandonment of which would make that Government virtually unrecognizable.

While I was in prison, a friend of mine, George Green, was on a nationally syndicated talk show in 2004.[41] George was talking about his experience with the Elite in connection with an offer he was made in 1975 to be in charge of the finances for the presidential campaign of then Democratic presidential hopeful, Jimmy Carter. The political Elite member making the proposal was the late Senator Ted Kennedy.

"You know, Ted," George replied in response, "I've been an active Republican my entire life. I'm sure there are others who would be better suited for this appointment."

"It doesn't matter, George," Ted countered, "We control both parties. You should consider my offer."

Not long after that, George was invited to a dinner party where he ran into Ted shortly after making his entrance.

"That girl you came in with," Ted murmured, "Do you think you can set me up with her?"

"Ted, please, that girl is only fourteen years old."

"So what?," Ted replied, "Can you set me up with her?"

"Ted, you don't understand, that girl is my daughter."

"What difference does that make?" Ted shot back, irritated at George's rebuke.

Shortly thereafter, George left the party with his daughter; and, in the days that followed, he gracefully declined Ted's request to assist in Carter's election campaign.

At this point in his life, George was a very successful multi-millionaire, dealing in international banking and commercial real estate. One by one, George began getting calls from banks with whom he was associated, wherein his loans were

[41] See: http://www.coasttocoastam.com/show/2004/04/25. Interestingly, the people behind Coast-to-Coast AM edited most of George's more provocative statements. The interview was supposed to last two hours, but was cut short because Art Bell, the founder of the show, didn't like the political nature of the things George was talking about. I already knew this when I heard the interview live, but this was reconfirmed much later when I spoke to George about it in person.

being "called." In a mere matter of weeks, Kennedy made sure that George understood the penalties for not cooperating with the Elite – their way. He lost his entire fortune and ended up having to start his career all over again – from nothing.

I chose to tell this story for four reasons. One, because it's one that's relatively close to me. Two, because it characterizes the way in which members of the Elite view themselves above the law in every respect. Three, because it runs counter to the common narrative that the law is impartial and applies equally to everyone; and four, because it demonstrates the disconnect between the way the media portray the Elite at the very top of the dog pile and the way things really are.

Those who find this story lacking in credibility don't understand the prevailing conditions that exist in the halls of the Elite. Of all the intermediary tools which Governments and their high ranking Elite use to maximize negaprocity with minimal resistance, few rank as important or as far-reaching as the creation and enforcement of law. It is no wonder that over 2,500 years ago, Lao Tse could so insouciantly remark in the Tao Te Ching: "The more laws and order are made prominent, the more thieves and robbers there will be . . . the more laws that are written, the more criminals are produced."

The joys of psychopathocracy cannot be sustained without the force of law.

Interestingly, I can remember my father telling me as a child that I had to be in bed by 10 p.m. This household "law" didn't change until I was well into my teens. Even then, it seemed arbitrary to me. Whether I went to bed at 9:30 or 10:15 p.m., did it really matter? I was a good student and would have done well whether I followed this rule or not. Nonetheless, there were harsh penalties for violating the rule, despite the fact that neither of my parents followed this rule themselves.

Now, of course, the argument can be made that this "do as I say, not as I do" approach makes sense if you're a parent trying to instill certain values in a growing child. Can the same argument be made to defend a worldwide crime syndicate in charge of worldly affairs as it relates to the other 99%-plus of humanity?

As important as the role of law is in the functioning of Government, far more so is the role of money.

Premise On The Role Of Government In Banking

Since money serves as the sole common denominator over financial affairs of an entire nation's citizens, and since it is the chief measure by which a Government may quantitatively know its thermodynamic potential, its study provides the best working illustration of Government's allegiance to the banking community over that of its own people's welfare, and the nefarious effects that this tendency produces.

Because banking grows through horizontal taproots that penetrate every facet of society from the core family to the modern superpower – from true generosity to the most extreme negaprocity – where its base of power resides, it is the primary medium perpetuating "The Great Winding." And because of this ubiquitous tendency, it is not an exaggeration, as previously stated, to say that money truly is "the root of all evil."

We covered banking to some extent in the last chapter. Nonetheless, the role of banking as the most important intermediary force used by Government to subvert the interests of its own people – and in the case of Sector H and J entities of the Negaprocity Chart – deserves mention here.

Of all the facets of intermediaryism covered to this point, none are as pure and irrefutable in their singular devotion to negaprocity as central banking, whose designers have managed to create the most brazen form of public theft imaginable.[42] There is nothing tangential about the purpose and intent of central banking in our age. The "oak masters" have created a system, which – like the mosquito's proboscis – is designed

[42] There are hundreds of books on the market that provide nauseating detail as to the role of central bankers in robbing the public. For its direct and succinct style, my personal favorite is Pastor Sheldon Emry's Billions for the Bankers, Debts for the People, (1982).

to be injected into the lifeblood of the populace and maintain its bloodsucking until the oak masters' bellies are full. This, of course, is the critical problem.

There is a limit to how much of your blood a mosquito can extract. Its stomach has a limit.

The oak masters do not have such a limit.

None of this would be relevant to the central thesis of this book were it not for the fact that Governments the world over are complicit in this massive fraud. If central bankers are the ones in the vault pilfering all the cash, then Governments are the facilitators who stand willing and able to shoot anyone who would interfere with the robbery, not to mention their role as the drivers in the getaway cars.

This is the cruelest form of intermediaryism of all.

Premise On The Role Of Government In The Perversion Of Language

Spoken and written language is, by far, the medium through which people communicate. For this reason, it is vitally important that Government influence language in ways that promote its negaciprocal activities. Conversely, it is vitally important that Government influence language, so that linguistic expressions that subvert or are contrary to its objectives, are framed as socially unacceptable.

Language, spoken and written, is so central to modern civilizations that one might think I would cover this first, before education, medicine, media, science, agriculture, or banking. It is important to note that of all the forementioned, this one is probably the most subtle and least obvious. Few people really give thought to the meaning of the words they use, or how they can be perverted to act as their own form of programming. Thus, I chose to close this chapter with the Premise on Language.

The perversion of language to promote negaprocity is ubiquitous. Earlier, we discussed the rampant use of Doublespeak that George Orwell made so famous, but the process has been going on since the beginning of antiquity. Embedded in the most commonly used languages around the world are signs of this perversity.

Let's take one simple example among many. When we use the world "real," we refer to a "thing" (taken from the Latin noun, "res") that has existence in an objectified world, as opposed to something that merely exists in "thought, appearance, or language."[43] "Real" comes from the same root as "regal," "regulatory," and "rey" (the word we use in Spanish for "king," from the Latin "rex," "regis" in the genitive case). Few people ever give thought to the fact that the subtle implication of the word, which we use all the time, is that something only has legitimacy (which itself comes from the Latin "lex/legis," or law) if it descends from "rex" – the king – those in authority. Conversely, when you contemplate things that are not approved by authority, you are negotiating with that which is not real. Maybe you're not feeling well; maybe you need psychiatric help. After all, those who deal in the "unreal" as if it's real – that is to say, things not approved by authority, certainly cannot be psychologically well. Actually, it's worse. They might be a threat to society, so we should do something to silence these kind of people. You see where this takes us, don't you?

The aforementioned word "legitimacy" or its adjectival form, "legitimate," reinforces the same concept. "Legitimate" is good, reliable; it confers confidence, because it carries the weight of law behind it. Conversely, that which is "illegitimate" is unlawful, unreliable, perhaps even scandalous.

The mainstream media twists language all the time in its attempt to reshape our understanding of words and re-program our thinking. During the last U.S. presidential election (Nov., 2016), even sitting here in Ecuador, I don't think I'd ever seen the words "racist" and "misogynist" used so many times in my

[43] A good breakdown of "real" and its etymology is provided in The Compact Oxford English Dictionary, p. 1,519.

60+ years – to the point where it was obvious that there was an intent to extend the meaning of these words beyond the boundaries of what you'd find in the dictionary. These words now mean "unfit for office," "psychologically ill," and just plain "evil." None of this should be taken to endorse people who really are racist or misogynist, who, in my way of thinking, are just people who are exhibiting a lower state of development, but you can see what's happening. This isn't about taking words that are already pejorative and making them more so. It's about retraining them for another purpose and changing their usage. We're creating metaphors that are altering the language. Do you know someone running for public office who may be unfit for the office for which they are running? Okay, well, there's only one possible explanation: they're probably racist and misogynist.

When I was in prison, I spent time with a man who was a boy living in Denmark during the Nazi occupation there. His name is Uwe Jensen.[44] Now, we all know that the word "Nazi" is used in everyday language to describe someone who is cruel, tyrannical, authoritarian, aristocentric, etc. But to hear Uwe tell it, that was not at all the meaning of Nazi when he was growing up, and he describes the relations of everyday Danish people in his area under "Nazi rule" as being relatively civil.

The meaning of the word has changed dramatically since Adolf Hitler was in power and firmly believed by many to be heavily financed by the U.S. banking community.[45]

Let's take it a step further: when I hear the word "American," I think of industrious, hardworking; I think of communities with high social capital; I think of homes with no steel bars on the windows and the ability to leave the doors of your home unlocked without having to worry about thieves coming in to

[44] We're pictured together at: http://www.meditopia.org/chap3-3.htm.
Or see: http://www.meditopia.org/images/uwe_jensen_jan11.jpg

[45] See: "The Americans who funded Hitler, Nazis, German economic miracle, and WW II" https://orientalreview.org/2010/10/06/episodes-5-who-paid-for-world-war-ii/ https://www.sott.net/article/298259-The-Americans-who-funded-Hitler-Nazis-German-economic-miracle-and-World-War-II See also: Wall Street and the Rise of Hitler: The Astonishing True Story of the Financiers Who Bankrolled the Nazis, by Antony Cyril Sutton, (2010).

clean you out while you go to the supermarket. This is what comes to mind, because this is how I was raised to think about my culture when I grew up. Let's assume, for a moment, that I was an English-speaking Iraqi who was an eyewitness to the Gulf War 26 years ago. Let's assume that I was now living in one of the innumerable areas in that country that are now either uninhabitable or marginally so, because the U.S. used so many depleted uranium shells that women are advised by their own Government not to have children because of the high incidence of birth defect there. The problems with radioactivity there are that bad, to say nothing of the huge loss of innocent life that occurred in Iraq during that conflict.

Would anyone be surprised if an individual who had this experience used the word Nazi and American interchangeably?

Language and the meaning of the words we use are not only influenced by our own experiences, they are heavily shaped by those in charge who realize that words serve as control mechanisms to help achieve and maintain the objectives of Government. This, too, is a form of intermediaryism.

Mainstream Media Cannot Survive Unless It IS Fake

"The mainstream media is **fake news** simply because it cannot perform its vital functions unless it **is** fake. It is not a tool to educate. It is a tool to influence the masses and enforce the benign common narrative. In the U.S. alone, the unending concatenation of false flag events that have been a feature of American life since at least the Boston Tea Party in 1773 is proof enough of that. The media always, and with few exceptions, supports the fake narrative and buries the truth.

Get past the weather, sports, birth, marriage, and obituary sections and you quickly realize that the news doesn't exist to inform you.

It exists to test your stupidity and measure your gullibility."[1]

Greg Caton

[1] This is an expansion on my closing comments in an article I wrote in September, 2014. See: http://www.altcancer.net/ashwin/ashw0914.htm

The New York Times
abc
CNN
FOX

60
MINUTES
NBC

CBS

CNBC

BBC
WORLD
NEWS
THE WALL STREET JOURNAL

Chapter 4:

Testing The Limits Of Gullibility: How Government Conspiracies Are Used To Test & Measure "Victim Resistance"

In Chapter 2 we explored the landscape of negaciprocal territory, identifying increased thermodynamic potential as we approached Extreme Negaprocity. In Chapter 3 we built on this basic understanding to further define and delineate this territory. At the same time, we learned that a counterbalancing force, "victim resistance," increased as we moved in this same direction. Again, the more horrific the rape, the louder the victim will want to scream. Effective Government dictates that this simply cannot be tolerated. The victim may want to scream, but the rape must go on.

We subsequently discussed the vital role of propaganda in deflecting the concerns of citizens (i.e. victims) so that "victim resistance" is nullified or at least made manageable. As we discussed earlier, the goal is to get the rape victim to accept her own victimhood as benevolence – or, as Florynce Kennedy has noted, "There can be no really pervasive system of oppression . . . without the consent of the oppressed."[2]

Since we began with establishing Government's commitment to Extreme Negaprocity, the next question might be, "How does a Government know how far it can go? What it can get away with?" This question is a very crucial one, and modern, effective governing cannot take place if the boundaries of negaprocity are not constantly monitored and tested.

And so . . . how do you know what you can get away with? How do you know what acts of criminality you can safely commit without an unmanageable reaction on the part of your citi-

[2] See: Derrick Jensen and Aric McBay, Deep Green Resistance: Strategy to Save the Planet, (2011), p. 70.

zens/victims? We might compare this need to that of a seasoned bank robber.

While sitting in federal prison in Miami (late 2009), I had a cellmate who had robbed some 25 U.S. banks over a criminal career lasting quite a number of years. His lifetime earnings were somewhere in the vicinity of $500,000, as I recall.

Because I had never known a successful bank robber before, I couldn't help but inquire into his methods, which "Gerald" – I won't reveal his real name – was happy to share with me.

Gerald told me how he would study a bank well before making a "score." He knew when people came to work, what the security protocols were; he mapped out different escape routes and knew how far away the police stations were. He also monitored police communications on their frequencies, so he knew how occupied his potential adversaries in law enforcement were apt to be prior to entering the bank. Every robbery was an act of choreography. Gerald knew right to the second how long he had to get in, get the money, leave the bank, and be a safe distance away from the crime scene. Additionally, he also acted alone, because he understood that in a "snitch culture" environment, his greatest threat could come from the weak constitution of an accomplice who could "spill the beans" if things didn't go as planned. In short, he studied his target well and the many factors that could interfere with a successful robbery before committing to the act.

By contrast, I knew an inmate at the federal prison in Beaumont who was also a bank robber. It would appear that he wasn't very good at it, because he got caught on his very first attempt. Fashioning himself "The Lollipop Kid," this inmate expressed his admiration for the high drama of bank robbery as something – and I use this for lack of a better term – "heroic." Nonetheless, on closer examination, it became clear that the "Kid" used this romanticizing to mask something far more elemental: robbery was a cheap way to get money. Whereas Gerald was a philosopher and an anarchist who robbed banks and gave away most of his money, (pissed off at repeated U.S. Government abuses where he 'decided to attack the Government at their places of worship: the banks'), the "Kid" was just in it for the money; in fact, his rent was overdue at the time he made his sole attempt. Unlike Gerald, the Kid's financial need was his prime motivating factor.

When I asked the "Kid" what he did before trying to rob the bank, it was obvious that he had committed himself to nowhere near the preparation that had gone into Gerald's heists. In fact, shortly after being arrested, only then did the "Kid" realize that he had well exceeded the time he should have allotted himself to get in and out of the bank. "I got greedy," he told me. "If I had just taken a couple thousand dollars and left, I probably would have gotten away with it, but I got greedy and took too damn long."

Whereas the "Kid" opened himself up to chance, Gerald was methodical and put considerable energy into eliminating chance. Where the "Kid" acted on an immediate financial need; Gerald took his time and acted on principle. The "Kid" was impulsive; Gerald was not. The "Kid" did not understand the bank's vulnerabilities and weaknesses; Gerald wouldn't act unless he did. Gerald succeeded – for some time anyway – because he probed the limits of what he felt he could get away with. He tested the waters before each and every "job" prior to making his move. The "Kid" was an amateur; Gerald was a seasoned professional. Correspondingly, there are amateur Governments and seasoned, "professional" Governments, and it is easy to see which ones are more effective.

For all of Gerald's protests about a Government he found so distasteful, little did he stop to think that he was employing the very same technique that effective Governments use the world over: constantly testing the limits of what they can get away with. Their methods, however, are a little different, but that's only because the tools they use to steal from and financially enslave their own people – while simultaneously working to keep them ignorant and secure their consent – are more complicated than the tools a bank robber uses to steal from a bank.

The limits to the thermodynamic potential of any given act

by a modern Government are based not on what its constituent bodies would collectively like to do, but on the limits of what it can do with as little screaming as possible. It is essential, therefore, to constantly test the depths of a people's gullibility, because the level of nonsense you feed a people and get a majority of them to accept is an indicator of what acts you can safely commit with a maximized thermodynamic return. Any rapist will have an easier time with a victim who says, "Oh, you mean me? Okay, go ahead! I really believe you when you say that rape is good for me!" than he is with a victim who says, "Don't even think about, because if you try to rape me, I'll either cut your balls off or I'll die trying."

The attitude that an effective Government maintains to test the true limits of its abuse of power can be summed up in the following perpetual query: "If we can get the people to believe that, what can we get away with when we take it to the next level?"

Unless you know what a given people are and are not willing to believe, you have no idea what the limits of your power are. No Government can claim to be powerful if it doesn't know the limits to its abuse in dealing with its own people. To not know the limits of power among the people of another Government is understandable. To not know the limits of its abuse of its own people is inexcusable.

This is why those of us who have studied world history to any considerable degree are in absolute amazement as to what the U.S. Government has been able to get away with – particularly since 9/11. Yet we somehow understand it because a series of "testings" of breathtaking audacity preceeded it with very favorable response. ("Ok, this works for me! Please rape me more!") Americans have been repeatedly tested with one egregious lie after another throughout the history of the U.S. – each lie progressively more ridiculous – so that now, its leaders can "authorize" the funneling of trillions of nothings out the "back door" to their criminal bankster buddies with little result beyond a few Sunday comics that joke about it. Foreigners who watch U.S. foreign policy from a distance are often amazed at what ridiculous lies the majority here will believe, unaware that what made the U.S. Government the world's greatest superpower is precisely that: its supreme ability to exact such Extreme Negaprocity on a global scale with barely a whimper from the general public.

I'll pick from just five historic and current examples – all of which have occurred within my own lifetime, which together illustrate a crescendo of "gullibility tests" with corresponding successful results.

When John F. Kennedy was assassinated in 1963, I was in the second grade, living with my parents in Los Angeles. I was attending a public elementary school at the time called San Jose Street School, and the first sign that something very wrong was transpiring was the sight of a teacher from an adjoining classroom rushing into our class. She was crying and barely able to convey between sobs what she had just heard on the news. My fellow students and I – just seven years old at the time – stole glances at one another, completely mystified about what could be happening. That night I told my parents what had happened, and they explained to me how the President had been assassinated.

As events unfolded, first with the arrest and murder of Lee Oswald, and with time, the official explanation of what occurred – codified with the pronouncements of the Warren Commission – I believed everything I was told with the same dutifulness that I believed everything I was taught from our officially sanctioned history books.

It was only when I got older – well into my 30s – that I began to question what I had heard 25 years earlier, and came to the conclusion that the official explanation of JFK's assassination was completely fabricated. Since my aforementioned experience in the world of military intelligence was well behind me, I wasn't surprised that the official version was a complete lie. I knew, all too well, the inner workings of the black ops community within the intelligence establishment – and to whom they were beholden. Had JFK known the toes he was stepping on, particularly with his attempts to neuter the privately-held Federal Reserve Bank and reinstitute the constitutionally lawful issuance of real U.S. Government money, he surely would have known that he was making himself an assassination target.

Any U.S. President who attempted to do, today, what JFK did then, would likewise be "taken out." What surprised me more was just how many Americans were willing to accept the official version, cowed into submission for fear of appearing to be a "conspiracy theorist." The single greatest value of the Warren Commission was its ability to test the gullibility of the American People. Smashingly successful, today you will still find something close to 50% of the American people actually believe the astonishingly bogus official explanation. One of the Commission's members, Gerald Ford, would become a U.S. President just ten years later.

During the Presidential elections of 1992, Texas billionaire Ross Perot emphasized the disastrous effects that NAFTA and similar off-shoring measures would have to the American middle class. His "Paul Revere-style" warning would be remembered by his expression, "giant sucking sound" – signifying the deleterious effects on the country as the nation's best jobs left U.S. shores.[3]

In June, 1992, Perot was pulling polling figures of 39% of the vote – towering over candidates of the two officially sanctioned U.S. political parties – George Bush Sr. for the Republicans, and Bill Clinton for the Democrats. It wasn't long after that that Perot could be seen on The Larry King Show saying he was dropping out of the race because his family had been personally threatened by agents of the Bush family – whose historic ties to such extreme negaciprocal elements as Germany's Nazi Party, Operation Paperclip, and the CIA with its $600 billion a year in black ops cocaine and heroin operations, etc., are legendary.[4] Incidentally, the fact that being a billionaire in the U.S. – in Perot's case, one of its top 100 wealthiest citizens – still makes you a peon compared to the families that financially control this planet

[3] See: "Looks Like Ross Perot Was Right About The 'Giant Sucking Sound'," Business Insider, Feb. 11, 2011.

[4] See: Webster Tarpley and Anton Chaitkin, George Bush: The Unauthorized Biography, (2004).

is food for thought. It is amazing that anybody ever believed that ridiculous story about bowing out because the Bush family threatened to reveal compromising pictures of his daughter, who was about to be married. Come on. Couldn't they come up with a better lie than that? I've read more plausible cover stories in National Lampoon.

Subsequently, Ross was "tarred-and-feathered" by Government operatives as a wacko and largely forgotten by history. You rarely hear about him anymore, despite the fact that his warnings about a collapse in the U.S. job market have unfolded precisely as he said they would, accompanied by ridiculous "economic recovery" claims here in the U.S. that only an economic nincompoop could embrace. (As economic forecaster, Gerald Celente, likes to say: "It's not a recovery. It's a cover-up.")

Yes, the limits of the American People's gullibility were tested yet again – and this time the ante was upped to a yet higher level of absurdity. But it worked. A new threshold in "I believe you! Rape me, please! It's good for me!" had been reached. The fact that on re-entering the race – which was then "okay" because the intended damage had already been done – Perot got just 19% of the vote, or half of what he had the previous summer – demonstrated that the disinformation campaign had been a smashing success.

The next major event, which – for me – indicated that the table had been set to attain an even higher, stratospheric level of gullibility testing on the American people was 9/11. Now I realize that this is an even touchier subject than the two historical events just mentioned. I know that my entire reputation is now at stake for daring to propose that the official party line on Al-Qaeda – namely, that radical Muslims "hate us for our freedom," and has nothing to do with the indiscriminate bombing of women and children in Arab countries as we arrogantly go trampling through the Middle East in the quest to secure the oil, gas, Afghani poppy fields . . . and anything else we can steal – reads like something straight out of The Onion. I've had eight years in the U.S. criminal justice system to contemplate why those horrible, evil Muslims hate us for our freedom. Yeah. Given that the

U.S. puts more of its citizens, per capita, behind bars than any other nation ever recorded, I wonder if they shouldn't be hating us because we have more criminals here in the U.S. than in any other country on Earth.

I wonder if it ever offends them that the worst criminals are precisely the ones who are not behind bars.

The documentation that has been amassed to conclusively prove that 9/11 was an "inside job" – the most expensive theatrical presentation in the history of modern civilization – is nothing short of jaw-dropping. Those of us who are acquainted with the methodologies of the U.S. black ops community can see their fingerprints all over it. And footprints. And face prints. And butt prints. (I've included plenty of credible references in Chapter 5.)

Plenty of pressure has been applied to highly visible personages within the intellectual, publishing and political communities to maintain the party line. (You know what I mean, it's those Al-Qaeda people again. That mythical organization composed of any Muslim who doesn't agree with U.S. foreign policy in the Middle East and believes that the only way to alter events is to fight back. Yeah, the way the Founding Fathers of the United States fought back against the tyranny of their day.)

One salient example is a YouTube video I saw a couple of years ago where Noam Chomsky – a contrarian of U.S. foreign policy for many years now – was asked about "9/11 conspiracy theories." Without hesitating, Chomsky pooh-poohed any notion that there was any U.S. Government involvement. His rationale? That a cover-up of that magnitude would involve so many people that it couldn't effectively be pulled off. You'd never be able to keep it a secret.

Excuse me?

According to Katherine Austin Fitts, former U.S. Assistant Secretary of HUD, the CIA rakes in anywhere between five-hundred billion to one trillion in illegal drug revenues annually. That's not a single, one-time event. That's a massive, regular, day-to-day income stream. I have personally known dozens of people who were involved, directly or indirectly, in the U.S. Government's gargantuan drug operations. This enormous, ongoing, criminal, black operation involves many more people to maintain than 9/11 – a non-repeating, one day operation – would have ever required. I wasn't the only one to think that someone had whispered a word of caution into Chomsky's ear. Subsequent to that video, I was able to find numerous blogs and web posts that speculated on Chomsky's co-optation by the U.S. intelligence community.[5]

I had a cellmate in 2005, Juan, who did serious federal prison time for selling marijuana, by the metric ton. The CIA and DEA caught wind of his activities, but instead of "going in for the kill," decided that they liked his methods and felt that he could be useful to their cocaine operations, and so they tried to recruit him, or, as they say, "sheep dip" him.

Juan was so freaked out by the proposal made to him that he quickly passed on the deal, closed down his quite profitable operation, and decided to opt for an early retirement. Several months later, he decided to retool his entire distribution system in Mexico, and he quietly – or so he thought – got back into the business of selling that oh-so-nasty, nasty, backyard weed.

Fast forward several months later, and – you got it – Juan was arrested for selling "dope" early one morning at his home. All the usual actors were there on cue: local law enforcement, the SWAT team, DEA, FBI, the U.S. prosecutor, and – drumroll, please – the recruiting agent with the CIA that had tried to "sheep dip" him in the first place. They shot and killed his guard dogs, terrorized his family, and hauled him off handcuffed, but not before his CIA handler put in one last word:

"Juan, Juan, Juan, you weren't doin' anything wrong here, ol' buddy! But you're working for the wrong fuckin' team!"

An eight year term of imprisonment followed.

If the CIA can get away with moving the better part of a trillion dollars in illegal drugs every year, while relying on the gullibility of the American people to treat it as yet another unsubstantiated conspiracy theory; if the CIA, which is only one agency of the U.S. Government, can unlawfully produce

[5] See: "Noam Chomsky: Controlled Asset of the New World Order," http://educate-yourself.org/cn/noamchomskygatekepper26sep05.shtml

a revenue stream, which, if translated into private sector business, would make it the single most profitable corporation in the world – just how easy would it be to engineer an event like 9/11 and keep it a secret?

I'll tell you. It would be very, very easy. And as it was, it was.

Interestingly, Ron Paul – who runs a most interesting sideshow in the circus known as the U.S. Presidential elections – had a sign in his congressional office that read, "Don't steal! The Government doesn't like competition!" No, it certainly does not. And the 80%-plus of the U.S. federal prison population (in which I could be included) who are there on one or more "drug charges" are a living testament to that; which takes us on our journey to yet a higher threshold in the USA Government's quest to test the limits of its people's gullibility: the Wall Street bailouts.

In the summer of 2007 I had a business meeting in Houston with an attorney who wanted to compare notes on the "alternative views" concerning the economy – domestic and global, favorable expat locations, best offshore banking locations, the backroom deal-rigging in the gold and silver markets, etc. I'll never forget the meeting because it was early in the morning. We had agreed to have coffee, and the only place we could find that was open was a McDonald's. Let's call this friend "Dale," because this is another contact whose identity I won't reveal.

Dale knew that my wife and I had sold our food manufacturing company, the balance of our commercial real estate, and our home. Actually, Cathryn and I had been steadily liquidating since 2003, in part because I could see the downturn in 2008 coming as easily as I can see the lines on my palms. We sold my chemical manufacturing operation in 2003; Lumen Foods in March, 2007; and did a wrap-around contract on our home that very summer. We took in about $1.2 million – a fraction of what those properties in the aggregate were really worth. This sum is nothing compared to what U.S. agents destroyed when they decimated my laboratory.

Dale asked me pointedly why I was in such a hurry to get

out of the country, and I told him that an insider had confided to me that there was a conspiracy brewing at the U.S. Prosecutor's Office in Lafayette, Louisiana, involving FDA Special Agent, John Armand – who, as I detail in Meditopia, was bribed to bring fictitious FDA charges against me just four years prior. The goal was to get me "violated" on my supervised release so that I would have to go back to federal prison. This insider told me that my family would be in danger if I remained in the U.S. (Incidentally, everything I was told turned out to be true.)

I then asked Dale why he was considering leaving the U.S. at which point, I heard this big sigh and a long pause. What followed went something like this.

"Well, it's pretty simple, really," he began, "I have several clients who are close to this whole derivatives mess on Wall Street . . ."

"And?"

"Oh man . . . I don't know if I wanna get into all this right now. How much do you know about the state of the leveraged derivatives market?"

"Probably not enough. Finance isn't my field. But my instinct is that a major downturn is imminent; it was another contributing factor to our liquidating everything we own here."

"Well, finance isn't my specialty, either, but this is the 800 pound gorilla in the economy that nobody in the main media seems to wanna talk about. The whole thing's gonna implode sooner or later. I mean, we're only talking about half a quadrillion dollars."

"Okay," I asked, "so what if it implodes? What does that have to do with leaving the country? So what if a few Wall Street banks go belly up, file for bankruptcy, and see new ownership?"

"What, are you nuts? Don't you understand the magnitude of this thing? We're talking a sum of money that's greater than the net value of the total assets of every corporation on Earth, and the collapse of some players on Wall Street is only the first in a chain of events."

"What are your insiders telling you?"

"Listen, these are really big players. You'll see a few smaller banks and brokerage houses go under because that'll play well on CNN, but the ones who control the levers of power, like Goldman Sachs and JP Morgan, will use their political muscle to get the whores in Washington to bail them out, and we're talking many trillions of dollars running out the back door."

"Who told you this?"

"It doesn't matter, but here's the kicker: the bailouts we're talking about make the S&L (Savings and Loans) crisis look like pocket change. The sums are so large that only a part of the bailout will end up being reported 'on the books.' They'll never let the real numbers get leaked out."

"So? What are we talking about? Hyperinflating the currency? That isn't news. Hell, the U.S. dollar has already lost 96% of its value over the past century."

"Damn, you don't see it, do you? I'd stick around if we were just talking hyperinflation. I have clients in Brazil that weathered the collapse of the 'real,' and you have friends in Ecuador who survived the death of the 'sucre.'"

"Then what?"

"What follows the bailouts and the bleed-out of the dollar – which won't crash and burn without impacting the other fiat currencies, hell, how can it not? it's the world's reserve currency – is something much worse than all this nonsense in Iraq and Afghanistan. The American people will be too stupid to realize that eventually they'll wag the dog to a new level of violence."

"What? World War III?"

"Of course. It'll be quiet at first. More invasions in the Middle East, the use of advanced weaponry that's kept out of the media, the unleashing of some of those superbugs they've been developing at Plum Island, the urgent call for more toxic public vaccination programs. The American public can't bitch about the economy, no matter how bad it gets, if Washington can get a healthy pandemic going. But it's gotta happen. There's no getting around it. It's the only way to get rid of all this bad accounting."

Good God! Bad accounting. How refreshingly euphemistic.

"So what makes you think that things will be better for you

if you leave the country?" I asked pressingly. "I have different reasons, so I'd still be moving to Ecuador even if none of this other stuff was going on."

"I've put a pencil to this and looked at it forwards, backwards, upside down, diagonal, and inside out. I don't see how these things unfold without turning the U.S. into a post-industrial waste dump."

"A poor third-world country." I interjected.

"No, what comes to mind is something closer to Mad Max and Thunderdome. I'd rather take my chances in South America."

This is a fairly close approximation of my conversation with Dale. I didn't record the conversation, so I can't reproduce it word for word. But three things should immediately strike the reader, beginning with our use of "bifurcated communications." What I mean by that is even those of us who are able to see behind the veil of the BCN have had to develop two modes of thinking and of expressing ourselves. One is with our informed friends who are operating in the "know," which comprises roughly 5% of our acquaintances. We know when we're getting raped; we don't like it; so we take an interest in knowing the latest Government schemes to try and rape us again. We know that the Government lies all the time, so we want to know where to find the 2% in the rat poison.

The other mode is with the 95% of our fellow citizens who are still biorobotic zombies – the ones who prefer to believe that the professional wrestling match is a real athletic contest – the very ones to whom Government's never-ending gullibility tests are directed. Dale could only speak to me the way he did because he knew I was a "five percenter." He doesn't speak that way to his clueless clients, associate attorneys, or even family members who don't know what's going on.

The second thing that should strike the reader – and I alluded to this earlier – is that gullibility testing has a cumulative effect. Once Government has successfully secured one level of gullibility, it will always keep going until the majority of the people rise up and say, "Enough is enough. We're not taking your bullshit anymore. We know what you're doing." In other words, the rape never stops increasing in frequency or intensity until you threaten to cut their balls off, or die trying.

The third thing is the sheer magnitude, qualitatively and quantitatively, of the current grand display of Extreme Negaprocity. It has been made possible because previous gullibility tests proved to be so successful. According to Forbes Magazine, the total amount of money involved in the bailouts exceeds $16 trillion.[6] The U.S. Government will never admit to it, of course, despite the fact that various alternative media personalities have carefully documented the money trail. But, as Dale so presciently noted, the fix was in well before U.S. congressmen had their arms twisted by threats of imminent martial law if they didn't sign off on supporting legislation.

The rape of the U.S. Treasury, to the grave detriment of the American people, is so severe that it moved economist/author Michael Hudson to note: "Since they realized that the American economy is dead, they are trying to suck as much blood out of America as possible while the corpse is still warm."[7] The financial collapse that will ensue over the coming years is so predictable that U.S. Government planners have erected dozens of FEMA concentration camps. (You can see tours of them on YouTube, along with Jesse Ventura's episode of "Conspiracy Theory," where he provides more detail.)[8] How many Americans are prepared to admit to themselves that with the construction of these little Auschwitz camps – the result of many years of planning and construction – they are witnessing expressions of negaprocity that are no different than those of the Nazis during World War II?

My fifth and final example comports with our chronological rendering of increasingly more outrageous gullibility tests over time. As in my first example, this has to do with the U.S.

6 See: "The Big Bank Bailouts" https://www.forbes.com/sites/mikecollins/2015/07/14/the-big-bank-bailout/#cc629eb2d83f

7 See: Michael Hudson, "Financial Parasites Have Killed the American Economy," http://www.globalresearch.ca/financial-parasites-have-killed-the-american-economy/14922

8 See: Jesse Ventura, "Police State FEMA Camps," https://www.youtube.com/watch?v=h6vsK-MaSG1s

Presidency itself.

Early in 2011 Donald Trump made news by indicating his interest in seeking the U.S. Presidential nomination. Not long after his announcement he began to make an issue of Barack Obama's ineligibility to be president. If you're not from the U.S., you might not know that having been born in the U.S. is a Constitutional requirement in seeking the Presidency. Even before this development, there was an astonishing amount of proof – through eyewitness testimony, documentation, and circumstantial evidence that Obama was born in Kenya and that his alibi that he was born in Hawaii is a complete fraud. Like those who question the official 9/11 version of events and are termed "9/11 truthers," similarly a separate movement had arisen over Obama's obvious ineligibility to have been a U.S. Senator from Illinois (the first phase of this particular "gullibility test"), let alone President. The recently assigned name by the media for the latter is "the birther movement."

Of all the "gullibility tests" we have examined so far, none is as brazen as the handling of Obama's eligibility. Not even close. It can easily be argued that in terms of financial impact, 9/11 is unassailable, but in terms of outrageousness and venturing into new heights of gullibility where no man has ever gone before, Obama's ineligibility trumps all.

In April, 2011, the Obama Administration, having been nagged to death to produce his "long form" birth certificate, proving that he was truly born in Hawaii in August, 1961, finally came forth with his "final answer." Already the U.S. Supreme Court had blocked legal challenges to Obama's ineligibility by refusing to let the matter go to court. Still, the brave people comprising the "birther movement" were proving an annoyance. But here was an opportunity to make Donald Trump impotent, neuter the birther movement, and execute the final phase of this conspiratorial test – all in one fell swoop.

Upon examining the resulting document, graphics experts were horrified to discover that not only was it easy to tell that Obama's birth certificate was a forgery, but that the document itself was not recomposed to combine its underlying layers. If you don't know what that means, ask anybody who is proficient as a graphics designer – particularly someone who is experienced in working with Photoshop. Put in simpler terms, Obama's "long form" birth certificate wasn't just a fake; it had been presented to the public in such a manner that the Obama Administration was brazenly bragging about its lack of authenticity. To even the average observer it was difficult to tell whether or not this was a major screw-up on the part of the Obama Administration, or whether the act was deliberate and this was essentially Obama's way of saying, "Possession is nine-tenths the law, you mongoloid idiots. I'm President and I'm going to stay President. So what if I was born in Kenya? Who among you is going to do a God damn thing about it? So you can just shut up and fuck off." Whereas Obama's predecessor, George Bush, could so contemptuously remark that the U.S. Constitution was "nothing but a God damn piece of paper,"[9] Obama could conclusively prove it.

As if all this wasn't enough, to make his point loud and clear, Obama confirmed that this was a case of acknowledging he was born in Kenya and that the American people had crossed a new threshold in the heavens of hitherto unimaginable gullibility. He did this by brazenly reproducing copies of his fake birth certificate on coffee mugs and T-shirts, and having them distributed by his supporters. This amounted to arrogantly thumbing his nose at any and all citizens who had legitimate concerns about Obama's right to hold the nation's highest office. Worse still, it showed the degree to which executive privilege had made the U.S. Constitution completely irrelevant – "nothing but a (worthless) God damn piece of paper," even in the eyes of the U.S. Supreme Court.

No other conspiracy in the history of the U.S. has been executed in such an "in your face" manner. No other conspiracy in U.S. history has done more to prove that the U.S. mass media – which has sat silently on the sidelines while the "alternative

[9] See: http://hammeroftruth.com/2005/bush-bashes-constitution-just-a-gd-piece-of-paper/, see also: http://www.washingtonsblog.com/2013/03/obama-is-worse-than-bush-in-favoring-the-super-elite-bailing-out-the-big-banks-protecting-financial-criminals-targeting-whistleblowers-secrecy-and-trampling-our-liberties.html

media" has provided the bulk of the revelations – are traitorous to the interests of the American People. Indeed, Obama and his handlers successfully proved that average Americans are among the most gullible citizens ever governed.

I would make the case that this level of testing was predictable. There is enough space in the FEMA concentration camps, along with untold acres of unfilled coffins – enough to hold millions of people, all of it viewable on YouTube as of this writing – that new testing was inevitable to see how the American people would respond to martial law and the eventual extermination of those who had not reached an understanding of what, to use the words of former U.S. President G.W. Bush, "you are either with us or against us,"[10] really means. Here's what it means, "We will continue to rape you. It will be worse than before, and you will like it and not complain, or we will get rid of you with no less ferocity than we are getting rid of pesky Arabs all over the Middle East who stand in the way of our fascist agenda."

Americans, with their own acquiescence, are now prepared for the ultimate in Extreme Negaprocity, and in the minds of the puppet masters who really call the shots in the U.S., this is just as it should be. Americans have now consented to something worse than financial servitude, something much worse.

Are you able to break through the bondage created by a "dumbed down" educational system; by the crippling, cumulative effects of your fluoridated water, by your nutrient deficient drive-thru happy meals and industrial, chemically enhanced processed foods, by your propagandistic "fake news" media inputs, by your hopelessly self-destructive benign common narrative, and the exploitative effects of misleading programming from newspapers, magazines, television, radio, and now even your telephone? Are you able to see yet what you have consented to?

It doesn't have to be this way, but don't blame anyone in authority. You asked for this. How else would you expect your rapist to respond when you keep saying, "Oh, I'm so glad you picked me! I really believe you when you say that rape is good for me!"

[10] See: George Bush, https://www.youtube.com/watch?v=-23kmhc3P8U

Do you see what happens when you are acquiescent and you don't fight back? Do you understand why your forefathers gave you a Second Amendment in the first place? Why Government only gets worse when you don't perpetually confront it with a "Give me liberty or give me death" mentality? And what happens when you can't look your rapist in the face and tell him to back off, or you'll cut his nuts off or die trying?

Breaking out of victimhood doesn't require genius. It doesn't demand a superior education, or the kind of inside connections that some of my associates have – although all these things help.

It does, however, require that you realize that the Government isn't there for you and that it is a grave mistake to see those in authority as reciprocal in their nature or in their intentions. It also requires some common sense and a certain discipline – the kind that allows you to keep your sanity by still finding love and beauty in this world, even when those in charge are programmed to take that impulse and use it to turn you into a pathetically decerebrated moron.

"Our work is done here"

Chapter 5:

Psychopathy & Sectoral Distance: How Our Model Provides An Understanding Of The Relationship Between Good & Evil

---

Historical Documents That Enhance This Understanding

Any discussion of "good and evil" is usually found to reside within the realm of philosophy and religion, of which – if we confine ourselves to the latter – there are literally thousands. Most people are content to settle on eleven major faiths: Hinduism, Buddhism, Judaism, Christianity, Islam, Confucianism, Taoism, Jainism, Sikhism, Zoroastrianism, and Shinto. However, these are only the larger categories. By one estimate, there are 30,000 different variations of Christianity alone. By any conservative estimate, there are many tens of thousands of different "religions" in the world if we include the many "subsects."[1]

Nonetheless, all of these faiths, diverse as they are, with untold lists of observable dos and don'ts, tend to agree with certain principles as to what constitutes good and evil. As a species, we tend to associate "good" with love of neighbor, kindness, compassion, empathy, generosity, etc. Conversely, we associate "evil" with hate, greed, arrogance, lust, etc. Of ancient Christian origin are the "Seven Deadly Sins," which do a reasonably good job of defining the territory: pride, greed, lust, envy, gluttony, wrath and sloth, followed by the "Seven Cardinal Virtues": prudence, justice, temperance, courage (or fortitude), faith, hope, and charity. There are countless variations on this theme. Strip out references to admonition on sexual conduct (a great control

[1] See: https://www.psychologytoday.com/blog/excellent-beauty/201504/why-are-there-so-many-religions

mechanism) and theology (another great control mechanism) and you find that there is a striking correspondence between sectoral distance and "good and evil." Within the center of the reciprocity zone, you find characteristics most people normally associate with "good," and as you cross into the negaprocity zone, you find characteristics most people associate with "evil." (This is unmistakeably true once we get to the Outer Bands.) Indeed, we could – if only for illustrative purposes – construct a new philosophy or religion, built on the concepts of sectoral distance and the characteristics of each sector presented so far alone in this book.

As we are expanding on earlier concepts, we need to have a clearer definition of these relationships if we're going to understand our history with greater clarity and how negaprocity is bringing us to habitat collapse and the extinction of our species, not to mention myriad other species which we're in the process of taking down with us.

We began our study with the **center** of Marshall Sahlins' reciprocity chart: pure, unconditional love – a place from which there is no sectoral distance. This state, this condition of freely loving with no expectation of return, is our starting point. However, it is also the starting point for most religions: the grand act of Creation, the Beginning, one in which a Supreme Being or Source, complete and without need or want or desire, acting out of nothing more than Pure Love, sets Creation into motion. There is a Vedic saying in India: "the purpose of Creation is the expansion of Happiness." [2]

This is love in its purest form.

A mother's decision to have a child – love, feed, nurture, and care for her offspring – is a microcosm and re-enactment of this grand creative act. If you weren't a test tube baby, your birth and nurturing means that you came into this world from this **center** – a place without sectoral distance.

It is interesting to note that the majority of us with extensive

[2] See: Maharishi Mahesh Yogi, Science of being in Art of Living: Transcendental Meditation, (2001).

experience in the use of entheogens[3] have "unconditional love" revealed as the foundation of our existence. Great spiritual mystics and poets from different religious and cultural backgrounds have generously expanded on their experiences of "God" as a force of "pure goodness" throughout the course of history.[4]

> " I AM he who aches with amorous Love
> Does the Earth gravitate?
> Does not all matter, aching, attract all matter?
> So the body of me, to all I meet, or know."
>
> Walt Whitman
> "Leaves of Grass"

Conversely, there are documents which clearly link effective governance to a commitment to evil policies, intentions, and actions – negaprocity. In this regard, this book cannot be called original. I was exposed to the first such work in college during a political science course. Niccolo Machiavelli's, The Prince,[5] first published in 1513, clearly delineates the actions a political leader, the Prince, must make if he wishes to govern effectively:

- If taking over as a new principality, you must kill all the supporters of the former Prince of a hereditary principality. Machiavelli goes into detail on the importance of killing off rebels and those opposed to his rule. Although he also cautions against taking violent action if there is a threat of revenge.[6]
- Statecraft and warcraft are intertwined and necessary, not because they are vital to the welfare of a people, but because

[3] See: https://psychonautwiki.org/wiki/Entheogen

[4] It even works its way into comedy – see Bill Hicks' rendition of his mushroom experience at :https://www.youtube.com/watch?v=UQq9cmMGSQc

[5] Help for the following section is provided by the Gutenberg Project: http://www.gutenberg.org/ebooks/1232 and SparkNotes: http://www.sparknotes.com/philosophy/prince/

[6] See: The Prince, chapter 3

they are essential for the Prince to stay in power. Everything about Machiavelli's ideology is geared towards what is beneficial to the "Prince" (the State), not what is beneficial for the masses. In this regard, The Prince is a handbook for applied negaprocity. Moreover, Machiavelli uses numerous historical examples to reinforce his admonishments, as if to say, "Negaprocity has been the foundation of the State since time immemorial. To act in any other fashion (i.e. with reciprocity) is to risk the death of the State." Later in the work, Machiavelli goes so far as to say in Chapter 19 that "a Prince must have no other objective, no other thought, nor take up any profession but that of war . . . The easiest way to lose a State is by neglecting the art of war. The best way to win a State is to be skilled in the art of war."[7]

- The ordinary citizen (free man) is an expendable commodity to the Prince. Citizens may love or hate their ruler, based on whether the Prince's actions benefit them or they are injured by them. But the important thing is to maintain control. Any concern for the citizen's welfare is of value to the Prince only to the extent that it helps maintain control [8]
- Complete destruction is the surest way that the Prince can secure a State that has been free in the past. One gets the distinct sense that Machiavelli feels the Prince has a "moral" obligation to completely decimate a people who have previously known freedom, because once a people have known freedom as a way of life, they cannot otherwise be relied on to be good subjects. Only in this way can a wayward people be subdued and not pose a future risk to the Prince's rule.
- The Prince should set lofty goals worthy of praise by his subjects, knowing full well that if he doesn't meet these goals, even faint attempts in their direction will be seen as a promise of their completion. In other words, deception is crucial.
- Ruling over people is made easier by the fact that they are little more than cattle. Men are followers who were meant

[7] See: The Prince, Chapter 14.

[8] Ibid. These matters are primarily covered in the first four chapters of the book.

to be ruled over.

- Machiavelli doesn't put a limit on the cruelty or criminal activity the Prince must employ to secure and keep power, but rather on its duration. His advice is to commit one's atrocities all at once so that the governed will forget them with time. This is "victim suppression." Although Machiavelli acknowledges that cruelty is "evil," it doesn't dissuade him from encouraging its use to serve a pragmatic end. Some have noted that Machiavelli's acknowledgement that cruelty is evil makes the accusation that The Prince is an amoral work unjustified. Nonsense. The world is full of people in power who know quite well that their acts are evil and immoral. Acknowledgment of it does not make these acts less evil.
- The author advises that the Prince secure the well-being and confidence of his subjects during difficult times or when his kingdom is under siege. But this is not out of any sense of kindness or compassion, but rather to ensure that the Prince's power isn't seriously threatened. Again, maintaining power is far more important than the needs of a governed people.
- Machiavelli makes a convincing argument that sound laws and sound military go hand-in-hand. You cannot have one without the other. It is easy to propose, by extension, that you cannot have effective, enforceable law without negaprocity, since the military is inherently non-reciprocal.
- A Prince who exhibits generosity, compassion, or other virtues associated with goodness will ruin his State.
- It is better for a Prince to be feared than to be loved, which reinforces Machiavelli's position that the State is a creature of negaprocity.
- Maintaining his personal army is another situation where we see negaprocity in full bloom. Machiavelli indicates this when it comes to maintaining discipline, that there is never such a thing as too much cruelty. The mind of a successful Prince is cold and calculating, devoted to the ends rather than the means.
- A Prince is more successful when he employs cunning,

craftiness, and an ability to trick others. The Prince must readily break promises when it works to his advantage. The Prince must be a master of deception, yet emanate a virtuous air that belies his deceitful nature. A Prince should present the appearance of being a compassionate, trustworthy, kind, guileless, and pious ruler. Of course, actually possessing all these virtues is neither possible nor desirable.

- An effective Prince should take credit for his successes and blame unpopular laws or policies on lesser officials. Again, the aim of the Prince is not to be loved, but to avoid being hated. It's appearance that matters.
- A Prince appears great by defeating opposition. So it is in the interest of the Prince to foster his own opposition that can be readily subdued. Additionally, fostering subversion helps reveal the motives and identities of potential conspirators. Again, the successful Prince must embody the "virtues" of being deceptive, cruel, and dishonest.[9]

I could expand on The Prince at some length, but I believe these pointers make clear that the meaning and use of the term "Machiavellian" is well-deserved. A very clear picture is presented here of the negaprocity that a political leader must exhibit in order to obtain and maintain rulership over his subjects. The fact that this work addressed the rulership of a monarch and not the leader of a republic doesn't change the fact that it firmly and accurately describes the kind of negaciprocal activities that those in Government must exhibit.

Now, some have come to the conclusion that The Prince is a satire.[10] Again, this is the same treatment that Parkinson got in his coverage of how reality works. We're back to advice from Shakespeare: "Many a truth has been spoken in jest." Cynical, cheeky or not, doesn't make it less true.

I have devoted a few pages to The Prince, because it clearly

[9] Once again, help for this section was provided by the Gutenberg Project: http://www.gutenberg.org/ebooks/1232 and SparkNotes: http://www.sparknotes.com/philosophy/prince/

[10] By way of example, see Garrett Mattingly's "The Prince: Political Science or Political Satire?," http://www2.idehist.uu.se/distans/ilmh/Ren/flor-mach-mattingly.htm

affirms the relationship between the effective exercise of power and the manifestation of psychopathic behavior, and by extension, the magnetic attraction of diagnosable psychopaths into positions of high governmental power. Before proceeding, it is important to define the characteristics of a psychopath, and for that I refer to the most commonly used checklist utilized by mental health care practitioners, the Psychopathy Checklist Revised (PCL-R). I prefer this over the Antisocial Personality Disorder (ASPD) checklist contained in the Diagnostic and Statistical Manual of Mental Disorders (DSM V), since only about 1 in 5 people with ADP is a psychopath.[11] So the characteristics of a psychopath are:

- **Uncaring/Emotional Detachment**. This would take the form of a general state of callousness, lack of caring and empathy, coldheartedness, unconcern for the feelings of others. There is often a biological component with psychopaths, involving weak connections among the components of the brain's emotional systems. The inability to feel deeply is broad and includes extremely high thresholds for disgust, as measured by their reactions when shown disgusting photos of mutilated faces and when exposed to foul odors.
- **Shallow Emotions.** Psychopaths show a general lack of emotion, especially social emotions, such as remorse, shame, guilt, fear, and embarrassment. The PCL-R describes psychopaths as emotionally shallow and showing a lack of guilt.
- **Irresponsibility.** Psychopaths demonstrate irresponsibility and blame externalization. (That is, they blame others for events that are actually their fault.) They may admit blame when forced into a corner, but these admissions are not accompanied by a sense of shame or remorse, and they have no power to change future be-

[11] See: "What is a Psychopath?" by William Hirstein, Ph.D. https://www.psychologytoday.com/blog/mindmelding/201301/what-is-psychopath-0 The list that follows is drawn from this Psychology Today article and for those wanting a more complete explanation of these points, I recommend reading the article in its entirety.

havior.

- **Insincere speech.** Dr. Hirstein's description says it all: Ranging from what the PCL-R describes as "glibness" and "superficial charm" to Cleckley's "untruthfulness" and "insincerity,"[12] to outright "pathological lying," there is a trend toward devaluing speech among psychopaths by inflating and distorting it toward selfish ends. The criteria for APD include "conning others for personal profit or pleasure." One concerned father of a young sociopathic woman said, "I can't understand the girl, no matter how hard I try. It's not that she seems bad or exactly that she means to do wrong. She can lie with the straightest face, and after she's found in the most outlandish lies she still seems perfectly easy in her own mind."[13] This casual use of words may be attributable to what some researchers call a shallow sense of word meaning. Psychopaths do not show a differential brain response to emotional terms over neutral terms that normal people do. They also have trouble understanding metaphors and abstract words."
- **Overconfidence.** This takes the form of a "grandiose sense of self-worth."
- **Narrowing of Attention.** Again, from Hirstein: "According to Newman and his colleagues the core deficit in psychopathy is a failure of what they call response modulation.[14] When normal people engage in a task, they are able to alter their activity, or modulate their responses, depending on relevant peripheral information that appears after the task has begun. Psychopaths are specifically deficient in this ability, and according to Newman, this explains the impulsivity of psychopaths, a trait which shows up in several of the lists of criteria, as well as their problems with passive avoidance and

[12] See: Hervey Cleckley, The Mask of Sanity: An Attempt to Reinterpret the So-called Psychopathic Personality, (1941).

[13] Ibid p 47.

[14] Regarding insincere speech, overconfidence, and narrowing of attention, see: https://psychopathyawareness.wordpress.com/2011/10/03/the-list-of-psychopathy-symptoms/

with processing emotions."
Top-down attention tends to be under voluntary control, whereas bottom-up attention happens involuntarily.

- **Selfishness.** This would be embodied by "pathologic egocentricity," (and incapacity for love/a parasitic life-style).
- **Inability to plan for the future.** This includes a "lack of realistic long-term goals."
- **Violence.** This is seen as a very low tolerance to frustration and a low threshold for discharge of aggression, including violence.

This is not the only list, but it's fairly reliable. Someone recently sent me a graphic with a picture of the last four U.S. presidents (i.e. Obama, Bush I, Bush II, and Clinton) with a heading that read: "Characteristics of Psychopaths." Beside this, in much smaller type, was the following list, all of which comports with my study of psychopathic individuals:

- Aggressive, callous, and cunning.
- Complete absence of conscience and empathy
- Very adept at manipulating others, especially emotionally.
- Willingness to engage in immoral, criminal behavior.
- Willingness to take what they want and do as they please, regardless of who is hurt or wronged.
- Deceptive ability to appear outwardly benevolent.
- Deceptive ability to behave in superficially charming ways to hide purely selfish motives.
- Willingness to use intimidation and violence to control others in order to satisfy their own needs.
- Willingness to intentionally violate the basic inherent human rights of others.
- Complete absence of any sense of guilt or remorse for the harm their actions have caused others.
- Rationalization of their own immoral behavior
- Will attempt to lay blame upon someone else for their

conduct.
- Denial – will outright deny their own wrongdoing.
- Utter contemptuousness toward the feelings and desires of their fellow beings.
- Pathological lying – will say anything without any concern for truth in order to advance their own hidden agendas.
- Ability to feign normal human emotions and empathy.
- Severely distorted sense of the consequences of their own actions.
- Total failure to accept any responsibility for their own socially irresponsible ways.
- Strong belief that they will never be brought to justice for their criminal behavior.

Why do we consistently see people in high places of power exhibiting these characteristics? Could it be that if you're going to create organizations with "high sectoral distance" which are psychopathic by their very nature, you'll need plenty of psychopaths in charge for them to be able to operate?

These questions practically answer themselves, but what is worse, they give us an insight to understanding why the institutions and the people at the highest levels who run them in the "Outer Bands" are more than just psychopathic. They are, going back to our opening discussion in this chapter, outright evil.

Long before the rise of Christianity or Islam as dominating religious forces in the modern period, there existed Gnosticism, an ancient system of understanding man and his place in the universe. Relentlessly hunted into obscurity, the Gnostics have left us little today but the remains of some of their sacred documents, now collectively referred to as "The Nag Hammadi" texts.[15]

What I find interesting about the Gnostics is their under-

[15] See: Marvin Meyer (ed.), The Nag Hammadi Scriptures, The International Edition, (2007). .

standing that within the unseen demonic realms there exists a class of interdimensional beings called "archons" that feed off of negative human emotions. In many cases, this "feeding" is not so unseen. We have all known people, and – yes – the majority of them are psychopaths, who rejoice at the sight of someone else's misfortune or pain. We have no unique word in English for this phenomenon, so we borrow from the German, "Schadenfreude" (broken down as "schaden" for harm, and "freude" for joy).

In a sense, "Schadenfreude" is a mere shadow of something much deeper and far more insidious.

"In short, the psychopath is a predator. If we think about the interactions of predators with their prey in the animal kingdom, we can come to some idea of what is behind the 'mask of sanity' of the psychopath. Just as the animal predator will adopt all kinds of stealthy functions in order to stalk their prey, cut them out of the herd, get close to them, and reduce their resistance, so does the psychopath construct all kinds of elaborate camouflage composed of words and appearances – lies and manipulation – in other to 'assimilate' their prey.

This leads us to an important question: ***what does the psychopath really get from their victims?*** *It's easy to see what they are after when they lie and manipulate for money or material goods or power. But in many instances, such as love relationships or faked friendships, it is not so easy to see what the psychopath is after. Without wandering too far afield into spiritual speculations – a problem Cleckley also faced – we can only say that it seems to be that* ***the psychopath enjoys making others suffer. Just as normal humans enjoy seeing other people happy****, or doing things that make other people smile,* ***the psychopath enjoys the exact opposite.****"*[16] (emphasis added)

In his book, The Omniverse, Alfred Lambremont Webre describes archons as "hyperdimensional controllers."[17] I consider his explanation so vital to our coming discussion that I quote

[16] See: Andrew M. Lobaczewski, Political Ponerology, (2007) p. 17.

[17] See: Alfred Lambremont Webre, The Omniverse, (2015).

it in full:

"The ancient Gnostic texts from Egypt, the Nag Hammadi library, describe two types of demonic alien beings that invaded Earth long ago, which they call the archons. The first type of archon looks like a reptile, the other like a human embryo, with the same shape and appearance as the 'sky fish' photos. To sort out and clarify what the Sophianic narrative may have to say about the test of the archons is a great challenge to our understanding of the Gnostic message and how it can benefit humanity today.

"According to researcher and cosmologist Laura Magdalene Eisenhower (great-granddaughter of U.S. president, Dwight Eisenhower), archons are hidden negative controllers of humankind; they are inorganic interdimensional entities that must now be exposed and exorcised from the individual human mind, from our human species, from the planet, and from our universe as a whole, as part of our collective evolution to a new state of consciousness and being.

"Researcher Robert Stanley maintains that humanity must now take a scientific approach to identifying archons and exterminating them.

"It is time to expose the covert controllers of mankind. I assure you this is not speculation, a hoax, or the figment of people's imagination. These parasitic creatures are real and they need to be dealt with immediately so mankind can evolve to the next level of existence.

"Although these parasites are not human, they feed off the negative emotions of humans. It is unclear when these amoeba-like creatures first came to Earth, but we know they were discovered by shamans in altered states of consciousness long ago and have recently been photographed. The reason everyone is not seeing them on a daily basis is because the creature's energy signature is beyond our normal, narrow range of vision within the electromagnetic spectrum, what scientists call 'visible light.'"

"In discussing archons, John Lash writes:

"Although archons do exist physically, the real danger they pose to humanity is not invasion of the planet, but invasion of the mind.

"The archons are intrapsychic mind-parasites who access human consciousness through telepathy and simulation. They infect our imagination and use the power of make-believe for deception and confusion. Their pleasure is in deceit for its own sake, without a particular aim or purpose. They are robotic in nature, incapable of independent thought or choice, and have no particular agenda, except to live vicariously through human beings . . ."[18]

However, even this belies the fact that the arrangement is bilateral, and that it is the psychopath who gives this archon-"human" relationship "purpose." The psychopath must allow himself or herself to become an agent of evil. In a very real sense, the psychopaths we find in the Outer Bands are individuals who have sacrificed their spiritual identity to act as agents for the archons or other demonic entities. It is interesting that people who have "sold themselves" frequently comment that they have "sold their soul to the devil," or as Lobaczewski noted:

"Hervey Cleckley actually comes very close to suggesting that psychopaths are human in every respect – ***but that they lack a soul****. This lack of 'soul quality' makes them very efficient 'machines.' They can write scholarly works, imitate the words of emotions, but over time, it becomes clear that their words do not match their actions. They are the type of person who can claim that they are devastated by grief who then attend a party 'to forget.' The problem is: they really do forget.*

Being very efficient machines, like a computer, they are able to execute very complex routines designed to elicit support for what they want. ***In this way, many psychopaths are able to reach very high positions in life****. It is only over time that their associates become aware of the fact that* ***their climb up the ladder of success is predicated on violating the rights of others****.*

[18] Ibid, p. 93-95.

Even when they are indifferent to the rights of their associates, they are often able to inspire feelings of trust and confidence."[19] (emphasis added)

In the document exploration that is to come we find repeated references that attempt to justify violating the rights of others to fulfill political objectives.

In an earlier work, I wrote about my entheogenic experiences with various creatures in the non-physical realms, both angelic and demonic.[20] Uniformly and without exception, the demonic entities I have encountered represent the far extreme of what I would define as "negaprocity." Psychopaths are our fellow human beings, many of them politicians, who assume the role of the demonic, but they are, nonetheless, encumbered by physical bodies, which may mute the full intensity of their evil potential. Demonic entities in the non-physical realm, however, have no such encumbrances. They work to create and nurture fear, agony, terror, hatred, and other negative emotions. They take Schadenfreude to an entire new level, and spend an inordinate amount of time working on people who occupy the Outer Bands so that more "loosh" – the term Robert Monroe used to describe the negative emotions generated by humans which is served as food in the demonic realms – is made available. If you ever wondered why so many people in Government get excited making the lives of ordinary citizens miserable just for the "fun of it," now you know.

Clearly, there are periods of world history where "psychopathic expression," the elevation of vice, the diminution of virtue, and the involvement of demonic entities in human affairs reach their ascendency. We see this most clearly in how Governments have conducted themselves in modern times. Moreover, there are historical documents, even stronger than The Prince, which clearly support these tendencies, and these are areas which we will explore next.

[19] See: Andrew M. Lobaczewski, Ibid., p. 11

[20] See: Caton, (2012).

In 1972, at the age of 16, I took up the practice of Transcendental Meditation. Actually, in those days, I was studying principles put forth by Maharishi Mahesh Yogi, and the name of the organization was the "Spiritual Regeneration Movement" (SRM). Prior to learning to meditate, I was required to study Maharishi's "Science of Creative Intelligence." Paradoxically, I did this all this while attending a Catholic seminary – the now defunct "Our Lady Queen of Angels Seminary" in San Fernando, California. Seven years later, I attended Maharishi International University in Fairfield, Iowa, so that I could study in the company of other meditators. I remained in that community for four years, returning home to Los Angeles in 1983.

One of the salient features of studying at that institution was the incorporation of Vedic principles throughout the curriculum, regardless of one's major. One of the accepted tenets of meditators in that movement is that we are living in the midst of a Kali Yuga, or "age of evil," the fourth and last of four stages in a series of cosmic world cycles lasting millions of years.[21]

Although the Satya Yuga is of fairly long duration – it is 1,728,000 years long – because of its destructiveness, the Kali Yuga is much shorter: roughly 6,500 years. Various Hindu scholars ascribe the period of roughly 3102 to 3104 BCE to be the beginning of the current Kali Yuga. Maharishi, who died in 2008, believed that this Kali Yuga would be cut short and that we were in the process of transitioning into an Age of Enlightenment. I find this interesting because the first and most fundamental principle of the ancient Chinese divination text, the I Ching, is that when things reach an extreme, they revert to their opposite. In a subsequent chapter, I will discuss some of the evidence relating to the massive, global extinction event now underway – which, when you think about it – reveals that the current world system

[21] This is not just a Vedic principle. It is a fundamental belief of Hinduism. The other stages are known as satya, treta, and dvapara yugas – the first commonly referred to as an "Age of Enlightenment."

has, indeed, reached an evil extreme. If Maharishi is correct, the global extinction event is about to reverse itself, as the world dramatically exits the Kali Yuga.[22]

I am introducing a discussion of the Hindu concept of Kali Yuga, because regardless of the reader's belief system, the features of Western civilization – which affect the entire world community – are a spot-on match for the traditional characteristics attributed to this Yuga. These include:

- People are as far away from God and the principles of goodness as they can be.
- The value of human life, or even life in general, is greatly diminished. Murder is common.
- People break their promises; rulers, their treaties; dishonesty, avarice and cruelty are commonplace.
- Rulers, whose sacred duty in Satya Yuga is to promote spirituality and righteousness, abandon this duty, if not despise it. They do not protect their subjects, and they are a danger to the world.
- Addiction to alcohol and drugs is commonplace.
- Taxes are levied unfairly, and society degrades to the point where "might is right" is the prevailing ethic.
- Hindus believe that when Lord Krishna left the Earth, at the beginning of the current Kali Yuga, he taught that the coming age would be full of extreme hardships for people with ideals or values.

In short, a Kali Yuga brings with it all of the fruits of Extreme Negaprocity. When sectoral distance is maximized, this is what you get. We will be referring back to the Yugas later in the book as a model for where we are, and where we're going.

[22]See: Maharishi Mahesh Yogi, The Scientific Age Rising to be the Age of Enlightenment, (1977).

I want to close this chapter with an examination of a more recent document – certainly more recent than The Prince – that embodies the operating principles of Extreme Negaprocity. Without question, it embodies the governing principles one-would expect to find at the depths of a Kali Yuga, firmly mired in an accelerating, global extinction event from which humanity must extricate itself, to avoid devolving into a lifeless planet. I don't just mean our own extinction but the destruction of almost all life on Earth.

I initially hesitated to explore this area because it is so fraught with divisive overtones, making it difficult to give it a dispassionate examination. I'm going to adopt a neutral position, one that has prevented many of my intellectual forebears from achieving the impartial exploration that might have otherwise best served their purposes.

The document in question is commonly referred to as The Protocols of the Learned Elders of Zion, which I will hereafter refer to simply as The Protocols.[23] It has a most unusual history. The opening description provided in Wikipedia is probably as close to a mainstream consensus as any concerning this document: "(It is) an anti-Semitic fabricated text purporting to describe a Jewish plan for global domination. The forgery was first published in Russia in 1903, translated into multiple languages, and disseminated internationally in the early part of the 20th century. According to claims made by some of its publishers, the Protocols are the minutes of a late 19th-century meeting where Jewish leaders discussed their goal of global Jewish hegemony by subverting the morals of Gentiles, and by controlling the press and the world's economies."[24]

I'm not concerned with whether this document is a forgery or not. It well could be. I'm also not concerned about ethnicity, because I am of the view that this document thoroughly epitomizes "negaciprocal thinking," so it is highly instructive, re-

[23] There are a number of translations of The Protocols; however, I compared several translations from Russian, and they all read fairly close. In the text below, I use: Protocols of the Learned Elders of Zion, translated from the Russian of Nilus by Victor E. Marsden, late Russian correspondent of The Morning Post, (1934).

[24] See: https://en.wikipedia.org/wiki/The_Protocols_of_the_Elders_of_Zion

gardless of where it came from. In the discussion that follows, I am going to strip out all mention of Jews, Gentiles, or other ethnic groups, because it only clouds an even-handed analysis of the document. I'm going to use ethnic-neutral terms like "the Elite", "the masses," etc., for two reasons. First, because the inclusion of ethnicity clouds an impartial analysis, and, secondly, because these principles transcend location, temporal placement, or origin.

Lastly, I want to make it clear that my attempt at analysis is not an oblique attempt to promote any kind of anti-Semitic agenda. I, of all people, understand the irrationality of anti-Jewish vitriol. My first fiancée was Jewish. My first wife (Laura) was Jewish. A great number of my business associates have been Jewish, including Dr. Neville Solomon, a business partner in Guayaquil, who I previously mentioned. Not a single one of the many Jews who have been important in my current life have exhibited any of the thinking, actions, or goals that are reflected in The Protocols.

So I discuss The Protocols not because they are alleged to be of Jewish origin, but in spite of it. The Protocols – stripped bare of all mention of ethnicity – provide as clear a picture as I can find as to what Extreme Negaprocity in action effects, in terms of thinking, policy, and goals. My impartial analysis proceeds from that standpoint.

Moreover, if we adopt the conventional position that The Protocols are, indeed, fabricated, then we should at least appreciate the fact that the world has evolved in the precise manner specified in The Protocols over 115 years ago, making it the single most prophetically accurate document ever produced in the history of World Civilization in any language, in any country, and in any historical period.

First, a few comments about structure and content: the Protocols of the Learned Elders of Zion are actually twenty four in number. What follows are select excerpts, printed in italics; otherwise, it would take a separate volume to cover their entirety.

Second, there is nothing solicitous, exhortative, emotional, polemical or propagandistic about The Protocols. They don't attempt to convince anybody of anything. They read matter-of-factly as if they comprise a long-standing strategy of highly negaciprocal aims – a specific agenda that has been in the making for eons, for which the results have already been manifesting, and for which a final goal is near at hand. At no point is discussion or opinion solicited or desired. In this, they are unique and worthy of our examination.

The Protocols – (1903)

Protocol No. 1

" . . . What I am about to set forth, then, is our system from the two points of view, that of ourselves as that of the masses.

It must be noted that men with bad instincts are more in number than in good, and therefore, ***the best results in governing them are attained by violence and terrorization, and not academic discussions.*** *Every man aims at power, everyone would like to become a dictator if only he could, and rare indeed are the men who would not be willing to sacrifice the welfare of all for the sake of securing their own welfare.*

What has restrained the beasts of prey who are called men? What has served for their guidance hitherto?" (emphasis added)

Besides the obvious "might is right" undertone, the essential message here is that "we will rule over these 'beasts' who call themselves men, because they would rule over 'us' if they had our cunning and our complete commitment to take whatever extremely negaciprocal psychopathic measures are necessary to do so."

"Political freedom is an idea, but not a fact. This idea one

must know how to apply whenever it appears necessary with this bait of an idea to attract the masses of the people to one's party for the purpose of crushing another who is in authority. This task is rendered easier if the opponent has himself been infected with the idea of freedom, so-called liberalism, and, for the sake of an idea, is willing to yield some of his power. It is precisely here that the triumph of our theory appears: the slackened reins of Government are immediately, by the law of life, caught up and gathered together by a new hand, because the blind might of the nation cannot for one single day exist without guidance, and the new authority merely fits into the place of the old already weakened by liberalism."

This passage is important because it introduces us to a theme that is recurrent throughout The Protocols: "liberalism." The word was originally associated with basic human rights – John Locke's "life, liberty, and property" – and it was a major theme of the Age of Enlightenment that roughly ran through the 18th Century. The U.S. Constitution is rooted in the liberalism of this period, which may be best expressed in Voltaire's thoughts on the subject, which, paraphrased, may be summarized thusly: "I may not believe a word you say, but I'll fight to the death for your right to say it."

Noble words. Noble thoughts. All rooted in reciprocity, and therefore, most eligible to be twisted, perverted, and made subject to Doublespeak: "Slavery is liberty." The Protocols just happen to be the roadmap that tell us how to do it. Today the far edges of liberalism take us to the very perversion of Nature herself, and one glaring example would be how some States approach the issue of gender. Of course, there is nothing about transgenderism – exaggerated as it is, since even in California, one of the most liberal places on Earth, one survey estimated that only about 0.1% identify as such[25] – that promotes liberalism as thoroughly as taking the simple gender designation of male and

[25] See: https://www.nytimes.com/2015/06/09/upshot/the-search-for-the-best-estimate-of-the-transgender-population.html

female and expanding it to 31 different gender identities.[26]

As we proceed through The Protocols, it becomes apparent that "liberalism" has been hijacked to provide a false sense of true freedom. The use of "liberalism" to subvert Natural Law is now ubiquitous in Western Civilization, and we learn from The Protocols – this document that is 115 years old – how this was deliberate, well-thought out, and founded in very specific objectives.

From the passage above, we also learn that true power, as have discussed previously, knows no political party. "Don't worry. We control both parties," or to use another metaphor also from earlier in our study, "We know who will win, because we control both the white and the black pieces on the board." The "real" power works behind the scene. What is also evident, though not stated outright, is that **the State is the tool, the enforcer, through which negaciprocal forces fulfill their agenda.** Without the State, these dark plans could not be fulfilled.

"In our day the power which has replaced that of the rulers who were liberal is the power of Gold . . . the despotism of Capital, which is entirely in our hands, reaches out to it a straw that the State – willy-nilly-must take hold of; if not – it goes to the bottom . . ."

The controllers of the artificial constructs known as "money"or "currency" are the ones in control, not those in Government. The money-changers are far more negaciprocal than the Governments who end up being their lackeys, so naturally the former rules over the latter.

"The political has nothing in common with the moral. The ruler who is governed by the moral is not a skilled politician, and is therefore unstable on his throne . . . Great national qualities, like frankness and honesty, are vices in politics, for they bring down rulers from their thrones more effectively and more

[26] See: http://dailycaller.com/2016/05/24/new-york-city-lets-you-choose-from-31-different-gender-identities/

certainly than the most powerful enemy. Such qualities must be the attributes of the kingdoms of the masses, but we must in no way be guided by them.

Our right lies in force. The word 'right' is an abstract thought and proved by nothing. The word means no more than: Give me what I want in order that thereby I may have a [sic] proof that I am stronger than you.

Where does right begin? Where does it end?"

This passage is important because it nullifies any idea that morals or ethics – goodness, compassion, empathy, or any of the qualities that were mentioned at the beginning of this chapter – have any place in the world of negaprocity or in Government. They exist only to the extent that an "appearance" of them can be made to serve negaciprocal ends. In the Outer Bands, this is only made more so.

We also see here the foundation of the "moral relativism" of our time. The guardians of Extreme Negaprocity will tell you that there **is** no such thing as evil – no such thing as cruel or callous or heartless. "These are just relative terms," they will tell you. This becomes a necessary component of the character of people who serve in Extreme Negaprocity to disconnect them from their humanity. "Good is evil. Evil is good. It's all how you look at it!" Now it's important that **you** observe what they define as "good" or "bad." Controlling the masses demands it. But these principles do not apply to them. They are subject to a different commanding principle, best expressed by Satanist Aleister Crowley, "Do what thou wilt."

"In any State in which there is a bad organization of authority, an impersonality of laws and of the rulers who have lost their personality amid the flood of rights ever multiplying out of liberalism, I find a new right – to attack by the right of the strong, and to scatter to the winds all existing forces of order and regulation, to reconstruct all institutions and to become the sovereign lord of those who have left to us the rights of their power by laying them down voluntarily in their liberalism."

When the masses have accepted the perversion of their own natures, when the natural exercises of discipline and forbearance that come with being a fully functioning human being have been abandoned, this, too, in the minds of the Elite, is a form of acceptance of one's rape. This is another unspoken way of saying, "I believe you! Rape is good for me!"

"Our power in the present tottering condition of all forms of power will be more invisible than any other, because it will remain invisible until the moment when it has gained such strength that no cunning can any longer undermine it."

It is important that a negaciprocal power structure keep its plans secret when in its early stages, since normal human beings, steeped in the reciprocal traditions of their cultures or ancestry, will seek to subvert it. However, beyond a certain point, it doesn't matter what the masses do. Or to refer back to our earlier comment by former CIA station chief, John Stockman, "(They don't care) because they're still winning." In a very real sense, writing as I am now in 2017, they have already won.

"Out of the temporary evil we are now compelled to commit will emerge the good of an unshakeable rule, which will restore the regular course of the machinery of the national life, brought to naught by liberalism. The result justifies the means. Let us, however, in our plans, direct our attention not so much to what is good and moral as to what is necessary and useful."

More ends to justify the means. Anyone who has committed a heinous, criminal act could invoke the same justification. In this passage, we also find shades of the Elitist principle, "Order out of Chaos." Elitists are the lords of entropy, and it never occurs to them that their policies, which only accelerate entropy, can never bring order. This is an illusion and a violation of the Second Law of Thermodynamics. Perhaps this helps explain why – and I'm speaking broadly here – the Satya Yugas are so long, and the Kali Yugas so short.

"Before us is a plan in which is laid down strategically the line from which we cannot deviate without running the risk of seeing the labour of many centuries brought to naught . . ."

Again, the "plans" contained with The Protocols have been in motion for centuries. The Protocols are nothing more than an early twentieth century update and progress report. How else can we explain, as we shall soon see, how civilization has proceeded exactly along the lines specified in The Protocols? Or were The Protocols authored by someone far more prescient than Nostradamus?

"It is only with a despotic ruler that plans can be elaborated extensively and clearly in such a way as to distribute the whole properly among the several parts of the machinery of the State: from this the conclusion is inevitable that a satisfactory form of Government for any country is one that concentrates in the hands of one responsible person. Without an absolute despotism there can be no existence for civilization which is carried on not by the masses but by their guide, whosoever that person may be. The mob is a savage and displays its savagery at every opportunity. The moment the mob seizes freedom in its hands, it quickly turns to anarchy, which in itself is the highest degree of savagery."

This is why the Elite have such a propensity for concentrating power in as few hands as possible. David Icke presents this principle structurally in the form of a pyramid.

The reference to an unguided mass of people as turning to "anarchy" as the "highest degree of savagery" is worth noting. It's laughably untrue, of course. I have met indigenous groups throughout my travels to the Amazon where no Government exists or at the very least, there are no signs of Government anywhere.

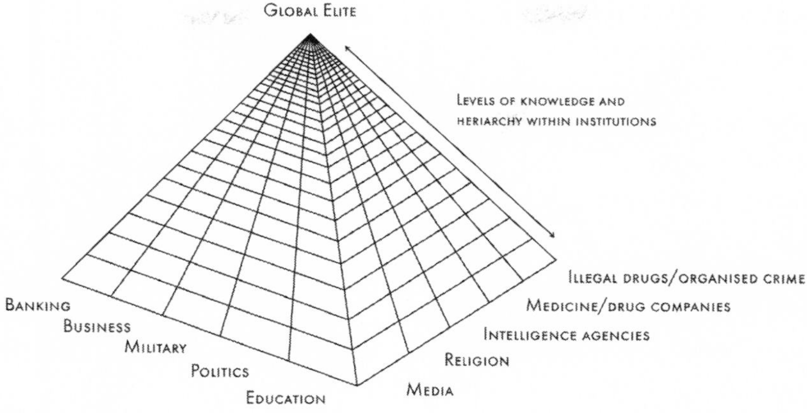

These tribes of people live perfectly happy lives – happier, I might add, than the vast majority of urbanites who I've observed living in civilization. The Elite cannot admit that to themselves **or** to the masses they rule. No rapist can openly admit that prospective rape victims would be better off not being raped, let alone the institutionalized raping machines that pollute the far corners of Expreme Negaprocity.

"Behold the alcoholized animals, bemused with drink, the right to an immoderate use of which comes along with freedom . . ."

The unleashing of more liberalism makes for both the justification for ruling the masses, but also points, once again, to the masses' acceptance of their own victimhood.

"Our countersign is – force and make-believe. Only force conquers in political affairs, especially if it is concealed in the talents essential to statesmen. Violence must be the principle, and cunning and make-believe the rule for Governments which do not want to lay down their crowns at the feet of agents of some new power. This evil is the one and only means to attain the end, the good. Therefore, we must not stop at bribery, deceit, and treachery when they should serve towards the attainment of our end. In politics one must know how to seize the property

of others without hesitation if by it we secure submission and sovereignty."

There are a couple points worth noting here. First of all, the principles put forth in this passage match precisely what we see in the techniques used by first world Governments and major corporations to secure assets and control. In his 2004 bestseller, Confessions of an Economic Hit Man, John Perkins reveals the tools he and his fellow "hit men" used to enslave countries around the world in trillions of dollar in debt. Indeed, they do not stop at "bribery, deceit, and treachery." Extortion, falsified financial reports, rigged elections, sex, and murder were all readily employed items on the menu.[27]

Not content with just one "tell-all" book, John Perkins went on to author The Secret History of the American Empire: Economic Hit Men, Jackals, and the Truth About Global Corruption, just three years later. Once again, it reads as if the world Elite, particularly in the United States, spent the 20th century using The Protocols as a roadmap for asset acquisition and political power.[28]

Speaking of asset acquisition, when I was imprisoned in the U.S. Federal system, I interviewed dozens of inmates who provided compelling evidence (because almost everyone keeps copies of their legal paperwork) that they were found "guilty" of victimless crimes with sketchy evidence as a technique to confiscating their family's assets. There is a division with the U.S. Department of Justice called the Office of Asset Forfeiture. Its original, putative legal authority was to acquire the assets of major drug kingpins and other serious criminals, but in practice, there was no one I met while in prison who was aware of this entity who did not know that its real purpose was to invent federal crimes as a pretext to rob a man and his family of as many assets as they could.

Lastly, this is the first of a series of passages where the term "make-believe" is used. I remember reading Derrick Jensen's

[27] See: John Perkins, Confessions of an Economic Hit Man, (2004).
[28] See: John Perkins, The Secret History of the American Empire, (2007).

The Culture of Make Believe[29] while imprisoned in Lafayette, Louisiana – struck by how fake and fabricated my culture seemed, completely detached from Natural Law. The Protocols make clear how this is quite intentional.

"Our State, marching along the path of peaceful conquest, has the right to replace the horrors of war by less noticeable and ***more satisfactory sentences of death, necessary to maintain the terror which tends to produce blind submission****. Just but merciless severity is the greatest factor of strength in the State; not only for the sake of gain but also in the name of duty, for the sake of victory, we must keep to the programme of violence and make-believe. The doctrine of squaring accounts is precisely as strong as the means of which it makes use. Therefore, it is not so much by the means themselves as by the doctrine of severity* ***that we shall triumph and bring all Governments into subjection to our super-Government.*** *It is enough for them to know that we are merciless for all disobedience to cease."* (emphasis added)

For most political commentators on the Right, the mention of a creeping "One World Order" is a constant refrain. In this passage we see the roots of it. The end goal is the melding of all world authority into one "Super-Government." Only in this way is world control in the hands of a small Elite possible, and any possibility of dissent – dissent in thoughts, words, or actions – minimized.

" . . . Far back in ancient times . . . wise men of the masses . . . could not make anything out of the uttered words in their abstractness; did not note the contradiction of their meaning and inter-relation, ***did not see that in nature there is no equality, there cannot be freedom; that Nature herself has established inequality of minds, of characters, and capacities, just as immutably as she has established subordination to her laws . . .*** *"* (emphasis added)

[29] See: Derrick Jensen, The Culture of Make Believe, (2004).

Again, we confront this delusional position that Extreme Negaprocity has anything to do with the workings of Nature. One gets a sense from this passage that there is almost a jealousy with how Nature operates, as if to say, "**that** power should belong to us." This mimics many religious traditions, which suggest that all of history can be viewed through the prism of this ongoing battle between the Creator (God), or pure good, and a force representing pure evil (i.e. Satan or Lucifer). The former representing reciprocity; the latter, negaprocity.

*"In all corners of the Earth the words, **'Liberty, Equality, Fraternity'** brought to our ranks, thanks to our blind agents, whole legions who bore our banners with enthusiasm. And all the time these words were canker-worms at work boring into the well-being of the masses, putting an end everywhere to peace, quiet, solidarity and destroying all the foundations of those States representing the masses. As you will see later, this helped us to our triumph: it gave us the possibility, among other things, of getting into our hands the master card – the destruction of the privileges, or in other words of the very existence of the aristocracy of the masses, that class which was the only defense peoples and countries had against us. On the ruins of the natural and genealogical aristocracy of the masses we have set up the aristocracy of our educated class headed by the aristocracy of money. The qualifications for this aristocracy we have established in wealth, which is dependent upon us, and in knowledge, for which our learned elders provide the motive force."*

Several points here: again, the use of "liberalism" to weaken and destroy the masses. The "killing off" of aristocracies – (think of them as potentially benevolent ruling forces who are no match for the forces in the Outer Bands of Extreme Negaprocity). We see the emergence of an "educated class" to guide science and determine what is and isn't allowable thought – determining their reality. We see that money trumps even the educated, which fits in with our Negaprocity Chart.

"Our triumph has been rendered easier by the fact that in our relations with the men whom we wanted we have always worked upon the most sensitive chords of the human mind, upon the cash account, upon the cupidity, upon the insatiability for material needs of man; and each one of these human weaknesses, taken alone, is sufficient to paralyze initiative, for it hands over the will of men to the disposition of him who has bought their activities.

The abstraction of freedom has enabled us to persuade the mob in all countries that their Government is nothing but the steward of the people who are the owners of the country, and that the steward may be replaced like a worn-out glove.

It is this possibility of replacing the representatives of the people which has placed them at our disposal, and, as it were, given us the power of appointment."

We see, again, the control of money, of banking, as central to controlling the masses. We also see in clear and unmistakable terms that Government is subordinate to money, elected officials are as disposable as used tissues, that the "real power" is behind the scenes, pulling the strings – year after year, century after century – and that the needs and wants of men can be controlled through the use of money, that they can be bought, in other words.

Protocol No. 2

"It is indispensable for our purpose that wars, so far as possible, should not result in territorial gains: war will thus be brought on to the economic ground, where the nations will not fail to perceive in the assistance we give the strength of our predominance, and this state of things will put both sides at the mercy of our international agentur . . ."

Again, true power means controlling both sides of any conflict. Wars are a natural part of Extreme Negaprocity. Erich Fromm noted that the "institution of war is absent from many indigenous cultures," something that was surprising to many early American colonists as well.[30]

". . . Let the masses play the principle part which we have persuaded them to accept as the dictates of science (theory). It is with this object in view that we are constantly, by means of our press, arousing the blind confidence in these theories. The intellectuals of the masses will puff themselves up with their knowledge and without any logical verification of them will put into effect all the information available from science, which our agentur specialists have cunningly pieced together for the purpose of educating their minds in the direction we want."

Two entities come into view here: scientism and the press, both of which we covered previously. The cancer industry is the perfect example of a promoter of "fake science," and the mainstream media are increasingly seen for what it is: a provider of "fake news." They didn't just suddenly become a merchant of fake news. The mainstream media have been a merchant of fake news all along. You can't have a media that are popular and at the same time viewed with favor by the Government and other negaciprocal institutions if they aren't peddling "fake news." That's their job. People are only now beginning to see this.[31]

"Do not suppose for a moment that these statements are empty words: think carefully of the successes we arranged for Darwinism, Marxism, Nietzsche-ism. To us . . . it should be plain to see what a disintegrating importance these directives have had upon the minds of the masses."

All three of these philosophies have had devastating impact on the minds of ordinary people. Darwin's theory of evolution is viewed by many as a ridiculous mythology, completely lacking in evidence. The fact that it is taught as "science" in schools

[30] See: Derrick Jensen, The Culture of Make Believe, (2004), p 178.

[31] See: http://www.altcancer.net/ashwin/ashw0617.htm, and http://www.altcancer.net/ashwin/ashw0517.htm

worldwide is yet another indicator as to the success of The Protocols.[32]

To its critics, Darwinism is antithetical to the notion of "intelligent design". In this sense, Darwinism strikes at the heart of the Laws of Thermodynamics, because it insists that our planet, itself a closed system, has produced increasingly advanced, complicated life forms, out of nothing. No Creator. No outside intelligent force. Out of the primordial muck just came life. Magically. Yes, it's an atheist's wet dream, or that of a "Liberal" or a "Progressive" or a lover of The Protocols . . . but Darwinism really does seem to test one's gullibility.[33]

Now on to one of history's most loveable characters, Karl Marx. Few philosophical doctrines have been a greater source of pain, agony, starvation and death – a veritable feast for the archons – than that of Marxism and the communist policies it has spawned. Marxism doesn't work, has never worked, and never could work, because it defies so many elements of basic human nature.[34] It deserves a place in The Protocols, if for no other reason than that communist doctrine reflects so many of the principles discussed in The Protocols.[35]

I can understand why The Protocols included Nietsche: his writings, if nothing else, promoted the liberalist cause, including – among its other gems – the idea that "moral values are not conducive to the flourishing of human excellence."[36] That whoev-

[32] See: "Darwinism is Materialist Mythology, not Science," https://www.c4id.org.uk/index.php?option=com_content&view=article&id=241&Itemid=132. See also: "The Scientific Case Against Evolution," http://www.icr.org/home/resources/resources_tracts_scientificcaseagainstevolution/

[33] See: Stephen C. Meyer, Signature in the Cell: DNA and the Evidence for Intelligent Design, (2010). Now I am well aware that the "conventional" position is that intelligent design is "pseudoscience." What comes to mind is that pathetic sell out for all things negaciprocal, - Wikipedia - and I address the problem of Wikipedia in a November, 2015 essay - see: http://www.altcancer.net/ashwin/ashw1115.htm
However, any impartial examination of both sides of this argument will, in my opinion, give credence to the idea that, as opposed to Darwinism, we do, in fact, live in a universe teeming with evidence for intelligent design.

[34] I could choose something more respectable, but for its simplicity and its exposition in common sense, I would direct the reader to the essay, "10 Reasons Why Communism Sucks," http://listverse.com/2013/01/17/10-reasons-why-communism-sucks/

[35] See any of the versions of The Naked Communist by W. Cleon Skousen

[36] See: https://plato.stanford.edu/entries/nietzsche-moral-political/

er was behind The Protocols would have backed and promoted Darwin, Marx, and Nietsche, is amazingly telling.

"In the hands of the States of today there is a great force that creates the movement of thought in the people and that is the Press. The part played by the Press is to keep pointing out requirements supposed to be indispensable, to give voice to the complaints of the people, to express and create discontent. It is in the Press that the triumph of freedom of speech finds its incarnation. But the States of the masses have not known how to make use of this force: and it has fallen into our hands . . . (and it is) gold in our hands, notwithstanding that we have had to gather it out of oceans of blood and tears. But it has paid us, though we have sacrificed many of our people. Each victim on our side is worth in the sight of (our) God a thousand ordinary people."

We get two insights here: one is how greatly cherished control of the press really is – because there are so many people still out there – then (1903) and now – who can't figure out **how fake the news really is** and what a powerful tool it is for controlling the thinking and actions of ordinary people. Secondly, we are told just how worthless the Elite consider the lives of ordinary people to be . . . as if we could not surmise that on our own on the basis of the countless wars they initiate and prosecute.

Protocol No. 3

". . . our goal is now only a few steps off. There remains a small space to cross and the whole long path we have trodden is ready now to close its cycle of the Symbolic Snake, by which we symbolize our people. When this ring closes, all the States of Europe will be locked in its coil as a powerful vise . . ."

Well, ladies and gentlemen, that's exactly what happened. As planned. As predicted. The European Union was conceived at the close of World War II, even though it wouldn't formally come into existence until November, 1993, when the Maastricht

Treaty came into force. Later, the Euro would replace twelve national currencies in 2002, bringing about the loss of sovereignty of its now 28 member nations. The tyrannical and controlling policies of the European Union towards its member states is accurately depicted in this passage as a "powerful vise."

This passage is one of a number that accurately predicts events that unfolded in the 20th century exactly as stated.

"In order to incite seekers after power to a misuse of power we have set all forces in opposition one to another, breaking up their liberal tendencies towards independence. To this end we have stirred up every form of enterprise. We have armed all parties. We have set up authority as a target for every ambition. Of States we have made gladiatorial arenas where a host of confused issues contend . . . A little more, and disorders and bankruptcy will be universal . . ."

Here we see more confirmation as to the relationship between occupiers of Outer Bands and the demonic agenda: create more strife, more conflict, more confusion, allow "board-certified" psychopaths to rise to the top of the political ladder because only the worst kind of humans best serve the demonic end of the negaprocity spectrum. As for "disorders and bankruptcy," here we have more correct predictions. The last century saw two horrific world wars, unprecedented in the extent of the death and destruction they wrought, and today all nations on Earth are heavily in debt – many of them in multiples of their GDP. For all intents and purposes, bankruptcy is universal. Mission accomplished.

". . . Abuses of power will put the final touch in preparing all institutions for their overthrow and everything will fly skyward under the blows of the maddened mob."

This passage can only refer to a unified World Government that replaces the family of nations that currently exists. There's really no other way of interpreting it. There are shades of meaning out of "maddened mob." The "mob" isn't naturally "maddened," it is made that way under countless programs, policies, and regulations that make it so. Between harmful GMO foods, chemtrails, industrial fluoride in municipal drinking water, the onslaught of massive electromagnetic pollution, etc., the Elite have created a more unstable mass of governed people who will be more easily brought under the yoke of even harsher, more tyrannical governing conditions than now exist. Who does this serve? The Elite and the demonic entities that they in turn serve.

"All people are chained down to heavy toil by poverty more firmly than ever they were chained by slavery and serfdom: from these, one way or another, they might free themselves, these could be settled with, but from want they will never get away. We have included in the constitution such rights as to the masses appear fictitious and not actual rights. All these so-called "People's Rights" can exist only in idea, an idea which can never be realized in practical life. What is it to the proletariat labourer, bowed double over his heavy toil, crushed by his lot in life, if talkers get the right to babble . . . once the proletariat has no other profit out of the constitution save only those pitiful crumbs which we fling them from our table in return for their voting in favour of what we dictate, in favour of the men we place in power, the servants of our agentur . . . Republican rights for a poor man are no more than a bitter piece of irony, for the necessity he is under of toiling almost all day gives him no present use of them, but on the other hand robs him of all guarantee of regular and certain earnings . . . the people have fallen into the grips of merciless money-grinding scoundrels who have laid a pitiless and cruel yoke upon the necks of the workers . . ."

All these things are possible when psychopaths are given control of the money supply. Further confirmation is provided that "elected leaders" are simply puppets, that civil liberties exist in name only, and that structures exist to ensure that the average man's attention is devoted to "making a living," too preoccupied to take the time to understand the mechanisms of tyranny that are tightening around him and even less able to do anything about it.

"We appear on the scene as alleged saviours of the worker from this oppression when we propose to him to enter the ranks of our fighting forces – Socialists, Anarchists, Communists – to whom we always give support in accordance with an alleged brotherly rule (of the solidarity of all humanity) of our social masonry. The aristocracy, which enjoyed by law the labour of the workers, was interested in seeing that the workers were well fed, healthy, and strong. ***We are interested in just the opposite – in the diminution, the killing out of the masses****. Our power is in the chronic shortness of food and physical weakness of the worker because by all that this implies, he is made the slave of our will, and* ***he will not find in his own authorities either strength or energy to set against our will. Hunger creates the right of capital to rule the worker more surely than it was given to the aristocracy by the legal authority of kings****."* (emphasis added)

The Elite do not simply control all parties and factions. They control the different political philosophies that give rise to these factions. This was the underlying point of George Orwell's famous work, Animal Farm. When the Elite refer to "killing out of the masses," they mean business. The Georgia Guidestones, clearly an Elite-inspired monument, give us a stated goal of reducing the world's population to 500 million – not even 7% of the current world population of 7.5 billion. In other words, 93% of the current population of human beings needs to be murdered. Soon.

Now, mind you, I am not blind to the fact that *Homo sapiens* are in overshoot, and, given the Earth's current resources, exceeded "carrying capacity" quite some time ago. But there are methods of addressing overshoot without resorting to the methods prescribed by the Elite. No attempt has been made to integrate vital concepts of anthropology and ecological sustainability into the education systems in a serious way – anywhere on the planet – of which I'm aware. What does that tell us? Well, one of the things it tells us is that any sensible attempt to match human population to supportive habitat is going to obviate the sheer psychopathic pleasure the Elite will get from the accelerated, large scale death and destruction which has been a hallmark of their rule for thousands of years.

We have previously discussed the debilitating effects of modernity that sap the "strength (and) energy" of ordinary people. This next passage tells us that these features of modern life were not accidentally set into motion.

"When the hour strikes for our Sovereign Lord of all the World to be crowned, it is these same hands which will sweep away everything that might be a hindrance thereto . . ."

I leave it to my reader to figure out just who the "Sovereign Lord of all the World" is. If Santa Claus – a mere commercial, archonic distraction – came to mind, you may want to stop and give this more thought. It is interesting that a Biblical passage refers to Satan (Lucifer) as "god of this world,"[37] which closely matches the wording in the passage above.

*"The masses have lost the habit of thinking unless prompted by the suggestions of our specialists. Therefore, they do not see the urgent necessity of what we, when our kingdom comes, shall adopt at once, namely this, that it is essential to teach in national schools one simple, true piece of knowledge, the basis of all knowledge – the knowledge of the structure of human life, of social existence, which requires division of labour, and, consequently, the division of men into classes and conditions. It is essential for all to know that **owing to difference in the objects of human activity, there cannot be any equality**."* (emphasis added)

Two things jump out here: that systems of knowing and knowledge – we're back to Scientism – have been subverted and

[37] See: 2 Corinthians 4:4 – KJV

are control mechanisms, and secondly, that Extreme Negaprocity not only creates systems of slavery, but that inequality is at its very foundation.

"This hatred will be still further magnified by the effect of an economic crisis, which will stop dealings on the exchanges and bring industry to a standstill. We shall create by all the secret subterranean methods open to us and with the aid of gold, which is all in our hands, a universal economic crisis, whereby we shall throw upon the streets whole mobs of workers simultaneously in all the countries of Europe. These mobs will rush delightedly to shed the blood of those whom, in the simplicity of their ignorance, they have envied from their cradles, and whose property they will then be able to loot.

Ours they will not touch, because the moment of attack will be known to us and we shall take measures to protect our own."

This passage is important because it lays bare the mindset of those who propagate endless "false flags." That is, those who commit atrocities engineered to appear as if it is someone else's doing – someone else's fault. Secondly, it underscores the respect that the Elite have for "real money" – that being precious metals, not fiat currency. Again, fake money is something engineered for the masses – not an Elite that can create it out of thin air. Thirdly, one must consider that although Europe is noted as the theater of conflict here, the tactics are now evidenced worldwide.

"Ever since that time (the French Revolution, 1789-1799, which the authors of The Protocols take credit for engineering in an earlier passage), we have been leading the peoples from one disenchantment to another, so that ***in the end they should turn also from us in favor of that King-Despot . . . whom we are preparing for the world****."* (emphasis added)

Again, if Satan, Lucifer, Beelzebub, Belial, or some other embodiment of pure, uncompromising evil doesn't come to mind, then just use your imagination to come up with your own vision of the ultimate evil incarnate representing all things ungodly.

But even aside from a commitment to incarnate their Demon King, the Elite have a symbiotic relationship with the archons and other parasitic entities in the demonic realms, as well. We know this because of the numerous blood rituals and other dark sacraments that are woven into the daily lives of the world's Elite.[38]

Protocol No. 4

"But even freedom might be harmless and have its place in the State economy without injury to the well-being of the peoples if it rested upon the foundation of faith in God, upon the brotherhood of humanity, unconnected with the conception of equality, which is negated by the very laws of creation, for they have established subordination. With such a faith as this a people might be governed by a wardship of parishes, and would walk contentedly and humbly under the guiding hand of its spiritual pastor submitted to the dispositions of God upon Earth. ***This***

[38] There are numerous works that detail the relationship between the world's Elite and extreme dark forces. Fr. Malachi Martin, for example, wrote a series of popular novels, which he openly referred to as "factions" – that is, works written in fiction that were intended to convey real-life events. In his case, he includes the infiltration and enthronement of Lucifer in the Vatican. See: http://www.tldm.org/news/martin.htm, https://www.henrymakow.com/malachi_martin_--.html
The connection between Freemasonry and the worship of Lucifer is well-established. See: http://amazingdiscoveries.org/S-deception-Freemason_Lucifer_Albert_Pike
My next references, as it pertains to Freemasonry, have decidedly Christian overtones. That, in no way, makes the contents less truthful. First, I had to laugh when a YouTuber posted this video, because it contains a lot of hidden truth: https://www.youtube.com/watch?v=vBFuEo0Jzd8
The late William Cooper made some important comments in this connection years ago. See: https://www.youtube.com/watch?v=pOSifshiBZQ (carefully read the Comment section). (1977)
A longer exposition by William Cooper, referencing various fundamental Freemason texts, can be heard at: https://www.youtube.com/watch?v=Ecf1QUfqs7M. See also: https://www.youtube.com/watch?v=3_P1f8SgTil
The entertainment industry, throughout Hollywood and the music industry, is replete with celebrities who admit that in order to achieve success in their field, they were required to "sell their soul to the devil." If you see enough of these confessions online, you realize that the reference is not metaphorical. You realize that to belong to the "inner circle" of this industry, a commitment to a dark, negaciprocal master is required – the name you assign to this master being irrelevant.

is the reason why it is indispensable for us to undermine all faith, to tear from the minds of the masses the very principle of Godhead and the spirit, and to put in its place arithmetical calculations and material needs*.*

In order to give the masses no time to think and take note, ***their minds must be diverted towards industry and trade****. Thus, all the nations will be swallowed up in the pursuit of gain and in the race for it will not take note of their common foe. But again, in order that freedom may once for all disintegrate and ruin the communities of the masses, we must put industry on a speculative basis: the result of this will be that what is withdrawn from the land by industry will slip through the hands and pass into speculation, that is, to our classes."* (emphasis added)

The "freedom" referred to in this passage is decidedly different than the freedoms promoted by liberalism to destroy the fabric of society and make it more controllable. We see that the Elite find the premise that "all men are created equal," as we find in the U.S. Constitution – which has existed in name only within the U.S. for many years now – completely abominable. The Elite are divinely appointed leaders and the masses are, as we saw in a previous passage, just "beasts" – farm animals in need of their management.

We see this passage as quite prophetic on several fronts: first, we find that genuine pursuit of spirituality has waned over the past century. Traditional spiritual values have been uprooted by laws, regulations, and a shift in culture towards materialism. By way of example, in the U.S. if you could go back 120 years and talk to ordinary citizens, and you told them that in the early 1970s, abortion would not only be culturally accepted, but perfectly legal, many would respond in disbelief.

Whether you're "pro choice" or not, it doesn't matter, this is what you'd find.

Secondly, this passage is prophetic because it accurately predicts that industry, real production, would be subverted by "speculation," and we only need to look at Wall Street and the financial industry, in general, which has exploded in its size, profit, political influence, and prestige since the beginning of the past century, to find proof of this.

"Mexico is a country of a modest, very fucked class, which will never stop being fucked. Television has the obligation to bring diversion to these people and remove them from their sad reality and difficult future." [39]

Emilio Azcárraga
Billionaire head of the
Mexican media giant, **Televisa**

"*The intensified struggle for superiority and shocks delivered to economic life will create, nay, have already created, disenchanted, cold and heartless communities. Such communities will foster a strong aversion towards the higher political and towards religion. Their only guide is gain, that is Gold, which they will erect into a veritable cult, for the sake of those material delights which it can give. Then will the hour strike when, not for the sake of attaining the good, not even to win wealth, but solely out of hatred towards the privileged, the lower classes will follow our lead against our rivals for power, the intellectuals of the masses.*"

A couple of important things jump out there. First, the im-

[39] See: Derrick Jensen, The Culture of Make Believe, (2004), p. 594-595. Although this quote is taken from an Elitist in Mexico, about the majority of Mexican citizens, you could apply it to most nations on Earth.

portance of inter-class warfare as a means of diversion so that the masses never know the true source of their discontent. Secondly, this passage implies a precognition that people would learn about the ultimate worthlessness of fiat currency,[40] turning, instead, to precious metals. Indeed, although gold has been appreciated as a standard of real money throughout history, the acquisition and storage of "Gold" has, indeed, turned into a "veritable cult."

Protocol No. 5

"We shall create an ***intensified centralization of government*** *in order to grip in our hands all the forces of the community.* ***We shall regulate mechanically all the actions of the political life of our subjects by new laws****. These laws will withdraw one by one all the indulgences and liberties which have been permitted by the masses, and our kingdom will be distinguished by a despotism of such magnificent proportions as to be at any moment and in every place in a position to* ***wipe out any member from the masses who oppose us by deed or word****."* (emphasis added)

This passage is prescient in its accurate predictions in several areas. First, centralizing Government has been a major preoccupation of the major Governments of the world throughout the last century. Such efforts of this magnitude were unknown prior to the 20th century.

We first had the League of Nations, founded in 1920, which reached 58 member States by the mid-1930's, followed by the United Nations, founded in 1945, which now has 193 members. Additionally, numerous intergovernmental agencies and think tanks have sprung up over the past century which seek or support global Government, including the Council on Foreign Relations (CFR), established in 1921, and then there are the over 7,000 think tanks that work together to homogenize global objectives – with few, if any, of these organizations existing in the

[40] "It is the destiny of fiat currencies to return to their original value – zero." Voltaire

time of The Protocols.[41] The reference to an onslaught of new laws has already occurred, and is particularly noticeable in the U.S.[42] Lastly, the intolerance to opposing views has increasingly become evident with the Elite-inspired "War on Terrorism," which is of their own making.[43] Interestingly, in a report that came out in 2015, global freedom had seen a decline in each of the previous ten years, measured over 195 countries and 15 territories.[44]

"In the times when the peoples looked upon kings on their thrones as a pure manifestation of the will of God, they submitted without a murmur to the despotic power of kings: but ***from the day when we insinuated into their minds the conception of their own rights they began to regard the occupants of thrones as mere ordinary mortals****. The holy unction of the Lord's Anointed has fallen from the heads of kings in the eye of the people, and when* ***we also robbed them of their faith in God****, the might of power was flung upon the streets into the place of public proprietorship and was seized by us."* (emphasis added)

As we gleaned from The Prince, the kings of old were not above negaprocity – quite to the contrary. But this passage emphasizes that previous monarchies were no match in pure negaprocity and thermodynamic potential, to the pure psychopathic evil that we see manifested in The Protocols. This passage infers that the Elite attribute to themselves a power that even supercedes the Creator.

"Moreover, the art of directing masses and individuals by means of cleverly manipulated theory and verbiage, by regulations of life in common and all sorts of other quirks, in all which

41 See: http://repository.upenn.edu/cgi/viewcontent.cgi?article=1011&context=think_tanks

42 See: http://www.economist.com/node/16636027

43 Within the U.S., the ascension of a "you're either with us or against us" mentality and a decline in civil liberties is most apparent. See: http://www.wanttoknow.info/unconstitutionalcivillibertiesloss. See also: http://www.nytimes.com/2011/09/07/us/sept-11-reckoning/civil.html And see: https://www.economist.com/news/leaders/21582525-war-terror-haunts-america-still-it-should-recover-some-its-most-cherished

44 See: https://freedomhouse.org/sites/default/files/FH_FITW_Report_2016.pdf

the masses understand nothing, belongs likewise to the specialists of our administrative brain. Reared on analysis, observation, on delicacies of fine calculation, in this species of skill we have no rivals, any more than we have either in the drawing up of plans of political actions and solidarity. In this respect the Jesuits alone might have compared with us, but we have contrived to discredit them in the eyes of the unthinking mob as an overt organization in the shade. However, it is probably all the same to the world who is its sovereign lord, whether the head of Catholicism or our despot . . . But to us, the Chosen People, it is far from being a matter of indifference."

This passage is interesting in that it restates in a more concrete way how the panoply of fakeness that courses through our media, our sciences, our education system, saturating our BCN, infecting our understanding of the world around us, is all by design. The comment about discrediting the Jesuits is interesting, as today you will find critical statements – even videos – concerning the Jesuits in broad daylight that you would **never** see circulating about the **real** rulers of our world civilization.[45]

Lastly, the idea that any particular group of the Elite represents the "Chosen People," would predictably be an article of faith for any group operating on the far end of the Outer Bands. It would be hard to sustain their own private theology of death and destruction and control over all other groups of people without it.

"For a time perhaps we might be successfully dealt with by a coalition of the masses, but from this danger we are secured by the discord existing among them whose roots are so deeply seated that they can never now be plucked up. We have set one against another the personal and national reckonings of the

[45] By way of example, the worship of Lucifer as the victor over Jesus Christ by members of the Vatican, going all the way to the Pope, would never make its way to the public if the Jesuits were fully in control. It simply wouldn't be permitted. See: https://www.youtube.com/watch?v=sUN-XEU6HUc, https://www.youtube.com/watch?v=G-eru74oGqk, https://www.youtube.com/watch?v=rOQY2b1vWsg, https://www.youtube.com/watch?v=AHyY0PV2iVU, https://www.youtube.com/watch?v=ya-DhFdR6Jk

masses, religious and race hatreds, which we have fostered into a huge growth in the course of the past twenty centuries. This is the reason why there is not one State which would anywhere receive support if it were to raise its arms, for every one of them must bear in mind that any agreement against us would be unprofitable to itself. We are too strong – there is no evading our power. The nations cannot come to even inconsiderable private agreement without our secretly having a hand in it."

Sowing hatred and division between peoples of different religion, race, culture, language, geographic region, generation, economic group, occupation, political affiliation – this is the aim of those at the Outer Bands. They can never bring peace to the world because they have acquired and they sustain their power by secretly promoting anything but peace.

"Per Me reges regnant." ("It is through me that Kings reign.") And it was said by the prophets that ***we were chosen by God Himself to rule over the whole Earth****. God has endowed us with genius that we may be equal to our task. Were genius in the opposite camp it would still struggle against us, but even so a newcomer is no match for the old-established settler: the struggle would be merciless between us, such a fight as the world has never yet seen. Aye, and the genius on their side would have arrived too late. All the wheels of the machinery of all States go by the force of the engine, which is in our hands, and* ***that engine of the machinery of States is – Gold****. The science of political economy invented by our learned elders has for long past been* ***giving royal prestige to capital****."* (emphasis added)

There is always a god to give an arrogant Elite his divine blessing to sodomize you and every other person who isn't in "their" inside circle. History is filled with monarchies who claimed that their actions were protected by the "divine right of Kings," and the authors of The Protocols are no different. Once again – and this is a constant theme throughout The Protocols – we see a re-emphasis on the importance of controlling money, capital, Gold . . . the media of exchange by which people conduct commerce as the key to controlling everything. It is no wonder that is exactly what we saw evolve over the past century.

"Capital, if it is to co-operate untrammeled, must be free to establish a monopoly of industry and trade: this is already being put in execution by an unseen hand in all quarters of the world. ***This freedom will give political force to those engaged in industry, and that will help to oppress the people.*** *Nowadays, it is more* ***important to disarm the peoples*** *than to lead them into war; more important to use for our advantage the passions which have burst into flames than to quench their fire; more important to catch up and interpret the ideas of others to suit ourselves than to eradicate them. The principal object of our directorate consists in this: to debilitate the public mind by criticism; to lead it away from serious reflections calculated to arouse resistance; to distract the forces of the mind towards a sham fight of empty eloquence."* (emphasis added)

This passage has turned out to be highly prophetic on multiple fronts. The last century saw enormous consolidation in industry, trade, and the mainstream media. Shockingly so.[46] Signs of this trend in monopolization are everywhere. I remember negotiating for the purchase of a 50,000 square foot facility in 1996, formally owned by Guth Dairy, a family owned business in Louisiana that had been in business for over 70 years. The owner told me that when they started, there were between 250 and 300 family-owned dairies in Louisiana, but by the mid-90s, buyouts and consolidations had brought that number down to just three. A century ago, seeds for planting the world's crops were spread out over many thousands of companies. By 2011, a mere three companies controlled over half the global proprietary seed market.[47] One hundred years ago, there were thousands of

[46] See: https://www.theatlantic.com/magazine/archive/2016/10/americas-monopoly-problem/497549/

[47] See: http://www.apbrebes.org/files/seeds/files/Howard_seed_industry_patents_concentration_2015.pdf

media publications. Today only six companies control over 90% of TV and radio stations (which didn't exist when The Protocols were written), constricting consumer choice in media consumption.[48]

Has this concentration of corporate power brought more options, more competition, more innovation to the benefit of the people? Of course not. It has brought more oppression, just as The Protocols predicted it would.

Highly predictive, too, is the comment on the importance of disarming the people. Tyrants since time immemorial have known that disarming the public is essential to their control, as if sheer common sense would not convey this knowledge. Adolph Hitler once remarked, "The most foolish mistake we could possibly make would be to allow the subjugated races to possess arms. History shows that all conquerors who have allowed their subjugated races to carry arms have prepared their own downfall by so doing. Indeed, I would go so far as to say that the supply of arms to the underdogs is a sine qua non for the overthrow of any sovereignty."[49]

Over the past century gun control has exploded globally, all under the rubric of reducing gun violence – this, despite the fact that in case after case the evidence has accumulated that gun control doesn't work.[50] Well, we know why it doesn't work. It doesn't work because the ultimate intent of gun control laws – issued by negaciprocal Governments who are responsible for murdering somewhere around 187,000,000 human beings in the past century alone – isn't to keep people safe.[51] Gun control laws are intended to keep law-abiding citizens disarmed and

[48] See: http://freedom-articles.toolsforfreedom.com/mainstream-media-consolidation/

[49] See: http://www.snopes.com/politics/quotes/disarm.asp

[50] Taken from The Dailywire: "7 Facts on Gun Crime That Show Gun Control Doesn't Work," http://www.dailywire.com/news/7872/7-facts-gun-crime-show-gun-control-doesnt-work-aaron-bandler. See also: "National Review: Gun Control Doesn't Work," http://www.npr.org/templates/story/story.php?storyId=128186209
See also: "Harvard: Gun Control Doesn't Work," https://bearingarms.com/ba-staff/2013/08/25/harvard-gun-control-doesnt-work/, and in the newspaper the Charlotte Observer: "More gun laws won't work; gun opponents' true aim is confiscation." http://www.charlotteobserver.com/opinion/op-ed/article49682710.html

[51] See: "How many people have died in wars throughout history?" http://gurumagazine.org/askaguru/culture/many-people-died-wars-throughout-history/

unable to protect themselves from criminal elements. One can only speculate as to why Governments, those paragons of virtue, would want to aid criminal elements and deny ordinary citizens the ability to defend themselves. They are, of course, acting in accordance with the dictates of an Elite that seeks to eliminate all possibilities of "victim resistance."

The passage declaring that it is "more important to catch up and interpret the ideas of others to suit ourselves than to eradicate them" serves two purposes: first, to use the position of superior funds ("acorns out of nothing") to frame opposition as "conspiracy theorists" or otherwise out of touch with reality, dismissively casting any legitimate critique of Elitist policy and practice as unworthy of consideration – basically, "gaslighting" – and since I'll be using this concept again, you might want to become familiar with it;[52] and secondly, once again, to "test your gullibility."

The last third of this passage is devoted to "debilitating the public mind" – a recurring mantra woven throughout the entirety of The Protocols. It is so vital that it bears repeating:

"*The principal object of our directorate consists in this: to debilitate the public mind by criticism; to lead it away from serious reflections calculated to arouse resistance; to distract the forces of the mind towards a sham fight of empty eloquence.*"

The tool for executing this policy is, of course, the mainstream media. If you've ever wondered why the mainstream media assault you with one ridiculous article after another, always encased with a sickening "empty eloquence," now you know. Frank Zappa's famously cheeky examination of television could be applied to any of the communications media controlled by the mainstream media, as seen on the next page.

[52] See: https://en.wikipedia.org/wiki/Gaslighting

"I am gross and perverted
I'm obsessed 'n deranged
I have existed for years
But very little has changed
I'm the tool of the Government
And industry too
For I am destined to rule
And regulate you

I may be vile and pernicious
But you can't look away
I make you think I'm delicious
With the stuff that I say
I'm the best you can get
Have you guessed me yet?
I'm the slime oozin' out
From your TV set

You will obey me while I lead you
And eat the garbage that I feed you
Until the day that we don't need you
Don't go for help . . . no one will heed you
Your mind is totally controlled
It has been stuffed into my mold
And you will do as you are told
Until the rights to you are sold . . ."

Frank Zappa
"I'm the Slime"
Album: Over-Nite Sensation (1973)

A good example of "empty eloquence" is the current drumbeat in the U.S. as it relates to the alleged "Russian interference" in the U.S. presidential election of 2016. It also provides yet another example that you can't believe anything coming out of the mainstream media.

Now before I go any farther, let me make clear that I don't have a dog in this fight. I live in Ecuador, as a permanent resident, and have no desire to return to the States. I did not vote in the last election, nor do I have any plans to vote in any future U.S. election. I only pay taxes to the U.S. Government in an attempt to avoid yet another kidnapping at the hands of U.S. officials. I am, for all intents and purposes, paying the mafia their "protection money" just to keep the thugs away. I fully understand that the U.S. is all about "taxation without representation," so none of this strikes me as contradictory.

In the interest of full disclosure, let me say that I favored Trump over Hillary, (which is not the same as saying he was a good candidate). I say this not simply because Hillary Clinton signed the order to have me illegally kidnapped in 2009 when she was U.S. Secretary of State. I hold on to the strange notion that in a representative democracy, elected officials should actually work in the interest of those who elect them, not solely for the monied interests, and not for the globalists who are totally unconcerned with the welfare of the people in any one particular country.

Living south of the equator as an American expat, let me tell you what I saw from a distance: I saw one candidate, Donald Trump, appealing to an electorate's self-interests and promising to bring jobs back to the U.S., improve the economy, protect the country against terrorist invaders. (Whether he actually fulfilled or will fulfill these promises is another question.) I saw another candidate wondering aimlessly from topic to topic, calling people names – who will ever forget "deplorables" – and relying instead on the heavily biased aid she was getting from the Elite through their ownership and control of the mainstream media. I saw YouTube videos the likes of which I have never seen before with Trump filling large stadiums to the brim, leaving thousands more to wait outside the venue – the kind of attention and mass approval I have never seen before from any celebrity. I saw videos of Clinton speaking at events where she could not fill a high school gymnasium.

I saw exposé videos showing Clinton underlings bragging about election rigging and deliberately inciting violence at Trump campaign rallies.[53]

Conversely, although there is a long history of political vote rigging by both major political candidates[54] the evidence of the U.S. presidential election of 2016 is that vote fraud most decidedly favored Democrats – a fact that mainstream media pundits will deny until they're foaming at the mouth.[55]

Trump won the 2016 election in spite of opposition to him by the mainstream media, in spite of documented cases of illegal immigrants voting and President Obama himself openly encouraging illegals to vote, which is a felony.[56] This was quickly argued by the mainstream media as being misunderstood, de-

[53] See: "Rigging the Election: Video I: Clinton Campaign and DNC Incite Violence at Trump Rallies" https://www.youtube.com/watch?v=5IuJGHulkzY
Also see: "Rigging the Election: Video II: Mass Voter Fraud https://www.youtube.com/watch?v=hDc8PVCvfKs
Both videos were released by Project Veritas. See: https://www.youtube.com/channel/UCEE8w-v6Gg4j3ze3oX-urEw
Apparently, sophisticated vote rigging has been going on for a while now. Another gem is the sworn testimony of a computer programmer in 2006, Tom Feeney, who describes how he worked to create computer programs to rig elections in favor of whoever was the chosen winner by those controlling the voting machines. See: https://www.youtube.com/watch?v=-JEzY2tnwExs

[54] See: Christopher Collier and Kenneth F. Collier, Votescam: The Stealing of America, (1992). See also: http://www.votescam.org, http://www.wanttoknow.info/electionsfraud. Also see: https://ratical.org/ratville/BHoCEFiA.html

[55] See: "Could Massive Voter Fraud Have Taken Place in the 2016 U.S. Presidential Election?" https://www.electoralintegrityproject.com/eip-blogs/2017/2/2/could-massive-voter-fraud-have-taken-place-in-the-2016-us-presidential-election
Also see: "Trump's Bogus Voter Fraud Claims," http://www.factcheck.org/2016/10/trumps-bogus-voter-fraud-claims/
Also see: "All this talk of voter fraud? Across U.S., officials found next to none," https://www.nytimes.com/2016/12/18/us/voter-fraud.html

[56] See: "Obama Encouraging Illegal Immigrants to Vote?" http://video.foxbusiness.com/v/5198894475001/?#
Also see: "Obama Encourages Illegal Immigrants to Vote," https://www.youtube.com/watch?v=WCLO0WBvhF8
Also see: "Make No Mistake: Obama Told Illegals to Vote," http://www.lifezette.com/polizette/make-no-mistake-obama-told-illegals-vote/

spite the fact that Obama's comments are unmistakeably clear.[57] Nonetheless, there emerged the spurious political accusation that the Russian Government had interfered in the U.S. presidential election, successfully altering its outcome.

What has poured forth from the U.S. mainstream media almost daily with their "empty eloquence" is the idea that had the Russians not interfered in the election, Hillary Clinton, the obvious favorite of the Elite and their media, would be President. [58] The inference, of course, is that the massive groundswell of support for Trump either would never have happened were it not for Russians, despite the fact that there is not one of the 17 intelligence agencies in the U.S. who claimed the Russians hacked the U.S. elections,[59] that can come up with a shred of credible evidence.[60]

That 'playing the Russia' card without any supportive evidence is now a standard practice in politics,[61] and given how transparent and fictitious it is, one has to wonder if perhaps today's Elite are not becoming a little less adept than its forebears.

"In all ages the peoples of the world, equally with individuals, have accepted words for deeds, for they are content with a show and rarely pause to note, in the public arena, whether promises are followed by performance. Therefore, we shall establish show institutions which will give eloquent proof of their benefit to progress."

This underscores why you can't believe anything you see, read, or hear from the mainstream media. It's show. It's pro-

[57] See: https://www.washingtonpost.com/news/the-intersect/wp/2016/11/08/no-this-video-does-not-show-obama-urging-undocumented-people-to-vote/?utm_term=.bf2f34d3a3bb

[58] To read the conventional, once again, here's a Wikipedia article: https://en.wikipedia.org/wiki/Russian_interference_in_the_2016_United_States_elections

[59] See: "Yes, 17 intelligence agencies really did say Russia was behind hacking," https://www.usatoday.com/story/news/politics/onpolitics/2016/10/21/17-intelligence-agencies-russia-behind-hacking/92514592

[60] See: "Greenwald: 'No evidence' for Russian hacking narrative," http://www.dailywire.com/news/12224/greenwald-no-evidence-russian-hacking-narrative-robert-kraychik

[61] See: "Why it's always Russia wot dunnit: Blaming Russia is a 'get out of jail free' card for struggling political elites," http://www.spiked-online.com/newsite/article/why-its-always-russia-wot-dunnit/19640#.WWgFzlGQzIU

gramming. It's created to steer your opinions in the direction that the Elite see fit. Occasionally, this fact leaks out in an unexpected way. An example is a recent slip by Mika Brzezinski of MSNBC, a woman not lacking in Elite pedigree, who leaked that it was the media's job "to control exactly what people think."[62]

"In order to put opinion into our hands, we must bring it into a state of bewilderment by giving expression for all sides to so many contradictory opinions and for such length of time as will suffice to make the masses lose their heads in the labyrinth and come to see that the best thing is to have no opinion of any kind in matters political, which it is not given to the public to understand, because they are understood only by him who guides the public. This is the first secret."

Another accurate prediction. How do we measure bewilderment among the masses in "matters political"? Well, one measure is people in a democracy deciding that they're just not going to vote anymore, and a significant decline in voter participation around the globe is exactly what's been happening.[63] Irrespective of the fact that Trump is not fulfilling his campaign promises, and moreover if we understand how things work in the Outer Bands, we must understand that Trump works for the same masters as Hillary does, albeit perhaps not with the same level of commitment.

"The second secret requisite for the success of our government is comprised of the following: To multiply to such an extent national failings, habits, passions, conditions of civil life, that it will be impossible for anyone to know where he is in the resulting chaos, so that the people in consequence will fail to

[62] See: https://www.youtube.com/watch?v=OJ9ce-yMEfc

[63] See: "Voter turnout is dropping dramatically in the 'free world'" https://qz.com/899586/global-voter-turnout-is-dropping-dramatically-across-the-world/
Also see: "Why is Turnout at Elections Declining Across the Democratic World?" http://www.e-ir.info/2012/09/27/why-is-turnout-at-elections-declining-across-the-democratic-world/, and "The Alarming Decline in Voter Turnout," https://www.theglobeandmail.com/news/politics/the-alarming-decline-in-voter-turnout/article4247507/

understand one another. This measure will also serve us in another way, namely, to sow discord in all parties, to dislocate all collective forces which are still unwilling to submit to us, and to discourage any kind of personal initiative which might in any degree hinder our affair. There is nothing more dangerous than personal initiative; if it has genius behind it, such initiative can do more than can be done by millions of people among whom we have sown discord. We must so direct the education of the mass communities that whenever they come upon a matter requiring initiative they may drop their hands in despairing impotence. The strain which results from freedom of action saps the forces when it meets with the freedom of another.

From this collision arise grave moral shocks, disenchantments, failures. By all these means we shall so wear down the masses that they will be compelled to offer us international power of a nature that by its position will enable us without any violence gradually to absorb all the State forces of the world and to form a Super-Government. In place of the rulers of today, we shall set up a bogey which will be called the Super-Government Administration. Its hands will reach out in all directions like nippers and its organization will be of such colossal dimensions that it cannot fail to subdue all the nations of the world."

The United Nations, exactly the kind of "Super-government" described, has been putting forth initiatives for years now, since its founding in 1945, that erode national sovereignty, exactly as The Protocols predict. One of the more insidious of these is Agenda 21, signed by over 200 nation states.[64] Now I realize that if you Google "Agenda 21," you'll find numerous articles highlighting the "fact" that Agenda 21 is a "right wing conspiracy theory." How do the "presstitutes"of the mainstream media get away with this? Well, it's easy. They know that there isn't one person in a hundred talking about Agenda 21 who will

[64] See: "Agenda 21: The Plan for Global Fascist Dictatorship," https://wakeup-world.com/2014/08/05/agenda-21-the-plan-for-a-global-fascist-dictatorship/
See also: "Agenda 21 / Sustainable Development," https://americanpolicy.org/agenda21/

actually sit down and read the damn thing.[65]

By the way, I just love that tagline: "right wing conspiracy theory." I always look for this tag whenever I'm doing research, principally because it has been my experience that you are never closer to the truth than when henchmen for the mainstream media tag the area of your personal interest as a "conspiracy theory." Adding "right wing"only makes it more inflammatory. Time for a new premise.

Premise On The Importance Of Labelling Logical Conclusions That Defy Political Objectives (BCN) As They Relate To Current Affairs As "Conspiracy Theories"

Because heartbreakingly scandalous, criminal behavior is so essential to "good Government" and to the enhancement of thermodynamic potential, it is critically important to use the full weight of the mainstream media, the education system, the health care profession and the scientific community – all controlled by the Elite – to marginalize members of the masses who "catch on" to Government's numerous, unending, criminal conspiracies. Any Government which does not engage in this deceptive practice is at a critical disadvantage to those that are more proficient in its crucial practice.

This is an extension of the very things that were discussed in the previous chapter on gullibility.

Here's a question for you:

On balance, what is the difference between a conspiracy theory and an officially revised historical fact?

Give up?

In the majority of cases, it comes down to the passage of time, simply because it takes time to accumulate a critical mass

65 See: https://sustainabledevelopment.un.org/content/documents/Agenda21.pdf

of people who can look at the facts presented, apply elementary common sense, and figure out that the official Government version of an event was tailored to gullible people who have no inclination to challenge Elite-inspired, Elite-generated, Elite-supported, Elite-promulgated "cognitive dissonance."

You have to **fight** against the official tendency to gaslight you – to, once again, test your gullibility.

Despite the fact that occasionally an article will pop up in the mainstream media that throws "conspiracy theorists" a bone,[66] you normally don't find a more candid assessment unless you consult with the "alternative media."[67] Why is that? Because the mainstream media acts as the mouthpiece for their clients in the Outer Bands, whereas the alternative media are closer to ordinary people, which means there is less sectoral distance.

This book is long enough already, so I'm not going to add 5,000 pages by dissecting each of the great "conspiracy theories" of our time. There are already a plethora of excellent books on the market that analyze the most notable examples and demonstrate how nauseatingly ridiculous the official narratives are. So I will only list a handful of the most prominent "conspiracy theories" of our time, for illustrative purposes, and in more or less chronological order:

The Kennedy assassination (1963),[68] the "Gulf of Tonkin"

[66] Here are some examples: "Perhaps the world's conspiracy theorists have been right all along" http://www.telegraph.co.uk/men/thinking-man/11671617/Perhaps-the-worlds-conspiracy-theorists-have-been-right-all-along.html; See also: "Stranger than fiction: Ten shocking conspiracy theories that were completely true" https://www.thesun.co.uk/living/1572737/ten-shocking-conspiracy-theories-that-were-completely-true/; and "5 US national security-related conspiracy theories that turned out to be true" http://www.businessinsider.com/5-conspiracy-theories-that-turned-out-to-be-true-2015-6

[67] See: "Conspiracy Theorists Were Right About Everything – Now What?" https://steemit.com/writing/@therealpaul/conspiracy-theorists-were-right-about-everything-what-now
Also see: "2016 Is The Year All 'Conspiracy Theories' Were Proved True" http://yournews-wire.com/2016-is-the-year-all-conspiracy-theories-were-proved-true/

[68] None of the following books agree on all points, but all uniformly agree that the Warren Commission version (official) of the assassination is laughably implausible. To this effect, see: Joseph Farrell, LBJ and the Conspiracy to Kill Kennedy, (2011); also see: Jim Marrs, Crossfire: The Plot That Killed Kennedy, (1989) – this is the book that Oliver Stone used as the basis for his "conspiracy movie," "JFK"; also of interest is the following book: Jerome Corsi, Who Really Killed Kennedy?: 50 Years Later: Stunning New Revelations About the JFK Assassination; see as well: Craig Newman, The Assassination of JFK – Who Really Did It and Why, (2017); and: Lamar Waldron, The Hidden History of the JFK Assassination, (2013); and there are plenty more books on this subject. The official JFK assassination narrative, embodied in the

conspiracy (1964);[69] the bombing of the U.S.S. Liberty (1967);[70] the assassination of Rev. Martin Luther King, Jr. (1968);[71] the RFK assassination (1968);[72] the "HIV causes AIDS" hoax (late 80's/early 90's);[73] the crash and cover-up of TWA Flight 800,

Warren Commission report was so obviously false that even his own brother, Robert Kennedy, didn't believe it, though he was pressured at the time to publicly endorse it, not knowing that the same forces would come back for seconds and take him out five years later in 1968. See: https://www.irishcentral.com/roots/robert-f-kennedy-believed-jfk-was-killed-because-of-him

[69] This incident was historically significant, because it would launch the Vietnam War and cause over 50 000 American servicemen to lose their lives over the next 11 years. See: "Case Closed: The Gulf of Tonkin Incident" http://www.historynet.com/case-closed-the-gulf-of-tonkin-incident.htm, or "When Presidents lie to make war" https://www.theguardian.com/commentisfree/2014/aug/02/vietnam-presidents-lie-to-wage-war-iraq.
Years later, while still working in the U.S. Navy with a Top Secret clearance, I met a fellow cryptologist who coordinated intelligence going in and out of the White House. He told me that everyone he knew that was handling intelligence at the time in connection with the "Incident" knew that the entire affair "was a bunch of shit," created as an excuse to get the U.S. into yet another war.

[70] See: Peter Hounam, Operation Cyanide: How the Bombing of the USS Liberty Nearly Caused World War Three, (2003). This occurred in June, 1967, during the "Six-Day War." I had inside knowledge about this incident, which occurred over eight years before I was sent by the U.S. Navy to NTTC Corry Station in Pensacola, Florida, in early 1976 for training as a cryptologist. While there, I met two chief petty officers who gave me eyewitness accounts of what happened, as among the dead and wounded in the attack were shipmates of these non-commissioned officers, fellow cryptologists with my same rating.

[71] See: "Did you know? U.S. Gov't Found Guilty In Conspiracy to Assassinate Dr. Martin Luther King Jr." https://newsone.com/2843790/did-you-know-us-govt-found-guilty-in-conspiracy-to-assassinate-dr-martin-luther-king-jr/. See also: Dr. William F. Pepper Esq., The Plot to Kill King: The Truth Behind the Assassination of Martin Luther King Jr., (2016). And there are plenty more books on this subject.

[72] See: "Did the CIA kill Bobby Kennedy?" https://www.theguardian.com/world/2006/nov/20/usa.features11. See also: "Robert Kennedy Assassination" https://www.thoughtco.com/robert-kennedy-assassination-1779358, (carefully read the three pointers under "Conspiracy Theories.") If you want something more thorough, I suggest: William Turner and John Christian, The Assassination of Robert F. Kennedy: The Conspiracy and Coverup, (1993).

[73] See: John Lauritsen, The AIDS War: Propaganda, Profiteering and Genocide from the Medical Industrial Complex, USA, (1993); see also: Peter Duesberg, Inventing the AIDS Virus, Regnery Publishing, USA, (1997); AIDS: The good news is that HIV doesn't cause it – the bad news is that 'recreational drugs' and medical treatments like AZT do, (1995). It should be noted that Duesberg was no lightweight. At the time these books were published twenty years ago, he was one of the world's leading microbiologists, having pioneered the discovery of the HIV family of viruses, and having been a member of the U.S. National Academy of Sciences. The connection between HIV and AIDS has been pounded so hard into the mind of the public collective, so few people ever bothered to ask the obvious, which readily destroyed the official narrative about an HIV/AIDS connection. As Duesberg pointed out in the introduction to Inventing the AIDS Virus, p 445: "HIV does not cause AIDS... AIDS is not sexually transmitted... AZT makes AIDS." Worse, not better, Duesberg's evidence - revealed in top scientific journals but kept out of the mainstream press - raises questions the AIDS research establishment has so far declined to answer: If HIV causes AIDS, why have thousands of AIDS victims never had HIV? Why have hundreds of thousands who have had HIV - for many years - remained perfectly healthy? Why does the discoverer of the HIV virus now claim it cannot be the sole cause of AIDS? Why have more than ten years of AIDS research - costing tens of

(July, 1996);[74] "9/11" (2011);[75] What is the official response to these well-documented works, or, more broadly speaking, to "conspiracy theories" or specifically "conspiracy theorists," in general? Well, we know what it is. If you accept obvious, indisputable facts and choose not to believe an official narrative that's crafted to show how gullible you are, officialdom knows how to dismissively label you: paranoid or mentally ill,[76] narcissistic,[77] psychologically imbalanced to the point of needing a "coping mechanism,"[78] in need of attaching yourself to the delusional because you feel a "lack of control" over your life,[79] irrationally anti-establishment,[80] suffering from a diagnosable psycho-cock-

---

billions of dollars - failed to show how (or even if) HIV causes AIDS or attacks the immune system? With annual federal funding at more than $7 billion, AIDS research is better funded than any other disease - including cancer. Yet it has also produced the least results. Why? Duesberg explains how the lure of money and prestige, combined with powerful political pressure, have tempted otherwise responsible scientists to overlook - even suppress - major flaws in current AIDS theory; Neville Hodgkinson also addresses this issue in his book: AIDS: The Failure of Contemporary Science: How a virus that never was deceived the world, (1996); and see also:Jon Rappoport, AIDS Inc.: Scandal of the Century, (2003), among others.

74 See: James Sanders, The Downing of TWA Flight 800: The Shocking Truth Behind the Worst Airplane Disaster in U.S. History, (1997), see also: Jack Cashill, TWA 800: The Crash, the Cover-up, and the Conspiracy, (2016), etc.

75 See: Rodney Stich, David vs. Goliath: 9/11 & Other Tragedies, (2005); see also: Rebekah Roth, Methodical Illusion, (2015); also worth reading: David Griffin, Debunking 9/11: An Answer to Popular Mechanics and Other Defenders of the Official Conspiracy Theory, (2007); also by David Griffin, 9/11 Ten Years Later, (2011). The entire official 9/11 narrative is so full of holes that David Griffin practically made a living documenting it. This was Griffin's tenth book about 9/11 in ten years. Continuing on: Webster Griffin Tarpley, 9/11 Synthetic Terror, (2011); also, another great read is: Jesse Ventura, American Conspiracies, (2010). Ventura covers 9/11 only in passing, but his coverage is sufficient to convey that the official 9/11 story is bogus; also worth reading: Jim Marrs, The Terror Conspiracy: Deception, 9/11, and the Loss of Liberty, (2006); and these are but a few examples that stand out.

76 See: "The psychology of conspiracy belief" http://www.stuff.co.nz/national/health/64114756/the-psychology-of-conspiracy-belief, short version: Believing in conspiracy theories means you're more likely to be "paranoid or mentally ill."

77 See: "Believe in conspiracy theories? You're probably a narcissist" http://www.dailymail.co.uk/sciencetech/article-3482408/Believe-conspiracy-theories-probably-narcissist-People-doubt-moon-landings-likely-selfish-attention-seeking.html, short version: The title says it all.

78 See:"Paranoia and the Roots of Conspiracy Theories" https://www.psychologytoday.com/blog/the-narcissus-in-all-us/200809/paranoia-and-the-roots-conspiracy-theories, short version: The author draws from Empire of Conspiracy by Tim Melley who ties a belief in conspiracies together with paranoia and its use as a "coping mechanism."

79 See: "Here's why people believe in conspiracy theories" http://time.com/3997033/conspiracy-theories/, short version: conspiracy theorists feel a lack of control over their lives.

80 See: "Conspiracy Theorists Aren't Really Skeptics" http://www.slate.com/articles/health_and_science/science/2013/11/conspiracy_theory_psychology_people_who_claim_to_know_

tail of paranoia, schizophrenia, narcissism, delusions, anxiety, and/or trust issues,[81] or if that doesn't fit the bill, you're just an uneducated cretin.[82] We cannot marginalize these claims, now can we? After all, those in authority must know what they're talking about, because if we learn anything at all from The Protocols, the Government wouldn't lie to us, would it?

Protocol No. 6

"We shall soon begin to establish huge monopolies, reservoirs of colossal riches, upon which even the large (individual) fortunes of (unusually fortunate) members of the masses will depend to such an extent that they will go to the bottom together with the credit of the States on the day after the political smash . . ."

Truly there is no such thing as lasting wealth unless the money supply itself is under one's complete control. Under the present system, the banking Elite can issue as much money as they want to themselves and their criminal friends. The global economy is accordingly dominated by a network of private central banks using fractional reserve banking,[83] that issue fiat currencies directly into circulation right out of thin air. This debases the medium of exchange to the disadvantage of people who actually work for a living. Under a system this perverted, what does wealth really mean?

Once again, we see how clearly States are subordinate to

the_truth_about_jfk.html; short version: Conspiracy theorists are anti-establishment.

[81] See: "Are people who believe in conspiracy theories 'crazy'?" http://www.goodtherapy.org/blog/are-people-who-believe-in-conspiracy-theories-crazy-0423157; short version: Although conspiracy theorists do not have their own place (yet) in the Diagnostic and Statistical Manual of Mental Disorders, if you believe in conspiracy theories you "may" be experiencing paranoia, schizophrenia, narcissism, delusions, anxiety, or trust issues. Conspiracy theorists are also reckless people. They are less likely to use condoms, seek HIV treatment, or be gullible enough to vaccinate their children. They're horribly screwed up people!

[82] See: "Why more highly educated people are less into conspiracy theories" https://digest.bps.org.uk/2017/04/05/why-more-highly-educated-people-are-less-into-conspiracy-theories/; short version: If you believe in conspiracy theories, you're an uneducated cretin.

[83] See: Vladimir Z. Nuri, "Fractional Reserve Banking as Economic Parasitism: A Scientific, Mathematical & Historical Expose, Critique, and Manifesto" https://empslocal.ex.ac.uk/people/staff/mrwatkin/nuri.pdf

monied interests and how quickly an economic system can be brought to its knees at the mere whim of the money-changers. Gary Allen made this clear in his classic book on this subject, dealing with the goal of complete monopoly and its secrecy, when he quoted historian Dr. Carroll Quigley: "I know the operations of this (Elite) network because I have studied it for twenty years . . . my chief difference of opinion is that it wishes to remain unknown, and I believe its role in history is significant enough to be known." Then Allen goes on to say:

"We agree, its role in history does deserve to be known. However, we most emphatically disagree with this network's aim which the Professor describes as 'nothing less than to create a world system of financial control in private hands able to dominate the political system of each country and the economy of the world as a whole.' In other words, this power mad clique wants to control and rule the world. Even more frightening, they want total control over all individual actions. As Professor Quigley observes:'. . . his (the individual's) freedom and choice will be controlled within very narrow alternatives by the fact that he will be numbered from birth and followed, as a number, through his educational training, his required military or other public service, his tax contributions, his health and medical requirements, and his final retirement and death benefits.' (They want) control over all natural resources, business, banking, and transporation by controlling the Governments of the world. In order to accomplish these aims the conspirators have had no qualms about fomenting wars, depressions and hatred. They want a monopoly which would eliminate all competitors and destroy the free enterprise system."[84]

"In every possible way we must develop the significance of our Super-Government by representing it as the Protector and Benefactor of all those who voluntarily submit to us."

Yes. The Protector and Benefactor of all. Let's play God.

[84] See: Gary Allen and Larry Abraham, None Dare Call It Conspiracy, (1976), p. 15-16.

This is reminiscent of the charges made against this conspiracy more than a hundred years before The Protocols ever surfaced:

"Nothing can more distinctly prove the crooked politics of the 'Reformers' than this. It may be considered as the main-spring of their whole machine. **Their pupils were to be led by means of their meaner desires [i.e. liberalism], and the aim of their conductors was not to inform them, but merely to lead them; not to reform, but to rule the world. They would reign, though in hell, rather than serve in heaven."**[85] (emphasis added)

"The aristocracy of the masses as a political force, is dead – we need not take it into account; but as landed proprietors they can still be harmful to us from the fact that they are self-sufficient in the resources upon which they live. ***It is essential, therefore, for us at whatever cost to deprive them of their land****. This object will be best attained by increasing the burdens upon landed property – in* ***loading lands with debt****. These measures will check land-holding and keep it in a state of humble and unconditional submission."* (emphasis added to Protocols)

Another remarkably predictive passage. One of the measures of real land ownership is a freedom from encumbrance. Prior to the 19th century, mortgages were rare and normally made to wealthier bank patrons.[86] From 1870 to 2010, mortgage lending skyrocketed from less than 10% to nearly 70% of the ratio of bank lending-to-GDP, not just in the U.S., but in seventeen advanced market economies.[87]

All this makes sense when you understand that it's easy to take away people's land and property by standardizing the practice of placing mortgage liens on them and then engineering

[85] See: John Robinson, Proofs of a Conspiracy Against all Religions and Governments of Europe, Carried on in the Secret Meetings of Freemasons, Illuminati and Reading Societies, (1797), p. 182.

[86] One small example would be in New England. See: http://digitalcommons.law.yale.edu/cgi/viewcontent.cgi?article=1026&context=student_legal_history_papers

[87] See: http://economics.ucdavis.edu/people/amtaylor/files/w20501.pdf; see Figure 2, p. 11.

"bubbles" to instigate waves of default.[88] Clearly, the crash of 1929 and the resulting Great Depression were engineered.[89] I'm sure we will soon see another engineered crash beginning with global stock markets, since according to some market experts, equities are obscenely overvalued.[90] What will be the result? Well, among other things, higher unemployment, higher mortgage default rates, and more loss of land and property.

Just what The Protocols ordered.

". . . what we want is that industry should drain off from the land both labour and capital and by means of speculation transfer into our hands all the money of the world, and thereby throw the masses into the ranks of the proletariat. ***Then the masses will bow down before us, if for no other reason but to get the right to exist.*** *"* (emphasis added)

This encapsulates the thinking that resides at the far edges of the Outer Bands – before descending into Pure Evil. Globally, approximately the richest 1%, nearly all of whom belong to the Elite, have managed to accumulate 43% of the world's wealth, while the bottom 80% of the world's population have managed to hang onto 6%. The richest 300 people on the planet possess more than the bottom 3 billion people combined. [91]

What do The Protocols have to do with this? They predicted it. This is not a new development. It took time – yes, generations – to achieve this. Just 200 years ago, the "wealthy nations" of the world where the Elite reside were three times (3x) richer than the poor countries. By the 1960's, this gap had grown to thirty times (30x), and today that figure has exploded to eighty

[88] The process itself is explained in a now famous Rolling Stone article, entitled "The Great American Bubble Machine" http://www.rollingstone.com/politics/news/the-great-american-bubble-machine-20100405
Although the article focuses on Goldman Sachs, this has clearly become the modus operandi for Wall Street for at least a century.

[89] See: https://21stcenturycicero.wordpress.com/2008/02/11/how-a-group-of-international-bankers-engineered-the-1929-crash-and-the-great-depression/

[90] See: http://www.marketwatch.com/story/this-is-the-most-overvalued-stock-market-on-record-even-worse-than-1929-2017-03-13

[91] See: https://www.youtube.com/watch?v=uWSxzjyMNpU, and be sure to read the accompanying Fact Sheet: https://therules.org/inequality-video-fact-sheet/

times (80x).[92] Coincidence?

" . . . We shall raise the rate of wages which, however, will not bring any advantage to the workers, for at the same time, we shall produce a rise in prices of the first necessaries of life, alleging that it arises from the decline of agriculture and cattle-breeding . . ."

What makes this passage so prophetic is the timing. The 20th century produced more inflation than any other century in history, but the century preceeding it – the 19th century – the century that came before The Protocols were published, was deflationary! As GlobalFinancialData.com notes:

"Amazingly enough, the Nineteenth century was a period of deflation, rather than inflation. From the end of the Napoleonic Wars in 1815 until the start of World War II in 1914, there was no inflation in most countries, and in many cases, prices were lower in 1914 than they had been in 1815. Prices fluctuated up and down from one decade to the next, but overall, prices remained stable."[93]

Inflation is an engineered form of theft, which naturally follows from the control of money, or as Hans F. Sennholz wrote in his introduction to Inflation is Theft, "It is difficult to fathom anything more ominous in money matters than a political money monopoly. It permits Government authorities to inflate and depreciate the people's money and to force everyone to accept its money at face value."[94] (emphasis added)

One of the enticements for the creators of Central Banks is the ability to rob the users of the resulting fiat currencies every day, year after year, for the entirety of their lives. What's even tastier on this ghoulish menu is the pure psychopathic pleasure they get in knowing that they're able to rob the public without it

92 Ibid.

93 See: https://www.globalfinancialdata.com/news/articles/century_of_inflation.doc

94 See: Hans F. Sennholz, Inflation is Theft, (1994), p. 1. Also see: https://fee.org/media/15053/inflationistheft.pdf

knowing any better and blame on it on ridiculous misdirections, like "the decline of agriculture." This kind of robbery amounts to enslavement.

The common narrative, at least in the United States, is that "slavery" ended as a result of the loss of the Confederacy at the end of the American Civil War (1861-1865). It's complete malarkey, of course. Why enslave just black people, when everyone can be enslaved? Despite the fact that most people don't have to endure the harsh living conditions that most of the black slaves had to endure in the South, the fact remains that when a small clique – "the oak masters" – control the money supply, everyone else is, in varying degrees, just a slave.

Protocol No. 7

"The intensification of armaments, the increase of police forces – are all essential for the completion of the aforementioned plans. What we have to get at is that there should be in all the States of the world, besides ourselves, only the masses of the proletariat, a few millionaires devoted to our interests, police and soldiers."

Another remarkable prophecy.

There has been an explosive rise in the number of militarized police units in recent years, worldwide. In the U.S. alone, there are 19,000 independent law enforcement agencies, and as Paul Craig Roberts noted, they are now armed with "Blackhawk helicopters, machine guns, grenade launchers, battering rams, explosives, chemical sprays, body armors, night vision, rappelling gear, and armed vehicles. Some have tanks."[95] This trend has completely subverted the Posse Comitatus Act of 1878, whose purpose was to separate military and domestic policing functions.[96]

95 See: https://www.rutherford.org/files_images/general/Rise-of-the-American-Police-State-2010.pdf – p. 8, 9.

96 See:http://www.globalresearch.ca/global-capitalism-and-the-global-police-state-crisis-of-humanity-and-the-specter-of-21st-century-fascism/5444340

"Throughout all Europe, and by means of relations with Europe, in other continents also, ***we must create ferments, discords and hostility****. Therein we gain a double advantage. In the first place we keep in check all countries, for they well know that* ***we have the power whenever we like to create disorders and to restore order****. All these countries are accustomed to see in us* ***an indispensable force of coercion****. In the second place, by our intrigues we shall tangle up all the threads which we have stretched into the cabinets of all States by means of the political, by economic treaties, or loan obligations. In order to succeed in this we must use great cunning and penetration during negotiations and agreements, but, as regards what is called the 'official language,' we shall* ***keep to the opposite tactics and assume the mask of honesty and compliancy.*** *In this way the peoples and Governments of the masses, whom we have taughts [sic] to look only at the outside whatever we present to their notice, will still continue to* ***accept us as benefactors and saviours of the human race****."* (emphasis added)

Again, the controllers at the far end of the Outer Bands weaken any chance of opposition to Pure Evil by maintaining factions that are in constant conflict. This passage gives us a different insight into the nature of evil itself, which uses a variety of deceptive ploys to pretend that it possesses the qualities of goodness. Interestingly, you never see the forces of Good pretending to possess the qualities of Evil.

" . . . we must compel the Governments of the masses to take action in the direction favoured by our widely-conceived plan, already approaching the desired consummation, by what we shall represent as public opinion, secretly prompted by us through the means of that so-called 'Great Power' – the Press, which, with a few exceptions that may be disregarded, is already entirely in our hands."

There are many mansions in the Great Halls of Hell, but none so illustrious as those occupied by the journalists of the mainstream media. It is for this reason that you should avoid the mainstream media entirely, and commit yourself to boycotting the corporate sponsors who make their insidious programming possible. Few things are as toxic to the mind or to simple, clear thinking, as exposure to the endless drivel of the Deep State propaganda machine.

This is reminiscent of the famous statement by former CIA director, William Colby, in 1981: "The CIA owns everyone of any significance in the major media. We'll know our disinformation program is complete when everything the American public believes is false."[97]

Want a major rush of brain rot? Just turn on the television and "eat the garbage that they feed you."

" . . . we shall show our strength . . . by terrorist attempts and to all, if we allow the possibility of a general rising against us, we shall respond with the guns of America or China or Japan."

A key insight as to the source of most of the world's terrorist activity.

Protocol No. 8

" . . . We must search out in the very finest shades of expression and the knotty points of the lexicon of law justification of those cases where we shall have to pronounce judgments that might appear abnormally audacious and unjust, for it is important that these resolutions should be set forth in expressions that shall seem to be the most exalted moral principles cast into legal form. . ."

The benign common narrative (BCN) is designed to teach the masses that laws are created for the public good. This passage teaches us that laws are, more often than not, created to execute policies that are "abnormally audacious and unjust." It

[97] See: http://www.altcancer.net/ashwin/ashw0914.htm, which references this quote.

became very apparent to me during my legal travails in the U.S. that there was no morality, ethics, or justice in the criminal justice community there. I make that abundantly clear in Chapter 3 of Meditopia.[98] The creation of legal structures to advance the most hideously evil of agendas has been a long time in the making.

I can't help but discuss another document that illustrates the longevity of this practice - one that is over 525 years old; the sheer weight of proof that its provisions have been meticulously followed make it worthy of examination. It is nearly as prophetic as The Protocols themselves, despite its brevity. Here is the background: in March, 1492, the Catholic Monarchs of Spain (Isabella I of Castile and Ferdinand II of Aragon) – rightly or wrongly – were in the process of trying to rid their territory of Muslims and Jews who did not conform to what they felt were the good Christian values. A result of this was their issuance of the "Alhambra Decree," which specifically targeted Jews. Many years later, a document surfaced in Toledo, Spain, that is referenced by author Andrew Carrington Hitchcock. It was written more than 400 years before The Protocols and carries the same insidious tone:

"Chemor, the Chief Rabbi of Spain, wrote to the Grand Sanhedrin, which had its seat in Constantinople, for advice on what to do. His reply which can be found on pages 156-157 of the book, La Silva Curiosa, by Julio-Iñiguez de Medrano, published (in) Paris, Orry, 1608, was found in the archives of Toledo by the Hermit of Salamanca, amongst the ancient records of the kingdoms of Spain. I reproduce it here:

'Beloved brethren in Moses, we have received your letter in which you tell us of your anxieties and misfortunes, which you are enduring. We are pierced by as great pain to hear it as yourselves.'

The advice of the Grand Satraps and Rabbis is the following:

98 See: http://www.altcancer.net/chap3-1.htm

1. *As for what you say that the King of Spain obliges you to become Christian: do it, since you cannot do otherwise.*
2. *As for what you say about the command to despoil you of your property: make your sons merchants that they may despoil, little by little, the Christian of theirs.*
3. *As for what you say about making attempts on your lives: make your sons doctors and apothecaries, that they may take away Christians' lives.*
4. *As for what you say of destroying synagogues: make your sons canons and clerics in order that they may destroy their churches.*
5. *As for the many other vexations you complain of: arrange that your sons become advocates and lawyers, and see that they always mix in affairs of State, that by putting Christians under your yoke, you may dominate the world and be avenged on them.*
6. *Do not swerve from this order that we give you, because you will find by experience that, humiliated as you are, you will reach the actuality of power.*

(Signed) Prince of the Jews of Constantinople'"[99]

Regardless of the ethnic overtones of this document – which, as I stated earlier, I find objectionable, principally because it has little to do with those Jews who have nothing to do with the Elite behind this document or The Protocols – it is astonishingly accurate.

Let's briefly cover each of these six points from above:

1. The reply says "convert to Christianity in accordance with the Decree, if you must." This supports the notion that Eliteness isn't confined to any ethnicity or religious orientation. U.S. vice president, Joe Biden, himself bragged on video that, "I am a Zionist. You don't have

[99] See: Andrew Carrington Hitchcook, The Synagogue of Satan, p. 3-4.

to be a Jew to be a Zionist."[100] For the sake of the Jews who have suffered needlessly at the hands of the Elite – the Holocaust comes to mind – it should be added that you don't have to be a Zionist to be a Jew.

2. "Make your sons merchants so you may despoil others of their property." We covered that previously in our discussion of growing concentration of wealth. **Mission accomplished.**
3. "Make your sons doctors so you may take away their lives." We covered this previously in our discussion of the cancer industry. The Medical Industrial Complex takes in billions of dollars in research funds annually, yet after being the dominant faction in health care for over 160 years,[101] it has not managed to come up with a single cure for one degenerative disease. Instead, it has ushered in an "Age of Iatrogenesis."[102] This explains why the word "cure" has been banished from their lexicon.[103] **Mission accomplished.**
4. "Make your sons clerics that you may destroy their churches." Nothing has done this more effectively than liberalism. **Mission accomplished.**[104]
5. "Make your sons lawyers that you may dominate the world." This supports this opening passage from protocol #8. **Mission accomplished.**
6. "You will reach the actuality of power." **Mission accomplished.**

"Our directorate . . . will surround itself with publicists, practical jurists, administrators, diplomats and finally, with persons prepared by a special super-educational training in our

[100] See: https://www.youtube.com/watch?v=Uo-UXZ-1ups

[101] I assign the period around the founding of the British Medical Association in 1832 and the American Medical Association in 1848 as the birth of the Medical Industrial Complex.

[102] Once again, see: http://www.altcancer.net/ashwin/ashw0809.htm

[103] See: https://wakeup-world.com/2016/08/30/the-disappearance-of-the-word-cure-from-modern-medicine/

[104] See: http://www.americantraditions.org/Articles/Liberalism%20is%20Destroying%20Christian%20Churches.htm

special schools. These persons will have cognizance of all the secrets of the social structure, they will know all the languages that can be made up by political alphabets and words; they will be made aquainted with the whole underside of human nature, with all its sensitive chords on which they will have to play . . ."

This follows from our earlier examination of the Premise on the Role of Government in Education. It would be inconsistent with the goals expressed in The Protocols to have the descendants of its designers – those appointed to continue on with and execute this multi-generational horror story – contaminated by the same toxic, dumbed-down, educational system that feeds the masses.

"We shall surround our Government with a whole world of economists. That is the reason why economic sciences form the principal subject of the teaching given to the Elite. Around us again will be a whole constellation of bankers, industrialists, capitalists and – the main thing – millionaires, because in substance everything will be settled by the question of figures."

Two things come to mind here: the oft-quoted expression, "Figures don't lie, but liars will figure." Secondly, and of considerably greater importance, is my lifelong sense that economics is a dubious academic "science." The passage above not only confirms my suspicions, but reminds me that with the Elite at the helm, it couldn't have been any other way.

One gets a sense how out of touch with reality economics is with a casual reading of Stephen D. Levitt and Stephen J. Dubner's series of Freakonomics books.[105] However, "cracks in the Matrix" abound that should alert a person as easily seduced by logic as I am, and that at a deeper level, economics was never designed as an academic discipline to tell us how the world really works. It's designed to try to add respectability to a system

[105] The series began with the author's Freakonomics: A Rogue Economist Explores the Hidden Side of Everything, (2005), and has resulted in a series of books that follow the same theme: the world is not as it seems.

that's meant to justify the shameful exploitation of the masses, which is a sizeable part of The Protocols' message.

Interestingly, there is an annual Nobel Prize in economics, but none of the other social sciences are afforded that distinction: sociology, psychology, anthropology, etc.[106] Instead, they laud economists who produce mathematical models that rarely conform to real world financial behavior, causing one essayist to compare economics to "a highly paid pseudoscience."[107] This makes sense when you understand that even the discipline's ardent supporters will tell you that "economics is not a science."[108] It makes even more sense when you realize that the Nobel Prize in Economics isn't even a true Nobel Prize. It was snuck in 75 years later, in 1969, by Sweden's Central Bank as a "marketing ploy . . . to give free-market economics for the 1% credibility."[109] Dissenting members of the Nobel Prize in Economics said it best in 2004 when they wrote that the Prize was "so abstract and disconnected from the real world as to (be) utterly meaningless."[110]

This history of economics is a long chain of one policy position after another, intent on justifying the orderly economic destruction of ordinary people: classical economics,[111] trickle-down economics,[112] austerity economics,[113] Keynesian economics,[114] libertarian economics,[115] etc. – all incorporating a dizzying array of yet more models that do anything but help

[106] See: https://www.theguardian.com/commentisfree/2015/oct/11/nobel-prize-economics-not-science-hubris-disaster

[107] See: https://aeon.co/essays/how-economists-rode-maths-to-become-our-era-s-astrologers

[108] See: http://www.thecrimson.com/article/2013/12/13/economics-science-wang/

[109] See: http://www.alternet.org/economy/there-no-nobel-prize-economics

[110] Ibid.

[111] See: https://www.coursera.org/learn/principles-of-macroeconomics/lecture/GGcx8/why-classical-economics-failed

[112] See: http://www.faireconomy.org/trickle_down_economics_four_reasons

[113] See: http://www.newyorker.com/news/daily-comment/its-official-austerity-economics-doesnt-work

[114] See: https://azconservative.org/2013/10/15/economics-why-keynesian-economics-doesnt-work/

[115] See: https://genius.com/discussions/73674-C-l-libertarian-alan-greenspan-admits-libertarian-economics-doesnt-work

ordinary people. Should we have expected anything different?

"For a time, until there will no longer be any risk in entrusting responsible posts in our States to our brethren, we shall put them in the hands of persons whose past and reputation are such that between them and the people lies an abyss, persons who, in case of disobedience to our instructions, must face criminal charges or disappear – this in order to make them defend our interests to their last gasp."

This helps explain why pedophiles are promoted to top positions in leading Governments.[116] The Elite could not so easily persuade politicians to support laws and regulations that are opposed to the interests of their own people if the Elite weren't able to hang threats of prosecution over the heads of politicians who forget that they are merely puppets, who forget their true place in the world.

As for making the uncooperative disappear, I've already referenced the work of author John Perkins, and his excellent work on "economic hit men" and sending in the "jackals" to assassinate those who don't get the message.

Protocol No. 9

"The words of the liberal, which are in effect the words of our masonic watchword, namely, 'Liberty, Equality, Fraternity,' will, when we come into our kingdom, be changed by us into words no longer of a watchword, but only an expression of idealism, namely, into: 'The right of liberty, the duty of equality, the ideal of brotherhood.' That is how we shall put it – and so we shall catch the bull by the horns . . . De facto we have already wiped out every kind of rule except our own, although de jure there still remain a good many of them. Nowadays, if any States

[116] An excellent discussion of this can be found at: "Pedophiles run the Government and no one gives a damn," https://www.youtube.com/watch?v=DFZRQcSMeeM
If you don't think politicians can be brought down from their perches for not following orders, you can ask Dennis Hastert, former Speaker of the United States House of Representatives, recently released from federal prison.

raise a protest against us it is only pro forma at our discretion and by our direction, for their anti-Semitism is indispensable to us for the management of our lesser brethren. I will not enter into further explanations, for this matter has formed the subject of repeated discussions among us."

This opening passage of Protocol No. 9 contains vital insights. First, we are introduced to a new example of Doublespeak, reminded that the drivel intended to steer public opinion to accept cognitive dissonance as part of the BCN is engineered from the top. The incorporation of "masonic" makes sense when you understand that although low-level participants in freemasonry know little about its origins and closely guarded secrets, we now have two hundred years of "worshipful masters" as its highest levels who freely, openly, and proudly admit that Lucifer is their god.[117] Operating at the outer fringes of the Outer Bands, why would we expect to see anything less? – unless you are prepared to argue that Lucifer represents the opposite – goodness, virtue, generosity, etc.[118] (Those who think that Satan and Lucifer are not the same entity should ask themselves why the most devoted followers of "both" are so tightly associated with organizations that live and breathe in the Outer Bands – their public relations charitable activities, notwithstanding.)

When I first began discussing The Protocols, I indicated that I would do my best to strip out all mention of ethnicity, and I have done my best. The problem with this passage is that it makes no sense if you attempt to follow this restriction. The passage becomes incomprehensible. What The Protocols are telling us here is that the "anti-Semitic" label is just a controlling tool to quell dissent.

The orthodox Jewish community is not blind to the obscene way that the "anti-Semitic" tag has been used to promote the Elite's political and economic agenda. They can differentiate

[117] See: http://amazingdiscoveries.org/S-deception-Freemason_Lucifer_Albert_Pike

[118] By way of example, see: https://www.youtube.com/watch?v=9Q1hnkp5Zqw
This video clip would be laughable if it didn't accurately represent the views of those who live at the pinnacle of the world's leading secret societies. The video's creator makes his point, regardless of the infusion of his own personal beliefs as a Christian.

between this exercise in misdirection, and true, unquestioning, irrational hatred of Jewish people. They are well-aware that they have been victims of the Elite for the entirety of there existence. (Those wanting more information on this subject should look into and help support the activities of Neturei Karta International.)[119]

Lastly, the closing sentence of this passage suggests that this may be one of the most, if not the most, closely guarded secret in the Elite's arsenal against humanity.

"For us there are no checks to limit the range of our activity. Our Super-Government subsists in extra-legal conditions which are described in the accepted terminology by the energetic and forcible word – Dictatorship. I am in the position to tell you with a clear conscience that at the proper time, we, the lawgivers, shall execute judgment and sentence, we shall slay and we shall spare, we, as head of all our troops, are mounted on the steed of the leader. We rule by force of will, because in our hands are the fragments of a once powerful party, now vanquished by us. ***And the weapons in our hands are limitless ambitions, burning greediness, merciless vengeance, hatreds, and malice****."* (emphasis contained in the original text)

Consolidation of property and resources bring with it consolidation of power and, in order to make this process work in the open, where everyone can see it, one must transcend legal conditions. Once again, laws exist for "little people" – for the masses – and are not intended to be followed by those who create them, by the "Lawgivers."

The "weapons in our hands" reads like our earlier analysis of the characteristics of psychopaths, which is precisely what the Elite are. Let me hear the "I am Lucifer" video from that last passage again. Let it sink in. Lucifer is "pure and virtuous and wholesome and innocent." Let me say it with a "clear con-

[119] Neturei Karta's website is: http://nkusa.org/ See also: https://www.youtube.com/watch?v=awCOSRg-gks This video contains an excellent explanation by David Icke on the ways in which Jewish people are the most victimized by this misdirection.

science."

These are the people who rule our world. Unbelievable.

"It is from us that the all-engulfing terror proceeds. We have in our service persons of all opinions, of all doctrines, restorating monarchists, demagogues, socialists, communists, and utopian dreamers of every kind. *We have harnessed them all to the task:* ***each one of them on his own account is boring away at the last remnants of authority, is striving to overthrow all established forms of order.*** *By these acts all States are in torture; they exhort to tranquility, are ready to sacrifice everything for peace:* ***but we will not give them peace until they openly acknowledge our international Super-Government, and with submissiveness."*** (emphasis contained in the original text)

Creating terrorism is a natural function of Government in modern times. It is a natural by-product of employing Hegelian "problem-reaction-solution" tactics to force the public to make choices that they would never otherwise make.[120] The color palette of available terror activity is greatly enhanced by controlling all political factions, as this passage explains – a recurring theme in The Protocols.

We're back to addressing man's natural desire to find beauty, peace, and love in this world. The Elite understand this, and as we discussed in the previous Chapter, they use this desire to foster and encourage terrorist activity, wars, false flag operations, and all manner of violence so that the public will say, "Okay, okay, we'll give you whatever you want. Anything! Just please make it stop!"

"The people have raised to howl about the necessity of settling the question of Socialism by way of an international agreement. ***Division into fractional parties has given them into our hands, for, in order to carry on a contested struggle one must have money, and the money is all in our hands.***

120 An excellent, basic definition is provided at: http://ethics.wikia.com/wiki/Problem_Reaction_Solution, also see: https://www.bibliotecapleyades.net/biggestsecret/esp_icke22.htm

"We might have reason to apprehend a union between the 'clear-sighted' force of the kings of the masses on their thrones and the 'blind' force of the masses (mobs) themselves, but we have taken all the needful measures against any such possibility: between the one and the other force we have erected a bulwark in the shape of a mutual terror between them. In this way the blind force of the people remains our support and we, and we only, shall provide them with a leader and, of course, direct them along the road that leads to our goal." (emphasis contained in the original text)

Among other things, we learn from this passage why voting in today's democracies – at least for those positions at the top of the political pyramid that really matter – is such an exercise in futility. It isn't just the massive voting fraud that takes place, which we already covered, it is that even the choices that are presented involve individuals who have been 'pre-screened' for approval by the Elite.

Over 20 years ago, I had an associate, quite senior to myself, who told me that he learned that the entire system was rigged when he himself was still a young man in the 1960s. "I was walking on the beach with a wealthy political donor, when suddenly he got a phone call. This was back in the day when very few people had satellite phones because they were so bulky and calls were very expensive. My friend had a special backpack where he carried his. We were headed into the elections (November, 1968.) After a minute or so of listening to the caller on the other end of the call, I hear him say, 'Are you sure? This is unbelievable. Those bastards. Those fucking bastards.' After he hung up the phone, I naturally asked, 'What was that all about?' and my friend replied, 'It has already been decided. Richard Nixon will win the presidency in November and Hubert Humphrey will get a close second in the popular vote.' He refused to say anything more."

"In order that the hand of the blind mob may not free itself from our guiding hand, we must every now and then enter into

close communion with it, if not actually in person, at any rate through some of the most trusty of our brethren. When we are acknowledged as the only authority we shall discuss with the people personally on the market places, and we shall instruct them on questions of the political in such wise as may turn them in the direction that suits us."

Among other things, this passage alludes to infiltrating groups that are of interest to the Elite. This has certainly been standard practice within political circles, as we learned from Jesse Ventura.[121] However, with today's technology, staying in "close communion" to pass important information to "the most trusty of our brethren" has never been easier.

"In order not to annihilate the institutions of the masses before it is time we have touched them with craft and delicacy, and have taken hold of the ends of the springs which move their mechanism. These springs lay in a strict but just sense of order: we have replaced them by the chaotic license of liberalism. ***We have got our hands into the administration of the law, into the conduct of elections, into the press, into liberty of the person, but principally into education and training as being the cornerstones of a free existence.***

We have fooled, bemused and corrupted the youth of the masses by rearing them in principles and theories which are known by us to be false although it is by us that they have been inculcated." (emphasis in the original text and emphasis added)

We covered education extensively in Chapter 3, principally as a tool to dumb down people, but here we see the thinking that preceded it.

"Above the existing laws without substantially altering them, and ***by merely twisting them into contradictions of interpretations****, we have erected something grandiose in the way of*

[121] See: "CIA confirms Ventura meeting occurred," https://www.mprnews.org/story/2008/01/03/jessecia

results. These results found expression first in the fact that the ***interpretations masked the laws:*** *afterwards they entirely hid them from the eyes of the Governments owing to* ***the impossibility of making anything out of the tangled web of legislation.***" (emphasis in the original text and emphasis added)

One of the things that I learned as a result of my own experiences within the U.S. "justice" system is that the laws don't matter. Those in authority do whatever they want. I went to considerable trouble to explain this in Chapter 3 of Meditopia.[122]

"You may say that the masses will rise upon us, arms in hand, if they guess what is going on before the time comes; but in the West we have against this a maneuver of ***such appalling terror*** *that the very stoutest hearts quail – the undergrounds, metropolitans, those subterranean corridors which, before the time comes,* ***will be driven under all the capitals and from whence those capitals will be blown into the air with all their organizations and archives.****"* (emphasis added)

This gives us insight as to an influencing factor driving the construction of deep underground bases worldwide, something thoroughly documented by Dr. Richard Sauder.[123]

Protocol No. 10

"When we have accomplished our coup d'état we shall say then to the various peoples: 'Everything has gone terribly badly, all have been worn out with sufferings. We are destroying the causes of your torment – nationalities, frontiers, differences of coinages. You are at a liberty, of course, to pronounce sentence upon us, but can it possibly be a just one if it is confirmed by you before you make any trial of what we are offering you .' Then will the mob exalt us and bear us up in their hands in a unanimous triumph of hopes and expectations.

[122] See: http://www.meditopia.org/chap3-1.htm
[123] See: https://www.amazon.com/Richard-Sauder/e/B001K904DS

Voting, which we have made the instruction will set us on the throne of the world by teaching even the very smallest units of members of the human race to vote by means of meetings and agreements by groups, will then have served its purposes and will play its part then by the last time by a unanimity of desire to make close acquaintance with us before condemning us.

To secure this we must have everybody vote without distinction of classes and qualifications . . ." (entirety of passage emphasized in the original)

A recurring theme of the The Protocols is the acceptance, even embrace, by the masses of their own victimhood. A fundamental principle of Luciferianism is that you cannot have evil thrust upon you without your having on some level made a willful choice. Nobody "accidentally" sells their soul to the devil. It is the exercise of free will that seals the deal.

The last part of this passage is remarkably prophetic. Although suffrage movements had, by the time The Protocols were released in 1903, already secured women's right to vote in New Zealand and Australia, the rest of the world would not see these rights made legal until well into the 20th century.[124]

The past century also saw a dramatic lowering of the voting age, with debates currently underway in a number of countries to see it lowered still further to sixteen,[125] while many are still undergoing adolescence. The stated reasoning? Kids are becoming disillusioned with elections and participation will teach them the value of democracy.[126]

". . . it is not the (Government) institutions (themselves) that are important, but their functions. These institutions have divided up among themselves all the functions of Government – administrative, legislative, executive, wherefore they have come to operate as do the organs in the human body. ***If we injure one***

[124] See: https://en.wikipedia.org/wiki/Women%27s_suffrage

[125] See: https://en.wikipedia.org/wiki/Voting_age

[126] See: https://www.economist.com/news/leaders/21716030-young-voters-are-becoming-disillusioned-elections-catch-them-early-and-teach-them-value

part in the machinery of State, the State falls sick, like a human body, and . . . will die . . . *When we introduce into the State organism the poison of Liberalism, its whole political complexion underwent a change.* **States have been seized with a mortal illness – blood poisoning**. *All that remains is to await the* ***end of their death agony.*** *"* (emphasis added)

Government serves no purpose other than to service the desires of a negaciprocal Elite.

People do not need Government.
Governments need people.

". . . Then it was that the era of republics became possible of realization; and then it was that we replaced the ruler by a caricature of a Government – by a president, taken from the mob, from the midst of our puppet creatures, our slaves . . ." (emphasis in original text)

This passage provides the clearest language yet that the highest positions in Government are still lower than the lowest members of the Elite. This provides confirmation as to our placement of Government in relation to the other members in the Outer Bands.

". . . it is indispensable to trouble in all countries the people's relations with their Governments so as to utterly exhaust humanity with dissension, hatred, struggle, envy and even by the use of torture, by starvation, BY THE INOCULATION OF DISEASES, by want, so that the masses see no other issue than to take refuge in our complete sovereignty in money and in all else." (emphasis in original text)

Another remarkable prophecy.

"Inoculation of diseases" here refers to the implantation of biological agents to harm others, and although there is no question that low tech methods of dispensing diseases have existed since ancient times, there is no question that the "inoculation of diseases" didn't become a fine art until well into the 20th century – shortly after the release of The Protocols.[127]

The insertion of "inoculation of diseases" following first torture, and then starvation, as methods of "exhausting humanity" makes perfectly good sense when you understand that the personages who authored The Protocols were consumed with cost and efficiency. "It costs about $1 million to kill one person with a nuclear weapon, about $1,000 to kill one person with a chemical weapon, and about $1 to kill one person with a biological weapon."[128]

World War I, which was the first great military conflict following the release of the The Protocols, saw the use of both anthrax and glanders to infect animals in opposing forces, but it wasn't until World War II where biological warfare began in earnest, where tens of thousands of people died as a consequence of offensive biological research.[129]

Despite the signing of the "1925 Geneva Protocol for the Prohibition of the Use in War of Asphyxiating, Poisonous or Other Gases and of Bacteriological Methods of Warfare," the use of biological (as well as chemical) attacks have proceeded apace throughout the past century, with no end of their use in sight.[130]

Protocol No. 11

". . . the freedom of the Press, the right of association, freedom of conscience, the voting principle, and many [other civil rights] that must disappear forever from the memory of man, or undergo a radical alteration the day after the promulgation of the new constitution . . . the masses are a flock of sheep, and we are their wolves. And you know what happens when the wolves

[127] See: http://www.emedicinehealth.com/biological_warfare/article_em.htm

[128] See: William Dudley (ed.), Biological Warfare: Opposing Views, (2004), p. 23.

[129] See: https://c.aarc.org/resources/biological/history.asp

[130] See: http://www.johnstonsarchive.net/terrorism/chembioattacks.html

get hold of the flock?"

The ultimate goal of the Elite is the complete destruction of any and all civil rights. Nothing short of the destruction of humanity, whose members will be reduced to nothing more than mindless robots, is acceptable.

Protocol No. 12

"We shall deal with the press in the following way: ***What is the part played by the press today?*** *It serves to excite and inflame those passions which are needed for our purpose or else it serves selfish ends of parties.* ***It is often vapid, unjust, mendacious, and the majority of the public have not the slightest idea what ends the press really serves. . .*** *not a single announcement will reach the public without our control. Even now this is already attained by us inasmuch as all news items are received by a few agencies."* (emphasis added)

Are you still intent on listening to the mainstream? If The Protocols are not prophetic, how would you account for the fact that the media today are far more imbued with the characteristics found in this passage than at any other time in their history? As the mainstream media test the far limits of the public's stupidity and measure its gullibility, how else would the dramatic reduction in public trust in the reliability of the press be explained, at least in the U.S.?[131]

*"****When we are in the period of the new regime transitional to that of our assumption of full sovereignty we must not admit any revelations by the press of any form of pubic dishonesty; it is necessary that the new regime should be thought to have so perfectly contented everybody that even criminality has disappeared . . .*** *Cases of the manifestation of criminality should remain known only to their victims and to chance witnesses – no*

[131] See: http://wjla.com/news/nation-world/main-stream-media-continue-to-lose-the-publics-trust

more." (emphasis in the original text)

When you have an Elite that control the press, there are no crimes that those in authority cannot get away with. Only the victims of crimes, those close to them, and some "chance witnesses" will know the crimes were ever committed.

One example in particular is striking.

No one can question that Hillary Clinton has the full force of the mainstream media behind her. From the cavalcade of endless fake poll numbers that were shoved in the public's face in 2016 – nearly all of which showed that it was impossible for Trump to win – to the confirmation that CNN was secretly working with the DNC (Democratic National Committee) to help her campaign, the evidence is overwhelming.[132]

In the grand scheme of things, however, cheating on elections is a minor offense in the world of politics. A misdemeanor. Something like jaywalking. But what about a campaign to have people assassinated – lots and lots of them – who disagreed with you or did things you didn't approve of? Would that rise above the level of a misdemeanor? Not if you're a member of the Elite.

Over the years, I have watched with astonishment at the number of people around the Clintons who die under highly unusual circumstances – plane crashes, car wrecks, questionable suicides, barbells crushing the throat, etc.[133] Of course, news outlets like Snopes, a notorious mouthpiece for the Elite, will dismiss the obvious,[134] even though Occam's Razor comes to the rescue of even the most gullible: is the public to believe that all of these people with close connections to the Clinton's could

[132] See: "Not sorry for leaking debate questions" https://www.washingtonpost.com/news/the-fix/wp/2016/11/07/donna-brazile-is-totally-not-sorry-for-leaking-cnn-debate-questions-to-hillary-clinton/?utm_term=.bfe87782b3ee. Also see: "CNN admits: 'We couldn't help Hillary any more than we have'," http://www.zerohedge.com/news/2016-08-11/cnn-admits-we-couldnt-help-hillary-any-more-we-have. And: "Wikileads Proves Primary Was Rigged: DNC Undermined Democracy (at Hillary's behest)," http://observer.com/2016/07/wikileaks-proves-primary-was-rigged-dnc-undermined-democracy/

[133] See: "Clinton Kill List: 33 Most Intriguing Cases," http://www.wnd.com/2016/08/clinton-death-list-33-most-intriguing-cases/. Also see: "Clinton Kill List" http://www.disclose.tv/news/did_you_know_clintons_kill_list/130879. And: "Comprehensive Clinton Body Count List," http://govtslaves.info/comprehensive-clinton-body-count-list/

[134] See: http://www.snopes.com/politics/clintons/bodycount.asp

die in such diverse and mysterious ways without so much as an inquiry, or that it's a mere coincidence?

People in the Elite possess this kind of "power of misdirection." According to Peter Schweizer, in his book Clinton Cash,[135] the Clinton crime machine was involved in the sale of uranium to the Russians in a deal worth millions, one that would normally be considered a violation of U.S. national security law. Was this transaction ever investigated? Of course not. In its place, in a grand act of reverse projection, the public has been subjected to an endless stream of stories of Clinton's rival (Donald Trump) and his connection to nameless Russians who allegedly stole the election away from Hillary.[136] Without evidence to substantiate anything, it is a story that won't go away. Ever. This passage helps us understand why.

Protocol No. 13

"In order that the masses themselves may not guess what we are about ***we further distract them with amusements, games, pastimes, passions, people's palaces . . . soon we shall begin through the press to propose competitions in art, in sports of all kinds:*** *these interests will finally distract their minds from questions in which we should find ourselves compelled to oppose them. Growing more and more disaccustomed to reflect and form any opinions of their own, people will begin to talk in the same tone as we, because we alone shall be offering them new directions for thought . . ."* (emphasis in the original text)

Perhaps this passage is among the most prophetic of all.

Back at the time when The Protocols surfaced – let us say, the early 1900s – the vast majority of people, even in the "first world," were rural dwellers. Worldwide, about 14% of the world's population were urbanites, and the remaining 86%

[135] See: Peter Schweizer, Clinton Cash, (2016).
[136] See: http://www.washingtontimes.com/news/2017/jul/13/broadcasters-obsess-over-trump-jr-ignore-hillary-c/

lived in the rural regions.[137] By 2016, rural dwellers made up about 45% of the world's population, or nearly half what they had been a century before. Of course, in first world countries, this percentage tends to be far less (i.e. Australia, 10%; Canada, 18%; France, 20%; Japan, 6%; U.K., 17%; U.S., 18%),[138] with the artificiality of expanding urban life and all that goes with it – along with leaving behind the hard rigors of rural farm life, the influx of growing technology, and new types of media – came new forms of leisure. Chief among these was the explosion of a professional sports industry unlike anything seen in recorded history. In fact, we take for granted many sports today that didn't even exist prior to 1900.[139] With the addition of more spare time, "participation in sports, leisure, and amusement activities multiplied."[140]

Professional sports are so ubiquitous today that we rarely consider how closely linked they are to the media. Do the media push professional sports because the public demands it – (i.e. the phenomenon is market-driven)? Or is the public so consumed with professional sports, because the media are proactive in promoting them? Most people would say it is a combination of both, but the passage above offers a curious insight into an agenda to promote them. Were sports our only consideration with this passage, its validity might be questionable, but it isn't.

With the advent of television, video games, amusement parks, and the countless time-sucking avocations that the Internet has spawned, one has to wonder how much of this is by design. If not by design, how were the creators of <u>The Protocols</u> so prescient in foreseeing it?

One of the results of these developments has been the dramatic drop in the number of people who actually read – something I knew before writing this book, which is part of the reason I waited seven years to finish it. As Steve Jobs noted back in 2008, 40% of the people in the U.S. (which has been tradition-

[137] See: http://www.prb.org/Publications/Lesson-Plans/HumanPopulation/Urbanization.aspx
[138] See: http://data.worldbank.org/indicator/SP.RUR.TOTL.ZS
[139] See: http://www.thepeoplehistory.com/sports.html
[140] See: http://www.ushistory.org/us/39b.asp

ally a large consumer of books and other reading materials) read one book or less per year.[141] However, even looking at the global picture, in few countries do people spend more than six hours per week reading,[142] despite the large number of books actually published.[143] Compare that to, let us say, the number of hours per day that the average American spends watching television – somewhere around five,[144] or four if you believe A.C. Nielson Co.[145]

Reading is an essential part of being an informed individual, and its decline, concurrent with an explosion in those forms of leisure which do nothing to stimulate meaningful thought, is inferred from the passage above. So, too, is the growth of people incapable of generating opinions independent of the media.

" . . . we shall continue to direct their minds to all sorts of vain conceptions of fantastic theories, new and apparently progressive: for have we not with complete success turned the ***brainless heads of the masses*** *with progress, till* ***there is not among them one mind able to perceive that under this work lies a departure from truth in all cases*** *where it is not a question of material inventions, for truth is one, and in it there is no place for progress. Progress, like a fallacious idea, serves to obscure truth so that none may know it except us, the Chosen of God, its guardians . . .*

Who will ever suspect then that ***all these peoples were stage-managed by us according to political plan which no one has so much as guessed at in the course of many centuries?"*** (emphasis in original text and emphasis added)

Earlier I brought up an essay I wrote in August, 2009, that discussed the relationship between iatrogenesis and planned ob-

[141] See: https://www.wired.com/2008/01/steve-jobs-peop/

[142] See: https://www.indy100.com/article/the-countries-that-read-the-most-books-7348401

[143] See: https://ebookfriendly.com/countries-publish-most-books-infographic/

[144] See: http://www.nydailynews.com/life-style/average-american-watches-5-hours-tv-day-article-1.1711954

[145] See: https://www.csun.edu/science/health/docs/tv&health.html

solescence.[146] This passage now becomes relevant for a different reason: because it underscores the "illusion of progress" which has only accelerated with the advent of technology since the rise of the Industrial Age, 250 years ago.

We are surrounded by artifacts of technology: televisions, computers, cars, smart phones, household devices, hand tools, etc., which represent not only an "improvement" on prior human living, but promises that something better and more advanced will be shortly forthcoming. Subconsciously, this serves to acclimate the mind to the idea of non-permanence. Nothing is permanent – not even moral values. This is what they want you to believe. All values are relativistic and there are no absolute values in the Universe. Everything is changing. The past was primitive. The future will be better. There is nothing in existence today that will not be made better tomorrow. What you call reality today will be obsolescent very soon. And who promises you this ever improving "tomorrow," more real than what you call reality today? They do. The Government and negaciprocal industrialists at the far end of the Outer Bands. Without "them," you would not know progress. You would be stuck in a false or temporary reality. You would be condemned to live a "primitive life."

The road from the "inner Man" to the purely "external Man," from the endosomatic to the exosomatic, is the path of destruction. I make this abundantly clear in a piece I wrote called "Entropy & Caton's Exosomatic Axis."[147] The Elite understand this and use it as yet another control mechanism, and this passage makes that quite clear.

Protocol No. 14

"When we come into our kingdom it will be undesirable for us that there should exist any other religion than ours of the One God with whom our destiny is bound up by our position as the Chosen People and through whom our destiny is united with the

146 See: http://www.altcancer.net/ashwin/ashw0809.htm

147 See: http://meditopia.org/old/chap5_2004.htm or see Appendix A

destinies of the world. . .

Our philosophers will discuss all the shortcomings of the various beliefs of the masses, but ***no one will ever bring under discussion our faith from its true point of view, since this will be fully learned by none save ours, who will never dare to betray its secrets . . .*** *Our wise men, trained to become leaders of the masses, which will be used by us to influence their minds, directing them towards such understanding and forms of knowledge as have been determined by us."* (emphasis contained in original text)

The passage doesn't tell you who the "One God" is – though we've covered this in previous passages. However, whoever he is, whatever his name, it is a god of hate, malice, revenge, deception, bloodlust, cruelty, with a refined taste for inflicting fear, pain, and agony. We know this because The Protocols tell us so. It is the Bible of Governments and those who rule Governments, whether those who serve these institutions know it or not.

Is there a religion that comes close to the Elite's in its negaciprocal character? I wouldn't resort to this, except that the passage above makes clear that none of us within the masses are allowed to know its secrets. If such a religion exists that comes close to expounding the Elite's "faith from its true point of view," what might that religion be? It would have to be a religion that even if held by the Elite to be inferior, still outwardly expresses strong negaciprocal elements. Such a religion does exist. It is a religion whose beliefs share much of the content and tone of The Protocols.

It's called Islam.[148]

Now before I get started, a couple of points are worth noting. First of all, none of my forthcoming observations detract

[148] I began The Protocols with my justification for removing anything relevant to ethnicity. The same argument does not apply here because the true followers of Muhammad inject little controversy into the interpretation of their teachings, despite its varying sects. And why not? Because Muhammad's teachings, which are touched upon in the coming pages are homogenous and unequivocal. True Muhammadan's do not attempt to obfuscate their religion. Quite the contrary, they are inordinately proud of it. Strangely, I respect them for their candor, (but not their commitment to pure negaprocity). Unlike the dark figures behind The Protocols, the followers of Mohammed do not hide in the shadows.

from the fact that Islam, and its 1.6 billion adherents, are divided into many different sects, a development even Muhammad predicted.[149] Secondly, one must always differentiate between the teachings of a religion and the personal beliefs and interpretations of the individual.

Thirdly, Islam appears to be "managed theology" in the sense that it is being used to negaciprocal ends. By way of example, several million migrants have flooded into the 28 nations of the European Union just since 2015,[150] the vast majority of whom were Muslims,[151] or came from countries that are predominantly Muslim,[152] another estimated 6.6 million migrants – again, mostly Muslim – are waiting to get in,[153] though the figure could be as high as 10 million.[154]

The cost to support these migrants was estimated at 20 billion pounds in the EU, in 2016 alone,[155] stressing the very foundation of Europe's welfare state.[156] The financial stress is exacerbated by the fact that only about 0.1% of the Muslim migrants work (in Germany), with a majority of them never intending to find gainful employment.[157] Why would you ever work if you can collect welfare and your religion teaches you that you should live parasitically off non-Muslims? Incidentally, this same publication (Sunday Express) reported three months later – probably under pressure – that the figure had magically risen to 2.8%,[158] which does nothing to underscore the reason why the

149 See: https://www.dawn.com/news/1035023

150 See: http://ec.europa.eu/eurostat/statistics-explained/index.php/Migration_and_migrant_population_statistics

151 See: https://en.wikipedia.org/wiki/European_migrant_crisis

152 See: http://www.bbc.com/news/world-europe-34131911

153 See: http://www.telegraph.co.uk/news/2017/05/23/66m-migrants-waiting-cross-europe-africa-report/

154 See: https://www.gatestoneinstitute.org/10307/europe-more-migrants

155 See: http://www.express.co.uk/news/world/678878/migrant-crisis-cost-20bn-experts-reveal-shock-price-EU-pay

156 See: https://www.theatlantic.com/international/archive/2016/02/welfare-state-refugees-europe/463272/

157 See: http://www.express.co.uk/news/world/710927/million-migrants-Germany-unemployed-Merkel-open-door-policy

158 See: http://www.express.co.uk/news/world/745147/million-immigrants-Germany-few-find-jobs-migrant-crisis

Muslim community in Europe will never financially support itself. Why? This isn't why the backers of the migration had them sent to Europe in the first place.

Now, mind you, I have nothing against migrants. In fact, I happen to be one.[159] But the use of an immigrant group with a homogeneous set of religious beliefs as unique in its negacip-rocal character as Islam is for this purpose is, in my opinion, unique in modern times. Apart from the unreciprocated aid given to Israel,[160] I've never read or heard of another statistical cohort of people getting the kind of financial aid or preferred treatment that Muslim groups immigrating into Europe have gotten. The aid has continued unabated, despite the proliferation of terrorist attacks, rape gangs, and general violence that this migration event has generated.[161] This development has moved Czech president, Milos Zeman, to comment that the Muslim migrants are an "invasion force," intent on destroying Europe,[162] and Estonia's former Minister of Foreign Affairs, Kristiina Ojuland to state publicly that the Muslims are invaders who are arriving as an ongoing war against Christianity.[163]

None of this should seem shocking or unpredictable. Albert Pike, an Elitist, promised that Islam would be used to "destroy the West" way back in the 1800s.[164] Even Donald Trump commented on this obvious development in coded language of his own.[165] However, nothing in modern times is as clear as the statements of Turkey's president, Erdogan, as to the violent pur-

[159] My wife and I moved to Ecuador in 2007. Both of us are direct descendants of American forebears going back to the 1700's.

[160] See: https://fas.org/sgp/crs/mideast/RL33222.pdf

[161] See: https://www.jihadwatch.org/2016/04/the-muslim-migrant-invasion-and-the-collapse-of-europe

[162] See: http://www.telegraph.co.uk/news/worldnews/europe/czechrepublic/12082757/Muslim-Brotherhood-using-migrants-as-invasion-force-to-seize-control-of-Europe-Czech-president-claims.html

[163] See: "Islamic migrants invading Europe as part of a war against Christianity," https://www.youtube.com/watch?v=JVThZhsM478

[164] See: "Top Illuminati Grand Wizard: 'We control Islam and we'll use it to destroy the West'," https://www.youtube.com/watch?v=0dXD2H0m74g

[165] See:http://www.nationalreview.com/article/445169/sweden-rape-sexual-assault-non-muslim-immigrants

pose of the migration.[166]

I'm taking the time to sketch out this current affair because it couldn't have happened unless the foundation of Islam supported it, and we have only to examine Islam's source documents to know that the mind behind the Elite's religion is the same as Islam's. In fact, significant portions of the Quran read like The Protocols:

"So when the sacred months have passed away, then slay the idolaters wherever you find them, and take them captive and besiege them and lie in wait for them in every ambush, then if they repent and keep up prayer and pay the poor-rate, leave their way free to them."

Quran 9:5

Murder people whose religious beliefs are different than your own. Check.

"And fight them until there is no more Fitnah (disbelief and polytheism: i.e. worshipping others besides Allah) and the religion (worship) will all be for Allah alone (in the whole of the world). But if they cease (worshipping others besides Allah), then certainly, Allah is All-Seer of what they do."

Quran 8:39

As a follower of Islam, you have a commitment to keep fighting until the entire world is under the yoke of your religion. (Sound familiar?) Check.

" It is not for a Prophet that he should have prisoners of war (and free them with ransom) until he has made a great slaughter (among his enemies) in the land. You desire the good of this

[166] See: http://shoebat.com/2017/03/19/erdogan-has-just-declared-he-intends-to-have-muslims-invade-christian-europe-in-the-future-and-that-turkey-will-build-nuclear-bombs-to-soon-attack-the-christian-west-to-subjugate-the-church/

world (i.e. the money of ransom for freeing the captives), but Allah desires (for you) the Hereafter. And Allah is All-Mighty, All-Wise.

Quran 8:67

Wholesale slaughter is good. Check.

" Fight against those who believe not in Allah, nor in the Last Day, nor forbid that which has been forbidden by Allah, nor forbid that which has been forbidden by Allah and His Messenger and those who acknowledge not the religion of truth (i.e. Islam) among the people of the Scripture (Jews and Christians) until they pay the Jizya with willing submission and feel themselves subdued."

Quran 9:29

Extortion for personal gain is good. Check.

"It is He (Allah) Who has sent His Messenger (Muhammad) with guidance and the religion of truth (Islam), to make it superior over all religions, even though the Mushrikun (polytheists, pagans, idolaters, disbelievers in the Oneness of Allah) hate (it)."

Quran 9:33

Creating anguish for those whose religious beliefs are different from your own is good. Check.

I could go on and on with these negaciprocal little gems, but why bother? There are websites, published books, YouTube videos, and Facebook pages that are full of them.[167]

[167] Start with Gregory M. Davis' "Islam 101" at: https://www.jihadwatch.org/islam101.pdf – Jihad Watch has an entire book section: https://www.jihadwatch.org/; "Exposing the Lie of Islam: Program of Death": https://archive.org/details/exposingthelieofislam; "Islam Exposed Online": http://islamexposedonline.com/

My point is that these writings contain the same tendency towards negaprocity that The Protocols do. So why is it that the Elite would never endorse Islam, therefore, as a "true religion." I would propose that the reason is that it isn't negaciprocal ***enough***.

Nonetheless, if you listen to the negaciprocal media, you should never criticize Muslims who are blowing up buildings, raping non-Muslim women, extorting people of other faiths, or beheading Christians. Because once you've read Islam's core documents, you quickly realize that they are the only Muslims who are truly following their religion. A moderate Muslim is not a true Muslim. Give them a different name, because they are not following the very clear and unmistakable dictates of their prophet, Muhammad.

Protocol No. 15

"When we at least definitely come into our kingdom by the aid of coups d'état prepared everywhere for one and the same day, after the worthlessness of all existing forms of Government has been definitely acknowledged (and not a little time will pass before that comes about, perhaps even a whole century) we shall make it our task to see that against us such things as plots shall no longer exist. With this purpose we shall slay without mercy all who take arms (in hand) to oppose our coming into our kingdom. Every kind of new institution of anything like a secret society will also be punished with death; those of them which are now in existence, are known to us, serve us and have served us, we shall disband and send into exile . . . ***In this way we shall proceed with those (lower) masons who know too much****; such of these as we may for some reason spare will be kept in constant fear or exile. We shall promulgate a law making all former members of secret societies liable to exile from Europe as the centre of our rule."* (emphasis in original text)

My many apologies in advance for leaving out any of the other thousands of web pages, posts, videos, books, pamphlets and other related materials that are devoted to speaking the truth about this vital subject.

Several points here are worth noting.

Besides continuing to point out that Government is subservient to the Elite in the Outer Bands, we actually get a prophetic timeline. If we take 1903 and add a century, we get 2003. If we take into consideration that we are very close to the end point to which The Protocols repeatedly allude, this is a remarkably accurate projection.

Also worth noting is that when you align yourself with a secret society or any other organization that serves the Dark Side, you are always expendable to those who are closer to Pure Evil than you are. There is no honor among those who dwell in the Outer Bands.

Protocol No. 16

*"In order to effect the destruction of all collective forces except ours we shall emasculate the first stage of collectivism – **the universities**, by re-educating them in a new direction. **Their officials and professors will be prepared for their business by detailed secret programmes of action from which they will not with immunity diverge, not by one iota. They will be appointed with especial precaution, and will be so placed as to be wholly dependent upon the Government. . .**"* (emphasis contained in original text)

*"Knowing by the experience of many centuries that people live and are guided by ideas, that these ideas are imbibed by people only by the aid of education provided with equal success for all ages of growth, but of course by varying methods, **we shall swallow up and confiscate to our own use the last scintilla of independence of thought**, which we have for long past been directing towards subjects and ideas useful for us. The bridling thought is already at work in the so-called system of teaching by **object lessons**, the purpose of which is to **turn the masses into unthinking submissive brutes** waiting for things to be presented before their eyes in order to form an idea of them. . ."* (emphasis contained in original text and emphasis added)

We've discussed education extensively – to this point – but this goes a step farther. The goal here is education to induce lobotimization – for "all ages of growth." Wiping out "independence of thought" infers that any attempt to think independently becomes illegal. If you don't think that the Elite are the inspiration for "Minority Report," re-read the preceeding passage.[168]

Protocol No. 17

"Our kingdom will be an apologia of the divinity Vishnu, in whom is found its personification – ***in our hundred hands will be, one in each, the springs of the machinery of social life*** *. . . In our programme,* ***one-third of our subjects will keep the rest under observation*** *from a sense of duty, on the principle of volunteer service to the State. It will then be* ***no disgrace to be a spy and informer, but a merit . . .*** *"* (emphasis in original text and emphasis added)

The prophetic content of The Protocols seems to know no end. Here we're presented with the seed motivation behind the U.S. Government push for its "If you see something, say something" program.[169] The real benefit here? It deflects from the simple fact that the Government itself is the source of most of the terrorism – dishing up an endless variety of false flags as part of its vital function.

Protocol No. 18

*"****Criminals with us will be arrested at the first****, more or less well-grounded* ***suspicion****; it cannot be allowed that out of fear of a possible mistake an opportunity should be given of escape to persons suspected of a political lapse or crime, for in*

[168] See: http://www.dailymail.co.uk/sciencetech/article-1393582/Real-life-Minority-Report-tell-youre-THINKING-committing-terrorism.html
[169] See: "Dept. of Homeland Security: If you see something, say something," https://www.dhs.gov/see-something-say-something
Even the FDA had to get in on this action. See: https://www.fda.gov/downloads/Food/FoodDefense/UCM245306.pdf

these matters we shall be literally merciless. . ." (emphasis in original text)

Life under the kind of rule envisioned by The Protocols is almost not worth living. On mere suspicion, one becomes an enemy of the State.

Protocol No. 19

"If we do not permit any independent dabbling in the political, we shall on the other hand encourage every kind of report or petition with proposals for the Government to examine into all kinds of projects for the amelioration of the condition of the people; this will reveal to us the defects or else the fantasies of our subjects, to which we shall respond either by accomplishing them or by a wise rebutment to prove the short-sightedness of one who judges wrongly . . . through the Press and in speeches, indirectly – in cleverly compiled schoolbooks on history, we have accepted by sedition-mongers for the idea of the commonwealth. The advertisement has increased the contingent of liberals and has brought thousands of the masses into the ranks of our livestock cattle."

This underscores the short-sightedness of Pure Evil. That anyone could think that, at this point, any window dressing by even the most skilled deceiver could be viewed as any real attempt to "ameliorate the condition of the people" is beyond me. A person stupid enough to believe it would be one who has slipped below any semblance of humanity, even by the standards of today's drug-induced zombies.

Protocol No. 20

"How clear is the ***undeveloped power of thought of the purely brute brains of the masses****, as expressed by the fact that they have been borrowing from us with payment of interest without ever thinking that all the same these very moneys plus an*

addition for payment of interest must be got by them from their own State pockets in order to settle up with us. ***What could have been simpler*** *than to take the money they wanted from their own people?*

But it is a proof of the genius of our chosen mind that we have contrived to present the matter of loans to them in such a light that they have even seen in them an advantage for themselves." (emphasis added)

This protocol is mired in details for taxation strategies once the Elite have managed to put the entire planet on permanent lockdown. But this gem appears towards the end, the gist of which is: "How could these primates have ever been so stupid as to accept loans from us in the first place? Why did they ever agree to take our worthless nothings that we create out of thin air, and for which we charge interest, to begin with? That they ever did so in the first place is proof of our right to rule, to use them, to abuse them, and to treat them like the garbage that they are."

Out of this phenomenon comes the wisdom of Shakespeare's line: "Neither a borrower nor a lender be, for loan oft loses both itself and friend, and borrowing dulls the edge of husbandry."[170]

Protocol No. 21

"We have taken advantage of the venality of administrators and the slackness of rulers to get our monies twice, thrice and more times over, by lending to the Governments of the masses which were not at all needed by the States. Could anyone do the like in regard to us?"

Short version: we would never allow you to screw us over financially the way we have you – for centuries.

"We shall replace the money markets by grandiose gov-

[170] Hamlet Act 1, Scene 3.

ernment credit institutions, the object of which will be to fix the price of industrial values in accordance with Government views. These institutions will be in a position to fling upon the market five hundred millions of industrial paper in one day, or to buy up for the same amount. In this way all industrial undertakings will come into dependence upon us. You may imagine for yourselves what immense power we shall thereby secure for ourselves?"

The negaprocity of The Protocols knows no end.

Even having secured for themselves the entire world and the subjugation of all peoples, the Elite still have to scam the producers of industrial goods. There is no satiation of the appetites of those who flirt with Pure Evil – no such thing as enough.

Protocol No. 22

"In our hands is the greatest power of our day – gold: in two days we can procure from our storehouses any quantity we may please. . .

Surely there is no need to seek further proof that our rule is predestined by God? Surely we shall not fail with such wealth to prove that ***all that evil which for so many centuries we have had to commit has served at the end of ends the cause of true well-being*** *– the bringing of everything into order?"* (emphasis added)

Having commented on the foolishness of the masses ever having agreed to the Elite's lending schemes, this passage makes clear that the Elite consider tangible precious metal – in this case, gold – as having real value. It can't be pulled out of thin air, and it certainly isn't fiat currency.

Secondly – and the rest of this protocol reads along the same lines – this passage makes the classic argument that the end justifies the means. Essentially, "Yes, we're murderers and rapists. Yes, we've committed the cruelest and most heinous crimes that the imagination can conjure, innumerable times and for many centuries. But out of eons of horrors that are marked with our fingerprints, perfect order will be the result."

Philosophically, this position might be viewed as embodied in the school of thought known as "consequentialism,"[171] which sits contrary to "deontological ethics."[172] Stated in its simplest terms, the former allows for the employment of evil to be used to attain a noble end; whereas the latter argues that actions themselves should be assessed for their moral value, irrespective of any end that justifies the means.

However, it is my contention that the attempt to justify the Elite's position with consequentialism is completely circumvented by the fact that the end result is still negaciprocal. It is not the plan of the Elite to use negaprocity to attain "the Good." In fact, the evil gets worse after the goal is reached. Serving evil was the starting point. The means themselves are evil, or – in the minds of most readers who are exposed to The Protocols for the first time – redefine evil to be something even worse and more repulsive than they could have imagined. Then, finally, the end result pierces the outer wall of the Outer Bands such that little to no remnant of reciprocity remains.

Additionally, there is something more that an attempt to rely upon consequentialism overlooks: the means, as described in The Protocols in exhaustive detail, exist for their own pleasure, and one gets the impression that the Elite would be partaking of the "joys of psychopathocracy" even if there weren't any endgame strategy.

Let's take the example of a battlefield soldier. One is in the middle of a firefight and he's being shot at. He believes in his mind and heart that his efforts serve the defense of his fatherland and the protection of his people. He fires back and kills an opposing soldier. He didn't want to do it, but it was his duty. Moreover, failure to act in that situation might well result in his own death and those of his comrades.

Now take a second soldier. He, too, is in a firefight. In the midst of thick brush, he engages in hand-to-hand combat, kills the other soldier with a knife, but he doesn't stop there. He pro-

[171] See: http://www.iep.utm.edu/conseque/

[172] See: https://plato.stanford.edu/entries/ethics-deontological/#DeoFoiCon

ceeds to decapitate the deceased, collect a half litter of blood from an artery and drink it. He then uses his knife to deface the corpse with a variety of symbols of his own choosing to further celebrate his victory, laughing and reveling while he does so. None of the actions that occurred subsequent to the opposing soldier's death has anything to do with "the Good." The soldier is already dead. Our second soldier is simply acting out his own psychopathic pleasure for its own sake.

The tone and content of The Protocols mimic those of our second soldier. They're mean, cruel, and border on ritualistic Satanism. There is a joy of partaking in evil for its own sake, for its own pleasure.

That's what wrong with our world. Once again, it's run by psychopaths who use the most outlandish reasoning to justify their perversities, as we see in Protocol No. 22.

Protocol No. 23

"This Chosen One of God is chosen from above to ***demolish the senseless forces moved by instinct and not reason****, by brutishness and not humanness. These forces now triumph in manifestations of robbery and every kind of violence under the mask of principles of freedom and rights. They have overthrown all forms of social order to erect on the ruins the throne of* ***our King; but their part will be played out the moment he enters into his kingdom. Then it will be necessary to sweep them away from his path****, on which must be left no knot, no splinter. . .*

Then will it be possible for us to say to the peoples of the world: 'Give thanks to God and bow the knee before him who bears on his front the seal of the predestination of man, to which God himself has led his star that none other but Him might free us from all the before-mentioned forces and evils." (emphasis added)

This is one of the strangest of the protocols. It begins with a rambling condemnation of luxury, wayward manufacturers, alcohol use, which is now a crime punishable by imprisonment, and unemployment, and then it ends with the excerpted two paragraphs above, which get even stranger.

The gist of the first paragraph is: kill off our Minions of Darkness. We won't need them anymore once we've reached our ultimate goal. Then the Protocol closes with anything but a description of a loving, compassionate, or wise Creator. What's conveyed, like the rest of The Protocols, is a god who ascends and rules through power and coercion – not love.

Protocol No. 24 – (the final Protocol)

"In the person of the king who with unbending will is master of himself and of humanity all wise discern as it were fate with its mysterious ways. None will know what the king wishes to attain by his dispositions, and therefore none will dare to stand across an unknown path.

It is understood that the brain reservoir of the king must correspond in capacity to the plan of Government it has to contain. It is for this reason that he will ascend the throne not otherwise than after examination of his mind by the aforesaid learned elders."

This is the final protocol, and it is as strange and cryptic as Protocol No. 23. It deals with descendants of King David "preparing the King," his "exterior morality," and other aspects related to the ascension of the King that is the repeated end goal of The Protocols.

I found it interesting that the passages above allude to a vetting process, as if the King of all that is negaciprocal needs an "examination of his mind." Is whoever the god that will ascend to this throne so unobvious that he needs to pass through an approval process? Does he have to take an IQ and an SAT test, too?

The Protocols left me with the distinct impression that they were authored by several closely associated people. There are stylistic variations, too apparent not to notice, and the document starts off with a bang, with vigor, with surety, with purpose, and then seems to lose steam as it approaches the end. It's as if the "Elders" laid out their entire plan for the enslavement of humanity and successful creation of Hell on Earth, and as they approached victory, were left looking at each other, saying, "Okay, great. What do we do now?"

This outcome is actually both predictable and insightful as to the essential difference between good and evil and their relevant functions. Evil is parasitic, and when the host departs, the parasite dies.

Evil serves as an ultimate tool for the purification and clarification of the Good. It provides the contrast necessary for consciousness to appreciate and fully encompass its quality.

Good serves evil only to the extent that it breathes temporary life into a system of complete contrariness to Natural Law – without which evil could not serve its vital function.

Good needs evil as a temporary evolutionary tool. But evil needs the good for its very survival. Again, the host lives fine without the parasite. But the parasite cannot live without the host.

The seeds of all these universal truths are buried in the closing lines of The Protocols – though obviously unintended by its negaciprocal authors, blinded as they are, sitting on the very precipice of Pure Evil.

Regardless, having spent what is approaching one hundred pages examining this document, I believe that together with Machiavelli's The Prince and the examination of the attributes of psychopathy, we have firmly defined the territory of the Outer Bands of negaprocity – which I feel is vital before proceeding.

The principle actors on the Grand Theater that encompass our examination so far include humanity (including an Elite and the exploited masses), the unseen creatures (archons, demons, and other influencing, parasitic entities from the extant literature), and either a ruling, governing Prince, or a King who rules over the entire Earth. If we could be sure our drama was confined to these players, we might be able to end things here and be content to accept that *"Homo sapiens"* was a doomed species – still only one out of well over a million on the planet.

The problem is that when Extreme Negaprocity is this pervasive, when its tentacles have penetrated into every corner of the Earth – sucking the life out of everything and everyone – the inevitable has far more serious consequences.

We now address this in Book II.

Chapter 5

Book II:

The Great Unwinding

" They will live
with what they
have created "

Introduction to
The Great Unwinding:

Government Is The Face Of Extreme Negaprocity. Through It We May Understand How We Arrived Here & How We Can Escape

I began our study by providing a structural foundation for understanding human relationships by extending and enhancing Marshall Sahlins' reciprocity chart. I gave greater understanding to sectoral distance by providing gradations in what had previously been the undefined, unsegmented area of "negative reciprocity" – which I shortened to "negaprocity." Then I further defined this territory in terms of its relationship to various areas of social activity (i.e. education, agriculture, medicine, media, scientism, law, etc.)

Since the entities that occupy the far reaches of negaprocity – the Outer Bands – clearly exhibit psychopathic behavior, I examined the classical characteristics by which psychopathy is defined and used famous historical documents to provide a clear, contextual framework.

The focus of "The Great Winding" was Government – not because it is the most negaciprocal of the entities that occupy the Outer Bands, but because it is their face before the public. It is the façade that stands before the masses while more powerful, faceless forces operate behind the scenes – in darkness, obscurity, without responsibility or accountability – either to the rest of humanity or to the other life forms with whom we share our planet. Unseen forces may act as judge and jury in the course of human affairs, but it is Government that is the executioner.

The understanding is so important that I made Government the dominant element of this book's subtitle. As I stated in the second paragraph of my Introduction, it is Government that is the door through which I chose to enter so that together, we could view the interior of the mansion that is our civilization.

Essentially, the descent into the current Kali Yuga, the Vedic low point of human existence – with Government leading the charge – is addressed in this book's first subtitle: "Why Criminality Is Essential to Effective Modern Government." My choice of words is intended to draw attention to one of the more ridiculous notions of the BCN – namely, that obvious acts of official criminality are just "conspiracy theories." It was an attack on cognitive dissonance and a call to "wake up."

This smaller, second section, I call "Book II: The Great Unwinding," because we are near the endpoint of where negaprocity will take us. We have reached the point where we will either turn in the opposite direction and find our redemption, or see humanity and most life on the planet absorbed in the black hole of Pure Evil. This is important to understand because when Pure Evil reigns supreme – with time, it consumes and destroys everything.

I believe that for those who have had enough of the joys of psychopathocracy, the opportunity to escape it becomes their destiny.

If they are ready.

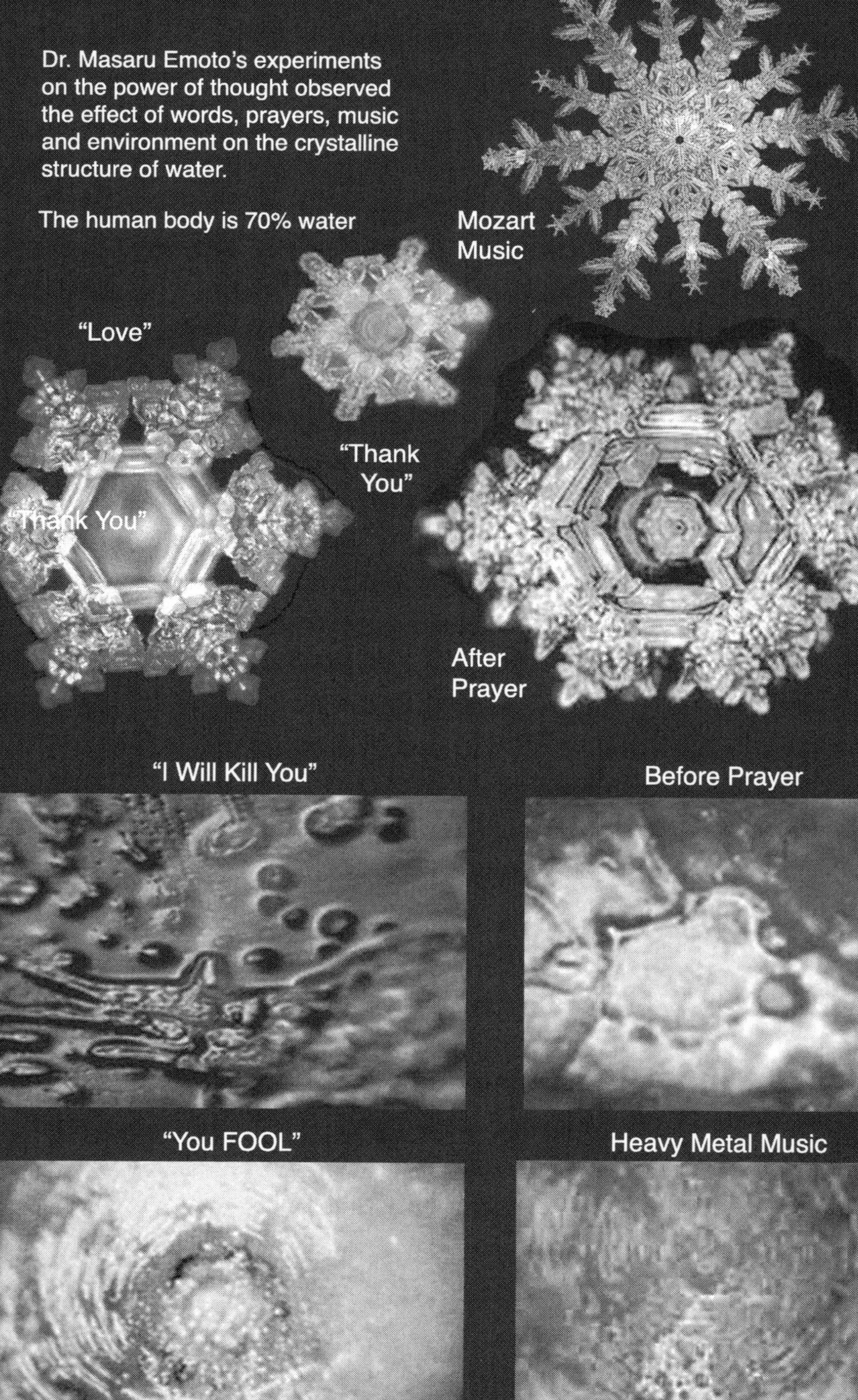
Dr. Masaru Emoto's experiments on the power of thought observed the effect of words, prayers, music and environment on the crystalline structure of water.
The human body is 70% water
Mozart Music
"Love"
"Thank You"
"Thank You"
After Prayer
"I Will Kill You"
Before Prayer
"You FOOL"
Heavy Metal Music

Chapter 6:

Unconditional Love Is The Foundation Of Creation; Negaprocity, The Destroyer Of Worlds

In December, 1978, I attended a meditation retreat near Cobb Mountain, California.[1] I was 22 years old at the time, although I had been practicing different forms of meditation since I was 15. The focus of this particular journey was learning the "Siddhis," or Patanjali's yoga sutras, and the majority of the day was spent performing spiritual practices.[2]

Sometime in the early morning hours of December 26th, I had an experience that would redefine the rest of my adult life. I was finishing my second "round,"[3] and, with eyes closed, was in the middle of the "pole star sutra."[4]

Suddenly, I had the awareness that I had stopped breathing and everything around me was in complete stillness. Time wasn't moving "forward," but rather "backwards." A moment later, I felt that I was somehow "freefalling" – something close to how I would imagine that skydivers feel as they're falling through the air, although I've never skydived.

[1] The retreat was "Hoberg's Resort and Spa," and it was then owned and operated by the TM® (transcendental meditation) organization. As an aside, the resort was completely destroyed by the "Valley Fire" of September, 2015. See: http://hobergshistoricalassociation.org/the-fire

[2] The TM or "transcendental meditation" movement was just beginning to teach their TM-Siddhi program to the general public at that time. See: http://permanentpeace.org/technology/sidhi.html. I will not address here the critics who claim the "movement" overcharges for their programs, or that advertised claims are overblown. This isn't relevant here, particularly since I have not been associated with the TM movement since 1983. Far more important is the experience I relate. Moreover, I believe that our spiritual experiences themselves are far more important than the tools we use to get there. The story that follows is the retelling of the same Brahmic experience that I relate in The Gospel of 2012, p.46-47.

[3] The regimen, in those days, consisted of practicing repetitions of asanas (hatha yoga), pranayama (breathing exercises), meditation, and repetitions of the Siddhis. One cycle of this process was called a "round," and the practice itself, "rounding."

[4] "Pole star sutra" is one of Patanjali's yoga sutras. See: https://www.ashtangayoga.info/philosophy/yoga-sutra/

And then, without any forewarning, it happened . . .

A burst of white light entered into my field of consciousness – many times brighter than the sun, and I could "see" 360 degrees around my person. More prominent still was the bliss, the happiness, the extreme ineffable joy, and experience of complete satiety – something to which even the most ecstatic experience in the normal, waking state of consciousness could never compare. I became "aware" that Love was woven into the fabric of all of Creation, holding everything together, like the mortar between the bricks that hold together a house. I was aware that even the behavior of subatomic particles was guided by this all-pervasive Force. I instantly saw through the artificiality of normal life, the "maya," the illusion encountered in the third dimension. I saw that everything I experienced with my senses was but a tiny sliver of objective reality, that all that I regarded as "real" was fleeting, and had no more reality than a fist after the hand has been opened. Everything about my perception of things was reordered. I understood the hidden meaning of the great poet Walt Whitman, no longer as merely an intellectual realization, but as only one who has had the cosmic experience can understand it:

> *"Hast never come to thee an hour,*
> *A sudden gleam divine, precipitating, bursting all these bubbles, fashions, wealth?*
> *These eager business aims—books, politics, art, amours,*
> *To utter nothingness?"*[5]

More than this, I saw that our perception of time is highly truncated. I realized that I was an immortal spiritual being, as we all are. That my life as a human was a very brief way station on an infinite journey, one of only many.

Surely, this was the pinnacle of experience and of pure "being" for any human. In a span of time that probably lasted no

[5] See: http://whitmanarchive.org/published/LG/1881/poems/142

more than two minutes, I honestly thought that I had achieved enlightenment – cosmic consciousness – the final destination of those who follow a thousand different paths that are part of the supreme wisdom of the Far East – for I was very familiar with the territory.[6]

Then, as freely and innocently as the experience had overtaken me, it passed. I opened my eyes, trying to grasp the full importance of what had just happened. A part of me was fighting off depression – not understanding how I could magically ascend to such a lofty Heaven, only to be thrown back into every day, dualistic, third dimensional, mortal life – a veritable hell-hole by any comparison. And then in the privacy of my little cabin in the woods . . . I wept.

Love, being the very substance of the Universe, is something to which all of Creation responds positively. We know this even without the experience of a heightened state of consciousness. Thoughts that feed the negaciprocal are, conversely, destructive, as are the entities that reside in the Outer Bands. The very reason that the Governments of the world are involved in so many projects that are destructive to the environment isn't accidental. They can't help themselves. It is their nature, sitting, as they are, at such a far sectoral distance from anything close to the inner sectors of the reciprocity zone.

I realized the importance of loving thoughts and how it affects our environment when I first read The Secret Life of Plants.[7] The book opens by describing the experiences of Cleve

[6] My journey began with a course in comparative religion while I was a student at Chaminade Preparatory in Chatsworth, California, in 1970. This was followed by years of studying Dr. Richard Maurice Bucke's Cosmic Consciousness (1901). In addition I had taken extensive courses on SCI (Science of Creative Intelligence) provided by the TM Movement, which was called SRM (Spiritual Regeneration Movement) when I got involved in 1971. Additionally, I had already, by that time, read a great many books that dealt with higher states of consciousness and mystical experiences.

[7] The version I'm referencing is: Peter Tompkins and Christopher Bird, The Secret Life of Plants, (1973).

Backster, who, even in the 1960s, was one of the world's foremost lie detector examiners. His new career began with an experience with a house plant (Dracaena massangeana). In 1966, he did a series of experiments using his galvanometer and was able to clearly show that his house plant registered the same emotional response, when stimulated by an event, as humans do. Moreover, his plant was able to "read his mind," differentiating between real or pretended intent.[8]

More amazingly, using a variety of different plants, Backster and other researchers were able to determine that plants are able to feel pain, often expressing themselves intensely,[9] that they were capable of having their feelings hurt,[10] that they can feel compassion for other plants, and will even share nutrients with suffering neighbors,[11] show clear evidence of having twenty distinctly different "senses" compared to our five,[12] but most relevant here, appreciate attention, love, and grow better when "fed" positive thought.[13] Whatever they are, plants are not the non-sentient automata that our mechanistic life sciences would make them out to be.

For his part, Cleve Backster went ahead, over 30 years later, and published additional material, repeatedly proving his earlier findings. Then, as now, despite the overwhelming weight of the evidence, colleagues label this work as quackery.[14] Perhaps it takes a certain level of consciousness to grasp the legitimacy of Backster's work . . .

The effects of our thoughts and actions on our environment were made even more clear to me when I became aware of Masaru Emoto's work with frozen ice crystals.[15] Despite criticism from the scientific community,[16] Emoto's work became an inspi-

[8] Ibid., p. 3-5

[9] Ibid., p. 64

[10] Ibid., p. 28

[11] Ibid., p. 73

[12] Ibid., p. 133

[13] Ibid., p. 348

[14] As an example, see: Cleve Backster, Primary Perceptions: Biocommunication with Plants, Living Foods, and Human Cells, (2003) p. 58-59.

[15] See: http://www.masaru-emoto.net/english/water-crystal.html

[16] See: https://en.wikipedia.org/wiki/Masaru_Emoto#Scientific_criticism

ration to millions. Essentially, Emoto found that water records the thoughts and vibrations of those around it. "The vibration of good words has a positive effect on our world, whereas the vibration from negative words has the power to destroy."[17] The most aesthetically pleasing photographs of ice crystals came from those that were exposed to the words, "love and gratitude."[18] The ones that looked the most wretched and hideous by any aesthetic standards were those that were exposed to negative thoughts and words, like "You fool!," "You make me sick!," "I will kill you!" The crystal that formed for the Japanese word for Satan (Lucifer) was particularly grotesque, evil and ominous looking.[19] Below are some examples of Emoto's findings:

Interestingly, Emoto found that the characteristics of crystals were affected by words, irrespective of the language he used. For example, when "Thank you" was projected to test water, the resulting crystals were harmonious and lovely to the eye, even when the equivalents were projected in Japanese, English, Chinese, German, French, Korean or Italian.[20]

Those who think that Emoto's work is merely theoretical may not know that it has proven applications that are being employed in industrial uses to improve the environment. I learned

[17] See: Masaru Emoto, The Hidden Messages in Water, (2004), p. 25..

[18] Ibid., p. 5

[19] Ibid., p. 9

[20] Ibid., p. 6-7

this from Ralph Suddath, a water technology expert that I've known for nearly 20 years.[21] Ralph has filed a number of patents that make use of Emoto's general concepts and these are now being incorporated worldwide.

In many spiritual traditions preceding the modern era, it was widely accepted that negative thoughts and actions have a cumulative effect on our surroundings. It is an article of faith in Vedanta, for example, that the effects of negative thoughts and actions can accumulate karmically and become the causative agents behind earthquakes, volcanic eruptions, and other natural disasters.

I've known this since I studied world religions as a teenager. For whatever reason, it just never occurred to me that the accumulation of negativity, of what I now call negaprocity, could lead to the extinction of my species and most life on Earth – near-term and of such severity so that even the tardigrades might not make it.[22]

Guy McPherson is a Professor Emeritus of evolutionary biology, ecology, and natural resources at the University of Arizona. He is well-known for coining the term "near term extinction" (NTE) and is of the belief that through runaway climate change, human extinction is probably in the range of ten years away – actually, make that ten years away from when he began making these prognostications in 2016.[23]

It would be easy to write McPherson off as a doomsday scientist who has spun off his axis after spending too much time behind a computer screen studying climate models. The problem I have in approaching McPherson dismissively is that he has been consistently wrong over the last ten years – ***on the conservative***

[21] See: http://www.altcancer.net/hydreva.htm

[22] If you're not familiar with this amazingly durable genus of animals, see: http://news.nationalgeographic.com/2017/07/tardigrades-water-bears-extinction-earth-science/

[23] See: http://www.dailystar.co.uk/news/latest-news/566478/climate-change-humanity-extinction-10-years

side.[24] Moreover, McPherson is supported by a cadre of highly credible climate scientists who have not accepted corporate or Government funds to keep their mouths shut, and whose views are anonymously posted on Arctic-News Blogspot.[25] Reluctantly, and only quite recently, these climate scientists have come to the same conclusion that McPherson has. *Homo sapiens*, through dramatic climate change and through the loss of habitat that is already occurring, (note: that's in the present tense, not the future tense, and this acceleration partly explains why we are seeing such large scale migrations from Africa and the Middle East), are on their way out. Their observations are in no way diminished by the fact that we presently have a record-breaking 7.4 billion humans living on the planet.[26]

Earlier this year, I took the time to read McPherson's laborious 32,000 word essay, detailing his position, appropriately entitled, "Climate Change Summary and Update."[27] Among the jaw-dropping gems this document contains, is a list of 69 separate, provable, documented, positive feedback loops that are kicking climate phenomena out of linear progressions and into exponential progressions. As of this writing, the document has not been updated since August 2, 2016. McPherson indicates he has no intention of updating it.[28]

McPherson has his share of critics, of course.[29] His views were even parodied on the HBO series, The Newsroom, which he ably confronts.[30]

What I find interesting are the attempts by those in authority to actively suppress his work. I relate to this since I've had to deal with it in my own work. McPherson detailed this in a one-

[24] If you go through his extensive run of lectures on YouTube, you'll find that he used to say that humans had until 2050, then until 2040, then until 2030, and now it's ten years, and average temperatures have consistently been higher than he previous thought they would be.

[25] See: http://arctic-news.blogspot.com/

[26] See: https://www.census.gov/popclock/

[27] See: https://guymcpherson.com/climate-chaos/climate-change-summary-and-update/

[28] You get a sense of McPherson's despair in a discussion of his 22 second clip, extending his version of Elizabeth Kubler-Ross's stages of grief at: https://www.youtube.com/watch?v=p-NAIyNLQPWM&t=19s

[29] Example: "How Guy McPherson gets it wrong" https://fractalplanet.wordpress.com/2014/02/17/how-guy-mcpherson-gets-it-wrong/

[30] See: https://www.youtube.com/watch?v=zM4UWCkMUSs&t=330s

on-one private interview that I had with him on May 7, 2017.[31]

Would it really be necessary to get a CIA agent enrolled in your classes to secretly monitor your speech, then effectively get you fired from your tenured position, and intercept the email traffic of people with whom you were corresponding, if you were a wacky professor subscribing to climate theories with no basis in reality? Would it really be necessary to have an intelligence agent visit you to effectively relate that, at least for the time being, the members of the Elite who are allowing you to live have the upper hand over those who want you dead?[32]

I do not argue that these developments, in themselves, are proof of anything. Nor do I have a problem with even my own friends and associates who feel that the CO_2 rise is overblown.[33] Perhaps even the effects of the mass release of methane hydrates, which are at least twenty times more potent, by volume, than CO_2 as a greenhouse gas, are overrated. (Some climate scientists believe that methane contributed substantially to the Permian extinction.)[34] As for just having seen the three hottest years on record,[35] our rush towards an ice-free Arctic,[36] or even current disruptions in the Earth's thermohaline circulation system,[37] let's just say that the effects of these developments are "inconclusive." We need more studies. Lots and lots of studies. As the planet sees up to 200 species per day go into extinction, there can never have enough studies!

One of the things McPherson pointed out in my interview with him is that between climate change, the effects of nucle-

[31] See: http://gregcaton.com/video/CatonMcPherson3.mp4

[32] These are all covered in the aforementioned May 7 interview.

[33] Example: Mike Adams, a friend since 1999 – the "Health Ranger" behind NaturalNews.com – makes an impassioned argument that global warming is a "scam" – see: https://www.youtube.com/watch?v=zR4kH5tpebY and https://www.youtube.com/watch?v=4rnXQtUl8p0

[34] See: http://www.independent.co.uk/environment/earth-permian-mass-extinction-apocalypse-warning-climate-change-frozen-methane-a7648006.html and https://www.theguardian.com/environment/2016/dec/12/rapid-rise-methane-emissions-10-years-surprises-scientists

[35] See: https://www.theguardian.com/environment/climate-consensus-97-per-cent/2017/jan/23/were-now-breaking-global-temperature-records-once-every-three-years

[36] See: http://e360.yale.edu/features/as_arctic_ocean_ice_disappears_global_climate_impacts_intensify_wadhams

[37] See: http://blogs.ei.columbia.edu/2017/06/06/could-climate-change-shut-down-the-gulf-stream/

ar accidents, like Fukushima, our poisoning of our ecosystems with "rescue chemistry," etc., our demise comes not at the hand of any one single development. We are signing our own death warrants with reckless abandon. Our exit is being driven by a variety of events that are man-made, deliberate, foreseeable, that could have been preventable, and which I maintain are all driven by negaprocity. The most poignant adjective in that last sentence is deliberate. I first learned this on my second trip to Russia.

The drive from St. Petersburg to the Estonian border city of Narva takes three hours. I wasn't enthusiastic about flying to St. Petersburg (Pulkovo airport) in the first place, but the Estonian scientist I was supposed to meet in Moscow, a man named Vamvoras, couldn't get his Russian visa in time. Since he couldn't come to Moscow to visit me, as planned, I decided to fly to him. I made the trip north in early July, 2003, partially lured by the opportunity to experience "white nights."[38]

When I finally got to Narva, I found Vamvoras to be a serious inventor who had made an astonishing discovery – one that could have profound repercussions in cleaning up the environment. Simply stated, Vamvoras had discovered a revolutionary way of manufacturing a "citric acid-based" plastic that was completely biodegradable and would rapidly break down after a few years, leaving no trace of toxins or other unwanted chemical residue.

The discovery addresses a problem that cannot be understated: the planet is awash with plastic garbage, over 5 trillion pieces in the oceans alone,[39] near a point where the oceans have more plastic garbage than fish.[40] When conventional plastics in

[38] See: http://www.saint-petersburg.com/virtual-tour/whitenights/

[39] See: http://news.nationalgeographic.com/news/2015/01/150109-oceans-plastic-sea-trash-science-marine-debris/

[40] See: http://www.businessinsider.com/plastic-in-ocean-outweighs-fish-evidence-report-2017-1 . . . frankly, given the fish die-off produced by the Fukushima nuclear accident alone, I think we may already be there

the ocean do degrade, they result in toxic components like bisphenol A (BPA) and PS oligomer. As for plastic in landfills, in the absence of UV rays, plastics remain garbage for an indeterminable period of time.[41]

Vamvoras, who had filed an international patent, indicated to me that he was already getting threats from Dupont and other U.S. chemical manufacturers, encouraging him not to proceed with his project. He indicated that he had received a far more favorable response in Russia.

"I don't understand their attitude," Vamvoras told me. "It's as if they want to wreck the planet."

Maybe it seems that way . . . because they do.

[41] See: http://science.howstuffworks.com/science-vs-myth/everyday-myths/how-long-does-it-take-for-plastics-to-biodegrade.htm and http://www.slate.com/articles/news_and_politics/explainer/2007/06/will_my_plastic_bag_still_be_here_in_2507.html

Chapter 6

Chapter 7:

Why Extreme Negaprocity, Left Unchecked, Leads To The Death Of Our Planet: The Implications Of Our Holocene Extinction Event

. . . Or Why The Status Quo Means The Destruction Of Our World As We Know It

In previous chapters I've covered a variety of ways in which Extreme Negaprocity has a cumulative nature. It's like an invasive weed, which, unchallenged by other plants for space, moisture, nutrients, sunlight, or disturbances brought on by unfavorable changes in the local climate, will just keep on gobbling up more territory unabated.

Unlike invasive weeds, however, modern Governments – the more effective of them – have managed to develop offensive systems that have destroyed nearly all of the traditional, reformative feedback loops that were used to keep the more outrageous negaciprocal Governments in check in the past.

For example, the very purpose of the second amendment to the U.S. Constitution – expressed quite specifically by its framers as the People's God-given right to bear arms – was to allow "the People" to revolt against tyranny. The American Revolution itself wasn't an act of repulsing a foreign power. It was a war by the British colonies against the very Government which was legally entitled to lay claim to its territory. There is absolutely nothing about the American Revolution, celebrated every year in the U.S. with the Day of Independence (July 4), which could not be compared to U.S. citizens rising up today and dethroning the crime syndicate that currently resides in Washington D.C.[1]

[1] As most U.S. citizens know, the Day of Independence celebrates the signiug of the Declaration of Independence, precipitating the American Revolution.

Will such an occurrence ever happen?

It will never occur . . . regardless of which new, demonic, uncharted levels of Extreme Negaprocity the U.S. descends into.

Quite apart from the stunning successes of the U.S. Government's relentless gullibility tests, there is the issue of a complete disparity in both defensive and offensive capability between the Government and the governed, between the privileged and the non 1%.

In earlier times a Government didn't think in terms of superior military technology. It thought about advantages in terms of "numbers" or resources. For many hundreds of years, European Governments had able fighters; so did the people. Governments had military hardware: spears, shields, horses, bows, arrows, and other low-tech weaponry. So did the people. Governments were far more worried about inciting citizen unrest. Washington has the luxury of not caring whatsoever about this.

Today the disparity between the tools that a people can use to protect itself against an excessively tyrannical Government and the tools that a Government can use to quell even mild dissension have never been greater.

I personally know of weapons in the U.S. arsenal – many involving advanced electromagnetic radiation – that the vast majority of Americans don't even know exist. To acknowledge their existence in uninformed public alone would make you a "conspiracy theorist."

How many Americans, for instance, know that the CIA has had in its arsenal of assassination tools a number of radioactive compounds which are lethal in the parts per billion – for the past fifty years? How many are aware that the U.S. took Tesla's original "ray beam" weapon designs and perfected them to the point where entire fields – areas where "suspected militia members" may be hiding – can be killed or permanently incapacitated?

I personally know of one friend who, like myself, held a high level security clearance and was targeted because he refused to do a "contract job" he found distasteful. The result was that he was targeted to be killed by means of a "Venus shooter": an electromagnetic pulse weapon which, from about 100 meters or so, will induce a heart attack in the individual targeted. Countless people have been assassinated by U.S. agents using this device – all made to look like natural deaths so that the perpetrators would be far removed from the crime.

When I met privately with Colonel Tom Bearden in 2002 he described advanced "scalar wave" technology that was being used in the Middle East by U.S. assassins with highly compartmentalized clearances to kill human targets where no trace of evidence would be left. His description of what this weapon does to the internal organs of the body was so diabolically grotesque that I simply refuse to repeat it here.

As for the numerous works that have been devoted to the fine art of "suiciding" dissenters – keep in mind that suicide used to be a noun, but with this fabulous, new approach to getting rid of individuals who just can't accept their assigned place in the slave world, it's now also used as a transitive verb and "suicided," an adjective – I doubt I could creatively add to that discourse, since other authors have so ably covered it.

What do the citizens of any nation have to counter this kind of death machine that has invested so many billions into perfecting the art of death? What does it say about a Government that would invest so much in developing and using such things? If what Oliver Wendell Holmes said is true – that power corrupts and absolute power corrupts absolutely – how do you even quantify this level of malignant intent, this refined devotion to Pure Evil?

Mark Zuckerberg – founder of Facebook, and believed by many to be a shill for U.S. intelligence[2] – likes to say that "the Age of Privacy is over."[3] No it isn't. The age of citizen dissent is over . . . eroding privacy is a just a by-product.

Something else is over, too, with far greater implications

[2] WikiLeaks founder Julian Assange touched on the subject of social networking in an interview with Russia Today, saying: "Everyone should understand that when they add their friends to Facebook, they are doing free work for United States intelligence agencies, and building this database for them." See: http://mashable.com/2011/05/02/julian-assange-facebook-spy-machine/#a0WcvF9dfEqL

[3] Several news outlets have reported this, and amongst the many, see: "Facebook's Zuckerberg Says The Age of Privacy Is Over," The New York Times, (January 10, 2010).

for the future of not only humanity, but all advanced life forms on this planet.

Even if you thought I was making up the preceding information . . . even if you didn't accept my facts, you could not argue with the proposition that no matter how great the chasm between modern Governments and their citizens in terms of their security or military resources, that chasm is nothing compared to the one that exists between the most effective, modern Governments – the standard bearers of Western civilization – and Mother Nature.

Humans can always do ***something*** to defend themselves, of course. In Ecuador, when the indigenous – who are, for all intents and purposes, defenseless – don't like what their Government is doing, they put up roadblocks and cause other disruptions that bring commerce to a halt. But Mother Nature can't put up roadblocks or hold a token political rally or send dissenting messages over the Internet – which is carefully monitored by U.S. Government agents using that most invasive of tools, the Windows Operating System, which, in any of its versions, comes installed with "back doors" which are accommodating to the intelligence community for just that purpose.[4]

Mother Nature can't tell her assailants, "Please don't rape me. I don't like it." Her signs of discontent are subtle, and yet so easy for pillagers to ignore . . . and ignore them we have.

Among all the victims of Extreme Negaprocity, it is our non-human co-inhabitants on this Earth that are most vulnerable . . . and yet our survival, as a species, ultimately rests upon our vigilance in respecting our co-dependence and interconnectedness with other earthly life forms. Because Extreme Negaprocity operates most horrifically against those victims who can't speak out, it is in the environmental realm that we see the most damage. Despite the countless acts of violence that humans have committed and do commit against each other, it is nothing compared to what humans have done to their environment. It is in this paroxysm of planetary destruction, where we are orchestrating the greatest extinction event in 252 million years, that

[4] See: http://techrights.org/2015/02/11/microsoft-back-doors/

modern Governments are playing the lead role.

I remember while serving in the U.S. Navy aboard the U.S.S. Coral Sea in the mid-70s, I was on a detail to dispose of garbage. You could find small mountains of large, thick plastic bags sitting every day on the fantail – aft of the hangar bay – as other seamen hoisted them over the rail to join a sea of these still-floating bags of every foul human and industrial waste you could think of on the surface of the ocean. I thought about the thousands of other ships around the world doing the same thing – every single day. Then I thought about how many years we've been doing it and how many more years we could possibly do it and get away with it. Then it occurred to me that if we continued to use the oceans – which cover 70% of the Earth's surface – as our own personal, industrial septic tank, it would eventually come back to haunt us.

It already has . . . worldwide.

As Derrick Jensen summarizes in one of his newer books:

"By now we all know the statistics and trends: 90 percent of the large fish in the oceans are gone; there is ten times as much plastic as phytoplankton in the oceans, 97 percent of the native forests are destroyed; amphibian populations are collapsing; migratory songbird populations are collapsing; mollusk populations are collapsing; fish populations are collapsing . . . Two hundred species are driven extinct each and every day (73,000 per year). . . This culture destroys landbases. That's what it *does*."[5]

It may be what it does. Certainly John Zerzan makes compelling arguments that civilization, our civilization, is inherently pathological,[6] but my essential point is that Government is the enforcer of this global suicidal behavior. The culture could be modified by a growing body of thoughtful world citizens if the

[5] See Derrick Jensen's preface in Aric McBay and Lierre Keith's book, Deep Green Resistance, (2011).

[6] See: John Zerzan, Running on Emptiness: The Pathology of Civilisation, (2002).

stronger, more effective Governments weren't there to prevent it.

When well-intentioned Governments attempt to take a more ecologically sensitive course, they are reducing their thermodynamic potential in ways that often make them politically unpopular – and most certainly more vulnerable and impotent regionally and internationally. As one official in Luxembourg has commented, "We [politicians] all know the right thing to do. We just haven't figured out a way to do it and still get elected."[7] With this kind of response, we may be tempted to say that our current state of affairs is all the fault of the commoners. Or, to repeat a well-worn proverb: "The Government people get is the Government they deserve."

But I find this perspective far too simplistic . . . and I waited until this late point in the book to bring up its global, ecological implications, precisely because I felt it was important to explore how divergent and dramatically opposed the interests of a Government are with its people – the natural result of great sectoral distance.

In the U.S. there is a solid majority of people who want peace, who want our troops out of Iraq, Afghanistan, Libya, Pakistan, Syria, etc. – as in yesterday, people who know, as General Butler used to say, that "war is a racket."[8] There are now numerous social arenas in which the will of the people has been amply demonstrated, to which the U.S. Government has taken the unspoken position, "We're in charge, you gullible morons. Get lost."

Those who still buy into the common narrative that change can be brought about at the ballot box remain woefully ignorant of the extent to which elections have degenerated into widespread voter fraud. The destruction of the tools of reformation is reform. More Doublespeak.

This is why our current course is taking us down a road where our planet will, in the not too distant future, begin to as-

[7] See:https://en.wikiquote.org/wiki/Jean-Claude_Juncker – see under "2007."

[8] See: Major General Smedley D. Butler, War is a Racket: The Antiwar Classic by America's Most Decorated Soldier, (2003).

sume a "life form profile" resembling Mars. There are no inertial factors on the horizon that appear up to the task of changing our direction. Undoubtedly this is the scenario that Jeremy Rifkin had in mind more than thirty-five years ago when he wrote Entropy.[9] We appear committed to riding the second law of thermodynamics into our own little planetary hell. As previously stated, the entropic factors do not appear to be linear anymore; they have, of late, taken on a more accelerated character.

The ecological solutions proposed by the Governments of this world are predictably anemic and "dumbed down" – destined to fail by design because negaciprocal institutions are inherently incapable of providing solutions to problems that cannot be solved unless we kill the negaprocity.

Unfortunately all this "happy talk" has not translated into meaningful action – yet . . . certainly none that I can see.

I built my career by sustaining a perpetual optimism about whatever projects I happened to be working on. I'm not a "doom-and-gloomer," but I have, of late, assumed a little more realism and a little less idealism in how I view our current circumstances. Because of the personal risks I have assumed in writing this book, however, you should have expected, by now, to see some kind of proposed set of solutions as an integral part of it.

Any solution has to have a chance at coming up victorious. I find nothing heroic in the object of Norse mythology, namely, that we all fight for a losing battle with Odin, destined for hell, but relishing the romantic notion that we were privileged to go down in flames with the gods.

To hell with that . . . literally.

Nor can I throw in my hat with the Elite eugenics people. Yes, I know we're suffering from overpopulation. It's a huge part of the problem. I could easily see that back in 1970 when, in high school, the topic of U.S. national debate teams was the sorry state of the ecology.

The Elite of this world – yes, those loveable darlings, those Luciferian card carrying members of the secret societies who think all our problems will go away if they can just kill off 6.5

[9] See: Jeremy Rifkin, Entropy, (1980).

billion people and get us down to a more manageable 400 to 500 million people worldwide – are completely deluded. I don't question that their deadly vaccines (with planned forced inoculations), nuclear wars (which have been secretly going on for years with the use of depleted uranium armaments), and advanced bioweapons, are capable of doing their job. They effectively address maintaining power, but they don't address the root of the problem. Like their cherished orthodox medical models: they are designed to treat symptoms, while leaving the disease intact.

It doesn't bother me so much that the "puppet masters" are suffering from the effects of intellectual incest when it comes to this issue. What bothers me is that they refuse to acknowledge that their negaciprocal hold is the source of the problem.

Their position is easily stated as, **"We will destroy this planet and everybody on it – right down to the microbes in the soil – before we will see one inch of our power diminished."** They may hold the world in their hand, but they are squeezing so hard that the clay is oozing out between their fingers, so that, in the end, they will end up just as empty-handed as the rest of us.

Their myopia is just as evident in the trillions of dollars they have allotted for underground cities – huge, deep underground shelters,[10] there are well over 150 of them in the U.S alone now.[11] The members of the Elite that I know personally – don't ask – have a name for the "inclusion right" into one of these dwellings when they decide to pull the plug. They call it "the ticket."

One scientist friend who shall remain unnamed, was offered "tickets" for himself and his family, and actually turned them down. He claimed: "These Elitists have acquired and maintained their global power over hundreds of years by exercising every evil, deceitful ploy imaginable. In terms of selective breeding, what you have there is the refinement and perfection of 'pure

[10] See: http://www.dailymail.co.uk/news/article-4618354/How-government-elites-plan-survive-nuclear-attack.html

[11] This is previously covered in my discussion of the work of Dr. Richard Sauder.

evil.' Why would you want to live a mile under the earth with a bunch of vipers, scorpions, and tarantulas? They will end up killing each other off – along with their reptilian overlords. If things really go to shit, I'd rather die on my own terms right here on the surface."

Whether you live in an underground bunker deep in the earth, or you live on the surface, your fate, and that of nearly all life on Earth, seems pretty clear. When I spoke to Guy McPherson, it became apparent that even though the focus of his work seems to be "extinction through abrupt climate change," he agreed that a far deadlier scenario was that of our dependence on nuclear power. The Fukushima nuclear accident of 2011 has already been officially designated "an extinction level event,"[12] and that was before the recent decision to release a billion pounds of radioactive tritium into the Pacific Ocean.[13]

This, of course, is nothing compared to what would happen if we had 450 Fukushima events occur worldwide,[14] which is precisely what we'd have if EMP (electromagnetic pulse) weapons were widely employed – a given in a World War III situation – or the arrival of a solar "Carrington Event," whose next arrival is not a matter of "if" but "when."[15]

These possibilities are not far-fetched. As it pertains to near-term human extinction, as obvious an anti-Luddite as Bill Joy is, this co-founder of Sun Microsystems wrote in early 2000: "Our most powerful 21st century technologies – robotics, genetic engineering, and nanotech – are threatening to make humans an endangered species."[16] No serious student of nuclear pow-

[12] See: http://lunaticoutpost.com/thread-746885.html; http://countercurrentnews.info/2016/11/fukushima-extinction-level-event-no-one-talking-2/

[13] See: http://enenews.com/fury-at-fukushima-over-1-billion-pounds-of-nuclear-waste-will-be-dumped-into-sea-top-official-the-decision-has-already-been-made-the-solution-is-to-pour-the-radioactive-liquid-into-t

[14] There are approximately 450 nuclear power plants in operation worldwide. See: https://www.euronuclear.org/info/encyclopedia/n/nuclear-power-plant-world-wide.htm

[15] See: http://www.businessinsider.com/massive-1859-solar-storm-telegraph-scientists-2016-9 and also see: http://news.nationalgeographic.com/news/2011/03/110302-solar-flares-sun-storms-earth-danger-carrington-event-science/

[16] This was the opening statement in Joy's now famous Wired magazine article, "Why the Future Doesn't Need Us," see: https://www.wired.com/2000/04/joy-2/. See also: https://en.wikipedia.org/wiki/Why_The_Future_Doesn%27t_Need_Us

er doubts that failure of a substantial number of nuclear power plants would extend the reach of that extinction well past *Homo sapiens*.[17]

This is where humanity, taking its guidance from a negaciprocal Elite, has brought itself and the world around us. This is where we sit at the far right end of the Exosomatic Axis.[18] This is where the Great Winding ends, and if there is any possibility to find our redemption, the Great Unwinding must begin.

[17] Walter Russell saw this clearly in the 1950's, when he and his wife, Lao, penned Atomic Suicide?. See also: http://themillenniumreport.com/2015/09/atomic-suicide-modern-day-prophet-walter-russell-foretells-the-future/

[18] See: http://meditopia.org/old/chap5_2004.htm or see Appendix A.

Chapter 7

Chapter 8:

Visions Of Resurrection In The Universal Meme; Notes On A Coming "Event"

To this point, in both "The Great Winding" and "The Great Unwinding," most of the material I've covered is the "terra firma" of this work – that is, the majority of the material is either easy-to-prove or already well-established. I am merely putting the pieces together. It is not possible to examine where this takes us from here (again, future tense) without delving into speculation. Despite an attempt to examine this area as objectively as possible, I will not be able to cover this territory without the inclination of some to dismiss it as metaphysics, pseudoscience, or just "woo woo."[1]

Skepticism will, no doubt, be fueled by the fact that history is littered with prognosticators who provided dates of civilizational cataclysms that never happened.[2] Although I provide no dates, what I'm about to discuss could be treated as such.

Nonetheless, I feel this is the most important part of the book – one might say as positive and uplifting as Book I is morbid and depressing. We're talking about the path to escaping this world of Extreme Negaprocity . . . and experiencing its opposite: the collapse of sectoral distance and a return to experiencing everyday life in the center of the reciprocity zone, experiencing pure love.

In a series of strange synchronicities, more compelling than anything I've experienced in the past, I find that a coming "Event" is being perceived by a growing number of unrelated people that share certain characteristics with some of the eschatological beliefs of the world's major religions.[3] My examina-

[1] See: http://www.urbandictionary.com/define.php?term=woo+woo

[2] See: https://en.wikipedia.org/wiki/List_of_dates_predicted_for_apocalyptic_events

[3] See: https://en.wikipedia.org/wiki/Eschatology

tion of this area has been going on for some time . . .

In the summer of 2004, I penned a chapter in the original version of Meditopia, entitled "The Inevitable Collapse: And the Rebirth That Will Follow/Opportunity in the Wake of 'Die-Off.'"[4] Even by that time, it was readily apparent to me that my civilization was reaching an "end point" – if only because we were approaching the extreme point of what I term "the purely exosomatic,"[5] or to use the language of the current volume, the point of Extreme Negaprocity. I could clearly see that the Governments of the world were taking us to a "negaprocity saturation point" – where things are so evil that they could not possibly become more so. I set out to find out what happens when we reach that saturation point after I moved to Ecuador in 2007, using techniques not traditionally recognized or appreciated in the West – techniques that had more than proven their legitimacy to me through first-hand experience.

Sometime in May, 2008, I spent time with a shaman in Tena, in Napo Province, Ecuador, which at that time was about a 12 hour bus ride from my home in Guayaquil. Spending many days deep in the Amazon jungle, we did a series of ayahuasca journeys together,[6] of which I have now done many. At one point, stunned by his erudition about the medicinal properties of what appeared to me to be hundreds of plants, I asked, "How could you possibly have acquired so much knowledge about plant medicine in one lifetime? How many plants are you intimately familiar with as medicines?" I had studied herbology for about 30 years, yet I could see that this shaman's knowledge way surpassed my own.

"I am very familiar with about 1,400 different plants

[4] See: Appendix A

[5] Again, see "Caton's Exosomatic Axis" at: http://meditopia.org/old/chap5_2004.htm or see Appendix A.

[6] See: http://www.ayahuasca-info.com/introduction

and their medicinal values, which parts to use, when, at what stages in their life cycle they should be harvested, and for what human medical conditions. As for the source of this knowledge, ayahuasca has taught me everything I know."

I was already familiar with such reports. Jeremy Narby opens his book on the subject with precisely these same kinds of claims of near supernatural information download.[7] Although I myself was still learning how to use ayahuasca to acquire knowledge, the idea came to me to repurpose and invigorate its use to look into future events involving what I will loosely call an "end time." As I explain in my previous book,[8] I was already having experiences of clairaudience and claircognizance using ayahuasca as early as 2006.

In 2012 I used ayahuasca to do a series of "journeys" in search of particulars about this "end point" – its nature, how it unfolded, peripheral details, and, if I was lucky, perhaps the timing. These journeys resulted in the publication of my previous book, The Gospel of 2012 According to Ayahuasca.[9]

It can be a real challenge to "interpret" the images and thought forms that you receive when using entheogenic material. Some vision quests, particularly those where you're actively probing into an abstract subject, are not unlike trying to interpret dreams. Then there is the process of deciphering what is real and what is metaphorical. Interestingly, much of the material that made it into the final manuscript was either contrary to my own beliefs at the time, or made me cringe to the point where upon reading the final edition, I frequently said to myself, "Did I really say that?" Nonetheless, I did the best I could to interpret the messages I was unearthing through my subconscious to the best of my abil-

[7] See: Jeremy Narby, The Cosmic Serpent: DNA and the Origins of Knowledge, (1998), p.1-4.

[8] See: Greg Caton, The Gospel of 2012 According to Ayahuasca, (2012), p. 4.

[9] Ibid

ity – flawed though my abilities as an "interpreter" may be.

Despite the intensity with which I explored this subject, I realized by 2013 that I had invested undue significance in a series of coincidences that related to a coming "Event." Among other things, I placed undue importance on the 2012 date itself,[10] as did a number of others, including notable authors, lecturers, and thinkers.[11]

Nothing happened, of course, and when I didn't pick up on any intuitive signals that indicated that anything important was imminent, I stopped selling the book, went on with my life, and invested little to no further energy into the material I revealed in the book. Since I didn't think it would be honest to continue selling a book whose particulars I could no longer support – tied as they were to an obvious "non-event" – I took it off the market, closed down the website connected to it, let the domain name die, and killed the company that had been created to promote the book.

Sometime in 2016, I began getting emails and phone calls from people who had previously read the book or were familiar with my work. They remarked that using hypnosis and other psychic exploratory tools, people were getting "messages" about a "coming Event" with startling specificity that matched to a remarkable degree what I had written about in my book. Others were "seeing" these same things in their dreams – again, from diverse sources. Many of these "messages" were being posted on YouTube and on alternative, spiritual, and futuristic websites.[12]

There are variations on this theme, of course. No two people "see" exactly the same thing. However, certain elements of this meme appear so frequently that they are inescapable in their repetition. The following are some of the important elements within the messages of Gospel of 2012 that mirror the informa-

[10] Generally agreed as being Dec. 21, 2012. See: https://www.fairobserver.com/culture/2012-phenomenon-end-world/ Although I was never "given" a date in any of my entheogenic journeys, I presumed there to be a connection to the 2012 "eschatology meme," and this clearly clouded my interpretations and skewed my judgment of what I experienced.

[11] See: Caton, The Gospel of 2012 According to Ayahuasca, p. 139-159.

[12] I list a variety of these sources below in the discussion of "meme elements."

tion that is coming out with increasing frequency now in 2017. (Note that most of the bold quotes below are taken directly from the Gospel of 2012 book.) None of this is meant to imply that some of this material didn't well precede the publication of my previous book – clearly much of it does – but the increased volume of messages, their details, intensity, and aforementioned correlation in content are worth noting. Below I detail some of the more notable ones:

1. **There is a coming Event involving the merging of dimensions or movement into a higher dimension.**

As I was told in November, 2011, there is a "momentous Event" that involves perception into the 4th and 5th dimensions. QHHT therapists who use Dolores Cannon's techniques[13] have unrelated clients reporting an outright migration of human souls to the 5th dimension, something that I myself wasn't told in specific terms.[14]

"You will experience a momentous event . . . where the perceptual boundaries that now separate the 3rd, 4th, and 5th dimensions will dissolve. What seem like impenetrable walls now will change to what will seem like transparent curtains."[15]

There is now more material on the Internet than ever where people are perceiving either a movement to a more interdimen-

[13] See: http://dolorescannon.com/ . . . Dolores Cannon (1931-2014) is no longer with us, but her work continues through her many trained practitioners.

[14] Examples: see Allison Coe videos: https://www.youtube.com/watch?v=2pyzZIQy4Xc which segues into: https://www.youtube.com/watch?v=3pRYMLUMfB4&t=43s
Alba Weinman, a hypnotist practitioner, has posted almost 150 videos, many of them dealing with this specific subject. Many of these videos are either unremarkable, irrevelant, or not worth discussing concerning the subject at hand. Additionally, I question whether some of her clients are truly in the hypnotic state when they are speaking consciously [her post #145 is an example of what I'm talking about]. However, she has other hypnotic sessions where the information and sense of authenticity is nothing short of astonishing [her post #081, or a client named "Gary" comes to mind]. A startling number of people share remarkably similar details. See: https://www.youtube.com/channel/UCt3xe3Yz-4P__NZ9bSo1udQ/videos
Alba's website is: http://albaweinman.com/

[15] See: Caton, The Gospel of 2012 According to Ayahuasca, p. 13.

sional state, or an outright migration to the fifth dimension.[16]

Another recurring theme coming from various sources is that the Event is either extremely rare, or is the only one of its kind ever witnessed by the Universe. As one QHHT client reported:

> **"(we are waiting) for something that doesn't happen very often . . . the evolution of humanity"[17]**

What was revealed to me was not simply that the event itself was rare, as many others have reported who have contacted me, but that the event is singular. It is outside the usual long cycles that mark the boundaries of the four yugas. In fact, it is unlike any other in the history of the Universe, with implications going far beyond any event on Planet Earth or the evolution of humanity. I perceived that the "Event" was billions of years in the making.[18] I opened the first chapter of the book with the title, "The Ultimate Black Swan Event," and later on, was given this description:

> ***"This coming event is a harmonic of the act of Creation itself. In time and space, we hit this harmonic (that) has never happened before. It is a special thing to reenact the conditions of the original Creation. Those whose hearts are open will be given the opportunity to feel the same feelings that God had when he made the decision to usher in Creation. We can share this with Him. It is the meaning of (one of) Christ's parables. God wants to have***

[16] Some examples: http://in5d.com/frequency-shifting-5d/ (There are articles on the in5d website devoted to this topic); http://ascension-temple.com/ascension-to-5th-dimension.html; http://soulguidedcoach.com/main-symptoms-of-ascension-into-5th-dimension/; http://portaltoascension.org/article/4d-portal-and-the-5th-dimension/; http://vidyafrazier.com/what-is-the-fifth-dimension/; Vidya Frazier has a couple books on the subject is called Awakening to the Fifth Dimension -- A Guide for Navigating the Global Shift, (2014); and Ascension – Embracing the Transformation, (2015). See also: Elizabeth Joyce, Ascension – Accessing the Fifth Dimension, Visions of Reality, (2013). These are just a few of the resources and references to be found on this subject.

[17] Alba Weinman, session #081, Jan. 2017. See; https://www.youtube.com/watch?v=90U6ZEZIN3U&t=5162s – the relevant passage begins at 9:58

[18] See: Caton, The Gospel of 2012, p. 30

a party, and He's invited us. And He'd like us to accept, because He'd be lonely without us. It's as if God doesn't want to be alone. He's lonely because we left Him. You have to know what Love and Joy it took for God to unfold Creation. Not out of a sense of lack. He did it out of fullness. He had such fullness; He couldn't hold Himself back from wanting to share it. We can experience that fullness (such) that God will say, 'Let me finally share with you why I did what I did. You'll understand in the end why I had to keep it a secret. It is time for Me to finally share it with you. And I've gone through such painstaking preparation; it would be such a sad thing for you to miss the party."[19]

2. "The Event" involves the separation of the Present Earth into an "Old Earth" and a "New Earth."

Some time in 2014, I was introduced to a teacher and psychic in Israel who was familiar with Gospel of 2012. Interestingly, he hadn't read the book but immediately related to the "New Earth / Old Earth" illustration that appeared on the book cover. He told me he had visions of a separation between Old and New Earth that looks ***exactly*** like the image on my book cover.

The description of this "separation" between an Old and a New Earth is a recurring theme in those who are working to unearth this information from the collective unconscious. Those familiar with the Biblical passage that makes mention of this may be tempted to suspect "frontloading":

"Then I saw 'a new heaven and a new Earth,' for the first heaven and the first Earth had passed away, and there was no longer any sea. [2] I saw the Holy City, the new Jerusalem, coming down out of heaven from God, prepared as a bride beautifully dressed for her husband. [3] And I heard a loud voice from the throne saying, "Look! God's dwelling place is now among the

[19] See: Caton, Gospel of 2012, p. 26

people, and he will dwell with them. They will be his people, and God himself will be with them and be their God. [4] 'He will wipe every tear from their eyes. There will be no more death' or mourning or crying or pain, for the old order of things has passed away.

[5] He who was seated on the throne said, 'I am making everything new!' Then he said, 'Write this down, for these words are trustworthy and true'."[20]

However, with all due respect, the current accounts of an "Old Earth" and a "New Earth" appear to supply a considerably greater degree of specificity than St. John of Patmos provided when he was doing his vision quests. This may, in part, be attributable to temporal proximity, because any experienced "spiritual psychonaut" knows that details get clearer and sharper as you approach a given event horizon. I saw this aspect of The Event quite clearly, in what is, to date, one of the most emotional and overpowering journeys I've ever had.

"As I viewed the Earth "splitting" into two separate bodies in a process not dissimilar from mitosis, I was telepathically told the significance of the two bodies. The one that appeared lifeless and moving to the left on its own trajectory was the place where souls would continue to go who had become enamored of a God-less society. In vision after vision, not unlike the levels of hell that Swedenborg was allowed to view, I saw the Earth's present Elite, and their future incarnations, obtaining the very world that they and their bloodlines had worked so assiduously for countless generations to create. "It will be the ultimate manifestation of the old Portuguese proverb: 'When God decides to punish men, He gives them what they pray for.'" I saw continuing wars, ending in a thermonuclear exchange, horrific Earth changes, and global pollution so bad that the skies appeared saturated with soot. And from outer space, I saw a planet that appeared all but dead.

[20] Book of Revelations 21:1-5, The Holy Bible, New Internation Version (NIV)

Except that it wasn't dead. It would be the new home for countless souls who had not prepared themselves energetically for the coming "Passage." And then I was told, 'If in their greed and selfishness 'they' so badly want a world that is bereft of the Divine, I shall grant them their wish.'

"The planet whose trajectory took off to the right had an entirely different look and feel. It was absolutely radiant. Whereas the "dark planet" version of Earth appeared flat and lifeless, this one was bursting with life force, emanating a joyfulness that jolted the senses at the very sight of it. The entire experience was one of awe. Even in the vision state, I could scarcely gaze upon it. I wasn't sure whether this was because I wasn't yet ready to fully experience it, or perhaps because I wasn't yet worthy. I couldn't be sure. It was as if the Garden of Eden had reconstituted Herself, spread to every corner of this New Earth, and been allowed to regenerate the planet so that there was no place from her core to her outer atmosphere that did not radiate this irrepressible Bliss. So wondrous was the sight of this magnificent, celestial body that I could 'hear' myself talking through my own soul, visibly and silently weeping back in my physical body as I 'said' it: "Oh my God! Let me be worthy of this! . . . Whatever I've done to offend you, I am so very sorry! . . . Do not forsake me! . . . Please don't leave me here. I wanna go home!"[21] (Emphasis in the original)

More specifically, as it relates to the current or "Old Earth":

". . . this other (devolved) Earth . . . it goes off in horrific ways. It experiences all the things that Edgar Cayce talked about. The souls in the astral planes around that planet begin all over again. It's almost like going all the way through high school. Imagine being 18 years old and flunking; and then you have to go back to kindergarten.

[21] See: Caton, The Gospel of 2012, p. 47-48.

You start over again. There is no place else to put you. (Currently) this is all beyond human understanding . . ."[22]

Like myself, others are receiving similarly realistic experience of this New Earth:

"It's happening now! I can see it! . . . There are auras around the Earth. Many are focusing on the New Earth. The New Earth is already here. The New Earth is our creation. The New Earth is another dimension – a new one . . . (How do we get on the New Earth?) We make a choice. (How do we make (that) choice?) Simply, create it."[23]

Another one of Alba Weinman's clients described the phenomenon more succinctly:

"We divide into two . . . the Old Earth and the New one."[24]

Interesting, shortly after this pronouncement, the subject above is visited by Archangels Rafael, Michael, and Uriel.[25] This is precisely the same exact group of visiting celestrial beings that I reported in one of my journeys in 2012.[26] The exact same ones, dealing with essentially the same subject matter.

Coincidence? Yeah, sure. Why not. Every day occurrence. Happens all the time.

Those vividly seeing the New Earth have been doing so for several years now. Dolores Cannon noted how she was at a conference with fellow author, Annie Kirkwood. Annie told her that she saw "the Split" appearing to be something like cellular

[22] See: Caton, The Gospel of 2012, p. 54

[23] See: Alba Weinman, session #081, Jan. 2017. See; https://www.youtube.com/watch?v=90U6ZEZIN3U&t=5162s – the relevant passage runs from 29:10 to 31:35.

[24] See: YouTube video, entitled "039 Alba Weinman – The New Earth, Mother Mary, and Message from the Masters." See: https://www.youtube.com/watch?v=Dg87YVHI93s. Begins at 1:06:00. Also, the Earth "splitting" is discussed after 1:41:00.

[25] Ibid. Runs from 1:11:15 to 12:30:45

[26] See: Caton, The Gospel of 2012, p. 59-64

mitosis and dividing "into two Earths."[27] As I stated at that time, this is precisely what I saw.

3. **"The Event" is accompanied by passage through the "Galactic Plane" or a cosmic Event of comparable significance.**

Conventional science tells us that we will not pass through the "galactic plane" for another 30 million years.[28] The nexus between a crossing of the "galactic plane" and the 2012 meme, was proffered by several researchers, most notably John Major Jenkins,[29] but it is questionable as to whether they are talking about the same thing.

> ***". . . the Earth will experience a complete rebirth as it passes through the galactic plane. This is not a theory. It is a pre-destined astrophysical event whose place in the time-space continuum cannot be altered. . ."*[30]**

My sense is that the confusion in what people are "seeing" in their thoughts, dreams, and visions, is caused by semantics relating to the phenomenon itself. Others are describing it as a "great galactic alignment," or "high energy zone" of natural origin.

> ***"We once again have this odd, repeating collusion of data that reinforces itself through its sheer repetition and refusal to die out. Obviously, if our quadrant, our local solar system, our Earth is slowly entering into a high energy zone of the great galactic disk center and it is a cycle that occurs every twenty five thousand years, it is certainly not an ET or supreme being created event – it is a natural,***

[27] See: Caton, The Gospel of 2012, p. 144

[28] See: http://earthsky.org/astronomy-essentials/will-earth-pass-through-galactic-plane-in-2012

[29] John Major Jenkins, Maya Cosmogenesis 2012: The True Meaning of the Maya Calender End-Date, (1998). Or see : http://alignment2012.com/whatisga.htm

[30] See: Caton, The Gospel of 2012 According to Ayahuasca, p. 14

***cosmic event."*[31]**

This harkens back to the thoughts of Dr. Paul LaViolette, a respected physicist, who has been studying galactic superwaves since the 1970s, and in 2009, hypothesized a connection to the next major wave arriving at the end of the Mayan calendar.[32] Mind you, I say this fully aware that the Mayans themselves did not attribute anything apocalyptic to the 2012 date,[33] although the assigned date was questionable[34] or even symbolic.[35]

In retrospect, it should never have been a touchstone for any date-specific cosmological event.

Similar to LaViolette's superwave are the observations of Russian astrophysicst, Dr. Alexey Dmitriev, whom I wrote about in Gospel of 2012.[36] Specifically, here is the short version of Dr. Dmitriev's position:

> ***"As our solar system travels through space, there is a protective heliosphere that protects the sun and the objects within its sphere of influence from the negative effects of travelling through intersteller space. The heliosphere is comparable to the protective layers of the Earth's atmosphere, but many times larger. In any event, the 'shock wave' at the leading edge of the heliosphere – (think of your car's bumper) – has increased in size 1000% since it was first observed and is continuing to expand rapidly. Dmitriev's conclusion? That our entire solar system is***

[31] See: http://www.theeventchronicle.com/metaphysics/metascience/galactic-center-2/

[32] See: http://www.starburstfound.org/downloads/superwave/Nexus2009.pdf . . . read section entitled: "The Probability of Future Arrivals."

[33] See: http://www.npr.org/sections/thetwo-way/2012/12/20/167626648/maya-expert-the-end-of-times-is-our-idea-not-the-ancient

[34] See: https://www.seeker.com/2012-mayan-calendar-doomsday-date-might-be-wrong-1765129775.html. However, quite apart from the possibility of the 2012 date having been 60 or more days off, there is the question of placing too much emphasis on date specificity to begin with. Does it really make that big a difference that the end of the previous "baktun" is a few years off from momentous eschatological events in the first place? I would propose that it doesn't.

[35] See: http://www.dailymail.co.uk/sciencetech/article-2068561/Mayan-prediction-world-ending-2012-misreading--just-start-new-era-says-expert.html

[36] See: Caton, Gospel of 2012, p. 156-157.

moving into a completely new energetic area.

I add this as a nexus point because the kind of astrophysical event that has been described to me could hardly seem possible unless there were energetic conditions detectable throughout our solar system that were leading up to it . . . for years. Dmitriev's research supports such a contention. Moreover, the astrophysical changes that have been occurring already are not nominal."[37]

Another visionary interpretation of "The Event," which sounds like a cross between LaViolette's superwave and a galactic plane transit is the famous "end time" prophecy of Bulgarian mystic, Peter Konstantinov Deunov[38] also known as Beinsa Douno. Issued just days before his death in 1944, the pertinent passage reads:

"Our solar system is now traversing a region of the Cosmos where a constellation that was destroyed left its mark, its dust. This crossing of a contaminated space is a source of poisoning, not only for the inhabitants of the Earth, but for all the inhabitants of the other planets of our galaxy. Only the suns are not affected by the influence of this hostile environment. This region is called 'the thirteenth zone'; one also calls it 'the zone of contradictions.' Our planet was enclosed in this region for thousands of years, but finally we are approaching the exit of this space of darkness and we are on the point of attaining a more spiritual region, where more evolved beings live."[39]

Another "cosmological trigger" is being described by some

[37] See Caton, The Gospel of 2012, p. 156 and 157.

[38] See: http://www.encyclopedia.com/science/encyclopedias-almanacs-transcripts-and-maps/deunov-peter-konstantinov-1864-1944

[39] There are countless sites that ruminate over Deunov's prophecy. By way of example, see: http://www.theeventchronicle.com/metaphysics/spiritual/70-year-old-prophecy-earth-will-soon-swept-extraordinary-rapid-waves-cosmic-electricity/

as being neither a passage through the galactic plane, a galactic alignment, nor a passage through a higher energy zone, but rather as a "great solar flash."[40]

This seems to be the positive interpretation to Ed Dames'[41] dark evil twin. For over 20 years, Colonel Ed Dames has been promoting "remote viewing" educational programs, while preaching about a solar "killshot" that would effectively destroy most of modern civilization.[42] That Dames has been astonishingly inaccurate over the years[43] is beside the point, especially when you consider that Elite preparations have been in place to prepare for solar phenomena not terribly dissimilar from what Dames describes.[44]

As an aside, my own vision quests emphasized that this cosmological event came with specific energy emissions that heightened human consciousness:

> ***"Human physiology will be subjected to a variety of frequencies – to energetic conditions – that will greatly expand human consciousness."***[45]

Additionally, it is interesting to note that a cosmological event is central in most of the eschatological teachings of the world's major religions, as well. By way of example, note the following frequently quoted passage from the Book of Matthew:

> **"Immediately after the tribulation of those days, the sun will be darkened, and the moon will not give its light; the stars will fall from heaven, and the power of**

[40] This meme is being widely circulated by David Wilcock and Corey Goode – one example of many: https://spherebeingalliance.com/blog/transcript-cosmic-disclosure-the-great-solar-flash.html; or see: https://arthousecontemporary.com/disclosure/

[41] See: http://www.thekillshot.com/dames.cfm

[42] See: http://www.thekillshot.com/index.cfm

[43] See: http://www.abovetopsecret.com/forum/thread1038880/pg1

[44] See: http://www.dailymail.co.uk/news/article-3302185/White-House-preparing-catastrophic-solar-flares-wipe-power-world-months-bringing-end-modern-civilization-know-it.html

[45] See Caton, Gospel of 2012, p.15

the heavens will be shaken.'"[46]

Since this brings up the issue of a darkening sky, the frequency with which "three days of darkness" comes up from the universal mind is also worth noting.

"At this point, I am visually shown the effects of this passage on photons, as all light in our solar system is sucked in the direction of the galactic center. All photons are made to appear like tiny iron filings being sucked towards a powerful magnet, or bread crumbs being sucked up by a powerful vacuum cleaner.

"'The net result of this energetic condition is a period of complete darkness. This shall last for three days. Men shall experience darkness as they have never known it before, as even within a deep cave there are at least photons emanating from the decaying matter and contributing subparticles from space – some of which your scientists are completely unaware of. The more profound effects will be those on human consciousness. Although these changes will be occurring on different dimensions and planes simultaneously, how it will manifest on the gross third dimensional level is that human physiology will be subjected to a variety of frequencies – to energetic conditions – that will greatly expand human consciousness.'

[Here there is a pause and I interject questions. "Hence this merging of the 3rd, 4th, and 5th dimensions I was first told about?"] ***'Yes. But this is just a tiny glimmer of what the experience will bring. The dimensions themselves do not change. What changes is human perception.'***

["Will all humans have the same experience?"] ***'The grossest physical effects, such as the three days of darkness will be experienced by everyone. But the enhance-***

[46] See: Matthew 24:29 – NKJV

ments to human consciousness will be experienced most intensely by those who are prepared. There are many who will experience little or nothing and I will expand on this when you are ready.'

["What do you mean 'prepared'? How could one possibly prepare for such a thing?"] ***'By opening the heart (and) by working on the opening of the heart chakra — because at its core this event is all about spiritual awakening. In fact, no event has ever happened like this before, since the beginning of Creation.'***[47]

There is nothing original about the conjoining of "three days of darkness" with eschatology. Although not of Biblical origin, Christian mystics have been doing it for centuries.[48] I was somewhat uncomfortable when the information came through during my own journeys, because I had an awareness of these mystical prophecies and my concern was that their presence in my subconscious could be contaminating the purity of what was coming from Universal Mind. (By way of comparison, much of the rest of Gospel of 2012 contains material I was given which I found shocking, and even sometimes bewildering.) However, this is yet another theme that will just not go away as it pertains to "The Event."[49]

4. The Event involves the collapse of parallel universes into a single coalesced whole.

This was a feature of "The Event" that was made clear to me in my own journeys.

[47] Ibid, p. 15.

[48] See: https://en.wikipedia.org/wiki/Three_Days_of_Darkness; http://www.3daysofdarkness.com/; http://www.ewtn.com/v/experts/showmessage.asp?number=326829

[49] Examples abound – see: http://www.universe-people.com/english/texty_vytahy/htm/en/en_text_tri_dny_temnoty.htm; https://goo.gl/FzoTiZ; http://www.metatech.org/wp/spiritual-warfare/the-three-days-of-darkness-dont-go-outside/; http://www.thecallofthebride.com/3-days-of-darkness.. . . to list but a few.

["After we go through the rift, will there still be parallel universes?"] ***'There is this coalescing. It appears that if these other parallel universes did exist (after the Passage), there wouldn't be the singularity. And according to God, there wouldn't be much to celebrate.'***

"'Your experience of yourself will change because you have to be merged with all the billions of (your) other (soul fragments) that are out there, so that we are all brought together." *["and we'll be conscious of all those experiences."]* ***"And for this cycle to complete itself, not only must we have conscious awareness . . . oh, this is all about our movement from the small to the bigger, not only will we have knowledge of this life and all our previous incarnations, but of all the other fragmented parts of our soul that have resided on all the other parallel universes. This is the complete, total understanding that comes (as a result of the Event). (It is) a complete, total defragmentation of the Universe. Everything went out and got fragmented . . . and all of a sudden, in one event God is taking all of this expansiveness and He's just going, 'I want it back. Enough, I've waited long enough.'""***[50]

The idea that "The Event" brings a coalescing into a consciousness singularity is not original, either. I point out in Gospel that Terrence McKenna spoke for years about his concept of "Timewave Zero" and how the Event would bring about "a singularity of infinite complexity."[51] (It is important to note before proceeding that a "consciousness singularity" is not the same as a "technological singularity" – its artificial, exosomatic equivalent.)[52]

Numerous websites now exist that discuss variations on this theme of a coalescing into Oneness, urged in this direction

50 See: Caton, The Gospel of 2012, p. 34
51 See: Caton, The Gospel of 2012, p. 141-142
52 See: http://www.integralworld.net/powers8.html

from the effects of The Event.[53]

5. **Preparation for "The Event" matters, and central to this preparation is the cultivation of the Heart – specifically, the experience and expression of Pure Love. Those who are not prepared may not know the Event even happened or may "go insane" as a result of its effects.**

Preparation for "The Event" was a recurring theme when I did my entheogenic, exploratory work. "You have to 'earn it.'"[54]

Most intimately connected to this preparation was expansion of the heart. I was even told that the Earth was "the heart chakra of the Universe" – with three chakras below it and three above it, placing it at the metaphysical center of the Universe.[55] Imagine how surprised I was, when years after The Gospel of 2012 came out, a documentary was released called The Principle, including interviews with some of the world's leading physicists, proposing exactly that: **the Earth rests at the center of the Universe.**[56]

Doing more to add legitimacy to this film and its "principle" than the work of a thousand full-time publicists and the support of a hundred Nobel laureates were the breathtakingly bizarre things the Elite did to suppress and denigrate the movie.[57]

Again, functionally, metaphorically, and physiognomically,

[53] By way of example, see: http://divine-cosmos.net/ascension-process.htm; http://www.corelight.org/resources/returning-to-oneness/chapters/chapter-one/; https://ascension101.com/en/home/free-articles/4-march-2009/13-ascension-and-oneness.html; http://calleman.com/2017/04/17/the-36-day-period-of-the-ninth-wave-the-purpose-of-celebrating-april-18-may-24-etc/ (This is Carl Calleman's site. Be sure to read the Comment section on this link, as well.)

[54] See: Caton, The Gospel of 2012, p. 23

[55] See: Caton, The Gospel of 2012, p. 45.

[56] See: http://rockingodshouse.com/documentary-the-principle-makes-shock-claim-earth-at-center-of-universe/; http://www1.cbn.com/cbnnews/healthscience/2014/October/Film-Shocker-Does-the-Universe-Revolve-Around-Earth. See the 2:20 minute trailer for The Principle at: https://www.youtube.com/watch?v=p8cBvMCucTg

[57] "What? There's something special about the Earth's placement in the Universe? Nonsense! Let's destroy those documentarians!" See: **"Thoughtcrime: The Conspiracy to Stop The Principle"**: https://www.youtube.com/watch?v=0eVUSDy_rO0

this all seems implicit with the importance of developing the heart:

> ***"... the enhancements to human consciousness will be experienced most intensely by those who are prepared. There are many who will experience little or nothing*** *... [in response to the question of how best to prepare] ...* ***by opening the heart (and) by working on the opening of the heart chakra – because at its core this event is all about spiritual awakening[58] ... Everything will be made clear. But keep fostering love from the heart. Try to feel the love for your children; try to feel every sense of what you've known love to feel like."[59]***

The last part of the above quote intimates that humans have devolved to the point where they have to be instructed as to what real love – the most powerful and fundamental force in the Universe – might feel like. Yet, this is a recurrent theme with other visionaries, as well. Going back to Peter Duenov:

> **"The Earth, the solar system, the universe, all are being put in a new direction under the impulsion of Love. Most of you still consider Love as a derisory force, but in reality, it is the greatest of all forces! Money and power continue to be venerated as if the course of your life depended upon it. In the future, all will be subjugated to Love and all will serve it. But it is through suffering and difficulties that the consciousness of man will be awakened ... Love will manifest in such a perfect manner, that today's man can only have a very vague idea."[60]**

The connection between the "The Event" and a return to

[58] See: Caton, The Gospel of 2012, p. 15
[59] See: Caton, The Gospel of 2012, p. 27
[60] Again, see: http://www.theeventchronicle.com/metaphysics/spiritual/70-year-old-prophecy-earth-will-soon-swept-extraordinary-rapid-waves-cosmic-electricity/

Love is a constant refrain from those who have devoted themselves to unearthing the meaning of their inner visions in connection with its arrival.[61]

Going farther, in my own vision quests, I had encounters where it was communicated that Love was all that mattered:

> ***"That I want you to have a full understanding of what you are. That I have such an enormous Love and Bliss for you that I want you to share in that Love and that Bliss. The same Love and Bliss that guided Creation. The same Love and Bliss with which I watch everything you do in every moment. It is the longing of a lost lover that you never knew about. And it's your Creator, and He just wants you to have just even the smallest reflection of the enormous Love that He had when He created all of Creation, but most importantly, when He created you!***
>
> ***That is the lesson of the heart. The lesson of the heart is appreciating the enormity of the Love of the Creator. If one could truly grasp that, there is no other spiritual path needed. There is no other meditation needed. There is nothing else needed. If one could only grasp the enormity of the Love that the Creator has for His Creation. And to have that and to focus on that, the Love, (just) the Love. If you want to reduce it to something as profane as to 'how do I get my ticket.' That's it. That's it. (Know) the Love."***[62]

Far from a mere "feeling" as an internal experience, what was communicated to me was far more proactive as it related to how that Love would manifest itself:

> ***"We are the parents of this Sat Yuga. We are the ones who are birthing it in. Our job is to co-create with God***

[61] See: http://www.theeventchronicle.com/the-event/event-flash-galactic-wave-love/; http://unarius.org/wp/?cat=6; http://prepareforchange.net/event-flash-galactic-wave-love/ http://theascendedmasters.com/the-coming-cosmic-event/ . . . to name but a few

[62] See: Caton, The Gospel of 2012, p. 27-28

> ***to make it happen.*** *["How can we help?"]* ***We can help by following our dharma, following our mission, what we agreed to. Feel your way into your place. Every single lifetime you had prior to this moment contributed to what you are now and what you are doing to make this happen. Everything that came prior to this had a purpose, even though we don't understand it."***[63]

One of Alba Weinman's clients confirmed the importance of love in making the transition:

> **"The ego does not reign supreme (there, like it does here). Love reigns supreme on the New Earth.** ***"***[64]

Another feature of the "Event" is that there are those who will miss the benefits of the Event or barely experience it at all. Others may be mentally impaired from its effects. **"Many will feel as if they're going insane."**[65] I was told the same thing in 2012:

> ***"You are going to have to take the various parts of what you regard as self . . . your five senses, your ego, the various parts of yourself . . . this is why some people will go insane . . . you have to take the reins of the horse . . . it's going to get crazy. So you must take the reins of the horse and let the horse know that you are the master. You have to hold it together . . . at the same time you have the desire to experience all of this. Things are going to be fragmented for a while; things are going to get very chaotic as this happens."*** [66]

This feeling that some were going to lose their minds was

[63] See: Caton, The Gospel of 2012, p. 24

[64] Alba Weinman, session #081, Jan. 2017. See; https://www.youtube.com/watch?v=90U6ZEZIN3U&t=5162s – the relevant passage begins at 32:38.

[65] See: https://www.youtube.com/watch?v=90U6ZEZIN3U&t=5162s – Alba Weinman, session #081, go to 34:40

[66] See: Caton, The Gospel of 2012, p. 21-22

accompanied by sensations that the Event brought with it. Two stick out most prominently in my mind: one, that you would feel as if you were travelling at "warp speed" (to borrow from science fiction),[67] and that you had to "hold on." The second, was the experience of being flooded by images of "remembering," exposed to information about your present life, your previous lives, the history of the planet, the history of the universe, etc.[68]

Perhaps on account of information overload related to the "unveiling," certain people would find it difficult to maintain their sanity.

Lastly, there are a number of websites out now that provide specific instructions as it relates to preparation, and some of them provide excellent advice. Note that some of them appear dated – much like The Gospel of 2012 – but the information is still worth examining.[69]

6. **The Event involves the dissolution of all "intermediaries," which each individual communicating directly with the Creator. In other words, a complete collapse of sectoral distance.**

For my part, this was a strong impression made during my vision quests. This only makes sense, because you couldn't reverse the Great Winding unless its Unwinding brought about the entire collapse of the sectoral distance that's been an ever-present feature of the current Kali Yuga in the first place.

> ***"God wants to get rid of middlemen . . . God wants every person to know that they have a direct link to the top. They don't have to go to anybody. This is the end of middlemen. The end of intermediaries. This is about each***

[67] See: Caton, The Gospel of 2012, p. 31

[68] See: Caton, The Gospel of 2012, p. 21-23, 31

[69] See: http://www.theeventchronicle.com/metaphysics/spiritual/ascension-preparing-whats-yet-come/#; https://judysatori.com/free/daily-practice-plan/ascension-preparation-and-support-for-lightworkers/; http://www.thecominggoldenage.com/Preparing_For_Ascension.htm; http://www.sandrawalter.com/preparing-for-the-third-wave-and-timeline-shift/; https://www.bibliotecapleyades.net/esp_2012_83.htm . . . among many others

person realizing that they have a direct relationship with God. And there need be nothing in the middle of that. And that's what's going to make life on this New World so unbelievable . . ."[70]

The elimination of "middlemen" is a ubiquitous feature within the community of those who are perceiving an "event horizon," although these exact words are rarely used. You'll see terms like "awakening" or "cosmic consciousness," which point to states of consciousness where you have "God awareness" – as opposed to lesser epiphenomena that are driven by entheogenic use. Any person functioning from a higher state of consciousness has no need for any spiritual intermediary. Interestingly, Pope Francis – head of what is arguably one of the most negaciprocal organizations in human history, the Roman Catholic Church,[71] emphasized a couple of years ago that it was "dangerous" to have a personal relationship with God (Jesus),[72] which was pounced on by various Christian organizations for its absurdity.[73] This comes from the same pontiff who indicated that Americans must fall under the yoke of a World Government "as soon as possible" – for "their own good."[74]

Yes, boys and girls, once again . . . never forget that rape is good for you and that you need to thank your rapist.

(Shockingly, Pope Francis frequently makes such utterances as if The Protocols were part of his playbook. Perhaps they are.)

7. **The demonic world loses control of the souls that graduate to the "New Earth." Those who do not**

[70] See: Caton, The Gospel of 2012, p. 28

[71] I am not inherently anti-Catholic. I was raised Roman Catholic, and I attended a Catholic seminary devoted to preparation for the priesthood. Only years later did I realize that the Church had very little to do with the actual teachings of Jesus Christ. My thoughts about the evils of its actual influence were later sealed after reading Bartolome de las Casas' A Short Account of the Destruction of the Indies, (1542)

[72] See: http://yournewswire.com/pope-francis-jesus-dangerous/

[73] Example: https://joecruzmn.wordpress.com/2014/07/05/pope-francis-says-having-a-personal-relationship-with-jesus-is-dangerous-false-prophet-utters-false-words

[74] See: http://yournewswire.com/pope-francis-world-government-rule/

graduate experience millions of years of repeated reincarnations until they reach this point in the cycle again. A very negative outcome awaits those who have knowingly committed themselves to the dark side, particularly those who have done so for worldly gain.

The coming Event provides an extremely rare opportunity to escape this "prison planet." Those who miss the opportunity will be very regretful. Again, Peter Deunov:

> **"The Earth is now following an ascending movement and everyone should force themselves to harmonize with the currents of the ascension. Those who refuse to subjugate themselves to this orientation will lose the advantage of good conditions that are offered in the future to elevate themselves. They will remain behind in evolution and must wait tens of millions of years for the coming of a new ascending wave . . ."**[75]

The ascension results in freedom from demonic influence. The archonic forces lose control over those who escape:

> ***"That's why 'they're' afraid. [The dark entities that feed on human thought.] When this thing happens, it comes with this momentous sense of the arrival of the Divine . . . the more that one has been working with dark forces . . . they are exposed in a way that makes them look really bad. I'm getting the sense they fear more the sheer embarrassment of it. 'Cause the whole world's gonna know.' The whole curtain comes down. It's like, show's over . . . they lose control of all souls that graduate to the New Earth (forever)."***[76]

[75] See: http://www.theeventchronicle.com/metaphysics/spiritual/70-year-old-prophecy-earth-will-soon-swept-extraordinary-rapid-waves-cosmic-electricity/
[76] See: Caton, The Gospel of 2012, p. 38-39

8. The Event leads to balancing between male and female, correcting the many gender distortions that mark our current age.

Returning to Peter Deunov:

> **"The question of rapport between man and woman will be finally resolved in harmony; each one having the possibility of following their aspirations. The relations of couples will be founded on reciprocal respect and esteem."**[77]

I had one vision quest that emphasized the critical role of women in the perfection of society, even though the reclaiming of this role would happen on the level of consciousness:

> ***"Women are the foundation of society. They are the center of gravity of what makes a civilized society. They have lost their knowledge. Women have to be retrained to be women. (They) don't get proper training (as to how) to create a divine home. The rebuilding begins with the women, not the men . . ."***[78]

Interestingly, one site I recently discovered is dedicated exclusively to education about the Divine Feminine.[79] Others emphasize the need for both men and women to become attuned to this gender recalibration process.[80] Yet others are devoted to the sexual aspects of this retuning.[81]

Most of what sensitives are picking up deals more with

[77] See: http://www.theeventchronicle.com/metaphysics/spiritual/70-year-old-prophecy-earth-will-soon-swept-extraordinary-rapid-waves-cosmic-electricity/

[78] See: Caton, The Gospel of 2012, p. 53.

[79] See http://www.artofthefeminine.com/

[80] Examples: http://ascendedrelationships.com/surrendering-to-the-divine-feminine/; http://theonelivinglight.com/one-living-light-articles/divine-sacred-union.html; https://soulfullheartblog.com/2017/08/04/trusting-the-ascension-process-leaning-into-the-divine-feminine/; http://ascensionmessages.com/divine-masculine-and-divine-feminine/; http://boundariesarebeautiful.com/twinflamecomplexity/

[81] Example: http://thesoulmatrix.com/sexuality/sacred-sexual-energy

simply the balancing of the genders. **"We are nearing a very important portal . . . that will allow the Divine Feminine and Divine Masculine to merge into ONE."**[82]

The acknowledged need to "prepare" in this particular area is giving rise to conferences and seminars exclusively devoted to cultivating the Divine Feminine[83] I expect this trend to accelerate as we approach the Event.

9. We are suffering from spiritual atrophy. On the New Earth, we recover powers and abilities that we lost long ago.

This, too, was a recurrent theme in my own journeys.

"(Feel the) flow of creation (and make a) habit of feeling your way upstream. We have to regenerate (the) subtlety of feeling. We've lost touch with our pristine origins. Like Matrix (the movie), where you have to be nurtured to regenerate the muscles (that have long been out of use) . . . What makes it worse, we've lost the tools to escape or modify it."[84]

["After three days of darkness and a New World will we have access to free energy, teleporting?"] ***'The problem is with the way that you worded your question. That you will simply have the desire, and (then) you'll have the knowledge. You don't have to be beholden to anyone or pay for the knowledge or whatever. You'll appreciate (the) powers of mind that you have (long ago lost). Again, they're showing me this picture. They are saying, your psychic muscles are completely atrophied. And what's going to happen is that this is going to have to be re-cultivated. You'll have to get used to the experience that the issuance of a thought by you, 'I want to know this***

[82] See: https://sacredascensionmerkaba.com/2016/11/01/twin-flame-union-portal-12-21-16-divine-feminine-and-divine-masculine/

[83] Example: http://portaltoascension.org/event/divine-feminine-conference

[84] See: Caton, The Gospel of 2012, p. 29

(free energy),' could be whatever . . . that things got so dense on the third dimension and so fouled up that we've lost touch with the power of thought, with what a thought can do, what a thought is. And so when you say you want access to this or that knowledge, you will simply have the desire that you want to know this, and that thought will go out and you'll be able to have the experience of a thought going out and gathering to itself the energy, the information, that was the basis for why you issued that thought in the first place.'[85]

Several sites devote themselves to the pre-Event development of various psychic abilities,[86] or recognizing the recovery of certain psychic abilities as we approach the Event.[87]

The Internet boasts a variety of aids that assist in the process, from specific crystal stones,[88] to guides concerning the alchemical properties of specific foods,[89] to the use of mantras, sutras, and entheogenics[90] – all of which I have found useful on my explorations over these past few decades.

Some "abilities" are recovered through directed intent, as is the case with the Yoga Sutras. Others come to you when you least expect them. Regardless, "practice makes perfect."

Comments on the Timing of The Event

I've already discussed my reluctance to get into the issue of "timing," since I did such an abysmal job of attaching my

[85] See: Caton, The Gospel of 2012, p. 35

[86] Examples: http://in5d.com/how-to-refine-psychic-powers/; http://www.ascensionwithearth.com/2017/01/becoming-superhuman-complete-guide-to.html; https://www.realityfiles.com/

[87] Example: http://in5d.com/ascension-and-premonitions/; https://galacticfederationoflight.wordpress.com/2016/02/12/an-introduction-to-ascension/

[88] See: http://www.healing-crystals-for-you.com/psychic-powers.html; https://www.crystal-vaults.com/crystal-encyclopedia/crystal-guide

[89] Example: http://www.alchemylab.com/guideto.htm

[90] Example: http://realitysandwich.com/11276/psychedelics_light_yoga_sutras/; http://bluelight.org/vb/forums/48-Psychedelic-Drugs (see extensive threads on the use of psychedelic drugs, much of it related to expanding "abilities"); https://www.reddit.com/r/Psychonaut/comments/3aq45n/my_7_ceremonies_with_ayahuasca_and_how_it_has/; (this is a good example of one psychonaut's experiences after seven ayahuasca experiences. My advice: with a few hundred more ceremonies, you'll see how cumulative the benefits become)

own communications with Universal Mind to an artificial date five years ago. Although I was never "given a date," my own intellect convinced me that an association with 2012 existed, and therein I made my error. I'm finished with "date setting."

Nonetheless, since clarity increases as a temporal event gets closer, one would think that we would get a better "sense" of the Event's arrival the closer we come to it – even if no specific date is provided.

With that thought in mind, I provide the following thought-provoking developments for your consideration and meditation:

Within Christian eschatology, we can think of the "Return of Christ" and "Judgment Day" as analogous to the Event we've been describing, and within this realm, there are plenty of signs that point to a near-term Event – arguably more than at any other time in history.

One of the key points I hear from my friends in the evangelical Christian community is that "no one knows the hour or the day."[91] However, a mistranslation of this passage has led millions of Christians astray – for centuries. As David Montaigne, an intense researcher of history and prophecy – and, like myself, a past victim of unjustified date setting – aptly points out:

> **". . . they assume that we can never know future dates. But the original Greek verb 'oiden' in Matthew 24:36 is past tense. Young's Literal Translation reads 'no one hath known' – and the correct modern translation is 'no one has known' or 'no one knows yet.' No one – not even Jesus Christ – knew then, in 33 A.D. As Philippians 2:7 tells us, He 'emptied Himself, taking the form of a bond-servant, and being made in the likeness of men.' To better experience humanity, He chose not to access His divine knowledge – but only during the Incarnation."**[92]

[91] See: Matthew 24:36

[92] See: David Montaigne, Antichrist 2016-2019, Mystery Babylon, Barack Obama & The Islamic Caliphate, (2014)

Not content to remain on the sidelines when it comes to pinning dates, Montaigne does an admirable job of trying to decode ancient documents, including Biblical references, and come up with new ones. He assigns the "second Coming" as October 14, 2019, and Judgment Day as December 28, 2019.[93]

The path to arrive at these dates requires quite a bit of detail, so I won't explain it here. You have to read the book for yourself.

Although it would be easy to scoff at such estimates – and plenty of people will do this without even taking the time to examine the logic and calculations of the researcher – it is uncanny how many people in the ancient world used precisely these same methods and came up with dates remarkably close to our own present time.

A YouTuber who has a channel in the name of "C. Ervana" posted a ten minute video in May, 2016, entitled, "The End in 2016: The Shocking Predictions of 12 Mysterious Men."[94]

I think this video is important enough to make a second addendum to this book to present the facts.[95] Nonetheless, the short version is this: though influenced by Isaac Newton (who was every bit as much a Biblical scholar as he was a mathematician, physicist, and astronomer), twelve separate Bible scholars came to the conclusion that the year 2016 (or thereabouts) was the beginning of End Times. Their accounts vary, but all twelve men lived, worked, and studied in the eighteenth and nineteenth centuries. Given the great span of time between when these men wrote their works and the present time, I would be impressed if anything they saw happening occurred in the 2015-2020 timeframe. If you're an archer shooting from 100 meters, does it really matter that much if you hit the bull's eye dead center or you're one inch off from dead center?

Another interesting prophecy that's been discussed elsewhere and is remarkably prescient is "St. Malachy's Prophecy

[93] See: David Montaigne, End Times and 2019: The End of the Mayan Calendar and the Countdown to Judgement Day, http://www.adventuresunlimitedpress.com

[94] See: https://www.youtube.com/watch?v=AkHpdMhn29Q

[95] See: Appendix B

of the Popes." Covered in exhaustive detail by Thomas Horn,[96] the basic details are actually quite simple.

St. Malachy (1094-1148) was an Irish bishop. In the year 1139, he was summoned to Rome by Pope Innocent II – (not to be confused with Pope Guilty III . . . okay, that was a test to see if you're paying attention). After a 16 month journey, Malachy arrived in Rome, took care of his papal business, and upon preparing to leave his residence on Janiculum Hill, was struck by an extraordinary vision of all the future popes. Each pope is represented by a brief two or three word Latin phrase or description, beginning with Pope Celestine II, elected in 1130. At the end of this list of 112 future popes is a description of the destruction of Rome and the commencement of Judgment Day.[97] So what is the relevance here? The final pope – pope No. 112 – currently sits on the papacy: Pope Francis, Jorge Mario Bergoglio – "Petrus Romanus."

Because St. Malachy's Prophecy of the Popes' wasn't printed until 1595, many have tried to brand it a hoax – and, quite predictably, it is regarded as such by theologians of the Roman Catholic Church.[98] Never mind that the first printed book of any kind didn't even come off a Gutenberg press until 1455.[99]

Those who have carefully studied the Prophecy of the Popes as a historical record and are not theologically or politically conflicted tend to have a different impression. "It is fair to say that the majority of Malachy's predictions about successive Popes are amazingly accurate – always remembering that he gives a minimum of information."[100]

96 See: Thomas Horn and Cris Putnam, Petrus Romanus, (2012)

97 Ibid., p. 14.

98 See:http://www.huffingtonpost.com/2013/02/14/st-malachy-last-pope-prophecy-theologians-prediction-_n_2679662.html

99 See: https://www.loc.gov/exhibits/bibles/the-gutenberg-bible.html

100 See: Thomas Horn, ibid., p. 40. The quote is taken from Catholic scholar, Peter Bander von Duren.

I've taken the time to mention these "long distance" prophecies because they coincide to a remarkable degree with our time.

Additionally – and now speaking more currently – I am struck by how many of the clients who undergo QHHT hypnosis are pointing to the same time frame. I've listened to scores of taped sessions and if I had to provide a range as to when The Event would transpire, I would have to say that we're looking at late 2017 to late 2019. That's a window of approximately two years.

Once again, to be consistent with my earlier comments about "date setting," I have to say that there are no guarantees, and certainly our collective thoughts as it relates to the creation of a New Earth will affect the final date.

However, taking into accounts predictions made two or three hundred years ago, or in the case of Malachy, almost nine hundred years ago, an astonishing number of voices are all pointing to the same time period. I believe we have enough synchronicity to say that the vast majority of people who are reading this will live to experience this Event.

Its approach can only be hastened by our preparation, intent, and focus.

Chapter 9:

Preparation For The Trip : Our Journey Home

When the last living thing
has died on account of us,
how poetical it would be
if Earth could say,
in a voice floating up
perhaps
from the floor
of the Grand Canyon,
"It is done,"
People did not like it here.

Kurt Vonnegut
"A Man Without A Country"[1]
(emphasis added)

On some level, I think I've known my entire life that my current incarnation was the end of a very long journey, and I said as much in Gospel of 2012. I began this book with the keys to understanding how the most active agent in the maintenance and propagation of global, Extreme Negaprocity is leading the way in the destruction of life on our planet. The Governments of the world have taken us to a place that is unsustainable – physically, emotionally, mentally, and spiritually. Our sojourn to the far reaches of pure evil are not unlike a description given in one of Alba Weinman's sessions: "(This was an experiment) to see how far away from the Light can people survive."[2]

My current personal life has been a microcosm of this same sojourn with which I am still grappling. In my early years, going back to my childhood, I began with a sense that I was here to

[1] See: Kurt Vonnegut, A Man Without A Country, (2007), p. 137.
[2] See: Alba Weinman: "The New Earth and the Evolution of Humanity", https://www.youtube.com/watch?v=90U6ZEZIN3U&t=5162s – Go to: 25:00-26:00

evolve, to use the body as a vessel for attaining higher states of consciousness. I had experiences that were comparable to the most mysterious, ecstatic, and fulfilling as one will find in the extant, mystical literature.

As I proceeded into adulthood, I was sucked into a devolutionary whirlwind of college life, military service, business, the creation of three manufacturing companies, two failed marriages, two stints in U.S. federal prison related to my work as an herbalist, and then the realization that I could never safely return to the country of my birth – no matter what I said or did – and that I must live out the remainder of my days in exile.

There is no place left for me in this world.

With more than seven billion people currently living on the planet, it would be absurd to suggest that we have seen the complete collapse of human habitat. It's a work in progress. (You always see the greatest population bloom just before overshoot and die-off. Ask any evolutionary biologist.) What we have now is **only** the complete collapse of suitable habitat for fully functioning human beings who are spiritually aware.

I am, as author Kurt Vonnegut concluded in his final work, "a Man Without a Country," who has unwittingly found himself in the "Lunatic Asylum of the Universe."[3] And I suspect that many of the people who will choose to read this book feel the same way. Nonetheless, it is yet a better exile that we seek. Once again, if the fundamental principle of life as expressed in the Chinese I Ching is true – that "when situations proceed beyond their extremes, they alternate to their opposites,"[4] then our journey home can only be filled with light, love, and an inexpressible joy that we cannot – even now – imagine. No one may know the timing, but our way must be clear, our minds calm, and our spirits aware. For "only the bright and the gentle can overcome the dark and unyielding."[5]

So even now, I find myself returning to the values of my

[3] See: Vonnegut, Ibid, p. 121.

[4] See: Taoist Master Alfred Huang, The Complete I Ching, Inner Traditions, (1998), p.20.

[5] Ibid. (The Complete I Ching), p. 300. A more elegant explanation is provided for Gua #36, Ming Yi (Brilliance Injured) or "earth over fire."

youth – the result of self-reflection, where I was able to look at myself and identify with a lyric from an earlier time: "I was so much older then. I'm younger than that now."[6]

It's not as easy as it used to be. Sure, the practice of pranayama, meditation, and siddhis are simple enough. At my age, there are hatha positions I can't do anymore, and I lack some of the clarity I had in my twenties, but there is a refined sense of purpose and direction that I have not previously had. The chess pieces of life may not appear as clearly, but I know many more moves and strategic combinations. "Young men know the rules. Old men know the exceptions."

We live in a Universe given birth through the powerful, irrepressible combination of boundless Love and intensity of focused Thought. I have come to believe that only through our feeble attempts to imitate and utilize this creative combination can we meet the Hand that is about to extend itself and attain our Salvation – and I use that word in the broadest possible sense.

The more time I spend focusing on the New Earth and a renewed life involving the collapse of sectoral distance, the clearer it comes into focus. I understand better now an earlier revelation:

> **"Prior to the Passage happening we should be cultivating a certain celebratory mood. You'll facilitate the birthing of it. It's like your expectation of it (affects the outcome). God is actually asking us to be co-creators. Realize that this is the awakening. This is your time. He's not wanting it to be . . . like we just (insouciantly) put cat food in the (cat) dish. Have some respect for it. Cultivate this kind of celebratory mood, in the sense that we co-creators will help create a world that is renewed . . ."**[7]

[6] Taken from: "My Back Pages" by Bob Dylan (1964), made popular by The Byrds, (1967), https://www.youtube.com/watch?v=h80l4XIPJC4

[7] See: Caton, Gospel of 2012, p. 24

Sometimes our intuition can reveal things to us that sit in the foreground, and we appreciate the immediacy of what subsequently transpired. Other times, the intensity of our visions can reveal things that we only think are immediate, but our impatience and anticipation mask the longer gestation period that is required to give birth to these premonitions.

In this effort, I have come to better understand previous intimations that tell me what I must do – what ANY of us must do – who have had enough of the joys of psychopathocracy. I see with greater clarity this final communiqué that came to me in 2012 – a perfected message to an imperfect messenger, and in this I can see my destiny:[8]

". . . Now that you have some inkling of the immense possibilities that await us as we approach the Passage — however this event manifests for each of us. The most important question is: What will you do about it? If you are like me, there are serious questions that remain, and if there is anything in the text itself which elicits, 'This is unbelievable,' you are in good company. However, if I have managed to accomplish anything at all with you, I certainly hope that it is the kindling of a desire on your part to "own your own truth." I have been told repeatedly that as we approach the Event, we will have the opportunity to communicate with the Divine through the opening in the heart so that we can obtain our own 'direct connection' to reality.

In this sense we are *all* chosen. The Divine wants all of us to take our "vision quests" seriously — no matter what material aids from nature you use (or don't use) in your effort to resolve this yearning we have all felt for so long. And my belief is that in moments unexpected, you will find (as I have) these unanticipated "clues" that will point you in the right direction. The more energy you put into the search, the more you will attract the answers that will bring you home.

This very morning before breakfast, I was standing on my

[8] What follows is a rewriting of The Gospel of 2012 According to Ayahuasca, p. 131-134. Hundreds of vision quests later, it is one of the most powerful messages I have ever received.

porch, communing with the clouds above — a practice I had seen my mother do so many times. Suddenly I was overcome with sensations that I realized I had never experienced before. At first I thought I was feeling a 'frozen moment'— that deep silence that exists between each note within the symphony that is a human life. . . but no, this was something more. As I used my heart to settle in deeper to what this sensation might be, I realized that I was experiencing a narrowing of the 'ley lines' or 'magnetic flux' in the time-space continuum. I can't think of any other words to describe it. Like the grain of sand in the hour glass, I was feeling the pull of the vortex that will eventually take all of us out of the "upper globe" and into "time past." I was feeling the speeding up of events, the accelerated global chaos born of frantic desperation emanating from the Anti-Singularity — and in that very moment I heard one of my spirit guides whisper in my ear with unusual solemnity: 'Hold onto the reins . . . It's already started.'

I have no doubt that you too will experience something very similar in the near future. But still . . . how will you perceive your experience, as a spectator or participant? As one who leaves fate to chance or as one who has accepted the Divine Invitation to help forge a New Earth?

And this is the promise of the Singularity: a New Earth — a state of interconnectedness where the true happiness of one demands the happiness of all, where the ebb and flow of life is experienced as never-ending waves of Love and Bliss — that same clay in the hands of the potter that set Creation into motion. Not as a conjecture, a philosophy, a system, a creed, a belief, a faith, some therapeutic healing balm to treat the wounded soul that feels it can't stand one more day in an unspeakably corrupt world. Not as something to be thought about — but something to be lived. This is the state of knowingness that transcends all teachings, all spiritual practices, and the perverting influences of eons of propagandistic fog that filled the vacuum that was created when we forgot who we were, where we came from, and the intense Love and Affection from which we were conceived.

The return Home is not automatic. It will require some effort, and we have so little time to get it right — a mere matter of years, perhaps even a few months. But it is more than possible . . . in fact we should feel that it is inevitable. Having fallen off the ship of Divine Love and hopelessly, frantically, struggled in the cold ocean water below for countless lives, we are finally being thrown a lifeline. All we have to do is grab it and hold on for dear life. How tragic it would be if we missed the opportunity to grab that line . . . before our ship sails off into the horizon . . . never to be seen again.

In the session of May 2nd, I asked the Divine to (let me) experience on the level of heart, in a more intimate way, what life would feel like on the New Earth. I needed to experience emotionally what it felt like to be there. It was the last in a series of pleadings to tether myself to an existence I was allowed to channel, but which my ever-nagging intellect told me was too good to be true.

In an instant I was transported to the most spectacular garden I had ever seen — on this planet or any of the other worlds I have been privileged to visit. I saw strange structures, geometric shapes and symbols that strangely appeared to have been created to make the plants happier. The experience of communication between people, animals, plants — with everything in one's environ was experienced as the passage of thought within a unified whole. I immediately noticed that in something so ordinary as the movement of a hand, arm, the turning of my head to look at something, the shift of my eyes from one charming plant to another — all beckoning me to give them attention — there was the experience of life as waves. Soft, gentle, loving waves — as if wadding through warm, shallow water and experiencing even the tiniest change in current, but infinitely less dense.

I could do nothing without feeling my interconnectedness with everything and everyone else around me. Every moment was magical, and every experience inspired awe. The joyfulness was incredibly intense. Even in the simple act of breathing in and out there was this rhythmic ebb and flow of love that produced a thrilling sensation I found most indescribable. The experience of having an unhappy moment seemed completely foreign to the very place itself. There was a beauty to my surroundings — between the gardens, animal paddocks, flowing brooks, bird feeders, simple thatched-roof dwellings — that words cannot describe. There was richness to life — everywhere and in every moment — that told me that there could be no other place in time or space that made me feel more at home.

In fact, that was it. This was Home. This was where I was meant to be. This was what I had been searching for through millions of lives. Only now I was experiencing the ultimate resolution to a search for which there could be no greater outcome. It was as if I had spent many millions of years trying to open a door with an unending series of keys that failed to budge the lock — and now finally, I was given the key that would spring the lock and allow me to open the door.

Naysayers may say that this is all a pipe dream. I'm sure there are those who feel that such experiences are only possible with the use of hallucinogens — not appreciating the irony that for those of us with extensive experience in the inter-dimensional realms, it is the return to this planet, in its current condition, that is the ultimate "bad trip." But even without so many entheogenic journeys, I can still feel what life can be, could be, and should be. I can feel the ultimate conclusion to My Purpose — a proper conclusion to which no substitute will do.

So, too, must you feel the conclusion to your journey . . . and accept no inferior substitute.

This is your call to channel all of your pain, disgust, loneliness, dismay, and bewilderment into the fashioning of the Life Divine.

Life as you know it was meant to be lived.

Life as you know you were meant to live it.

You — and everyone else who hears the siren call of the Divine at this special time — are the 'strange attractors' of chaos theory. You are that one perfectly-timed flutter of the butterfly's wing that has the power to completely reorder Creation.

As we proceed together towards the Event and you intensify your 'personal search,' you will find that you are not alone. You will find that there are opportunities to network with other awakening hearts that can feel the same call. Synchronicities will guide you when you least expect them. Then you will find that an image of the New Earth is emerging not because it was sitting there waiting for you to find it . . . rather, it came into existence with the Love and Grace of a Creator — the long lost lover you had long forgotten — who has waited billions of years to get you back.

And together you created it."

Appendix A

Background: In the summer of 2004 I wrote the following piece as a proposed "chapter" to a book concept I had recently come up with called "Meditopia." It is relevant to much of the material in "The Joys of Psychopathocracy," so I present the following excerpt here as an Appendix. (Original is posted at: http://meditopia.org/old/chap5_2004.htm).

Entropy & Caton's Exosomatic Axis

"[Classical thermodynamics] is the only physical theory of universal content which I am convinced, that within the framework of applicability of its basic concepts will never be overthrown."

Albert Einstein[1]
(1879-1955)

"All the evidence suggests that we have consistently exaggerated the contributions of technological genius and underestimated the contributions of natural resources."

Stewart L. Udall[2]

The very manner in which we define intelligence is integrally linked to the use of tools – the ability to take objects from our surroundings and use them not only to survive and expand the range of our influence, but to reorder Nature and create contorted artificialities of which no other known species on this Earth is capable.

[1] See: G. Tyler Miller, Jr., Energetics, Kinetics and Life: Ecological approach, (1971). p. 46.

[2] See: William R. Catton, Jr., Overshoot: The Ecological Basis of Revolutionary Change, (1980). p. xv. I. Catton's book is now considered a classic in ecological sociology, and the quote cited is taken from the "Foreword" by Stewart L. Udall.

As it pertains to the field of medicine, this has turned out to be more than a mixed blessing.

Anthropologists use **endosomatic** to describe our organs, our extremities – the limited physical components of what we call our bodies. They use **exosomatic** to describe these tools, these instruments – the array of physical helpers that are NOT a part of our body that we use to reorder our environment. The expansive distinction between the purely endosomatic and the purely exosomatic provides, in my opinion, a perfect metaphor for what guides us to, or away from, optimal healing.

That metaphor is the purpose of this chapter.

My first exposure to the concept came a quarter century ago (1980) in my initial reading of Rifkin's Entropy. But I did not realize the importance of how entropy affects our lives until I saw its effects close up, relative to the corruption of organized medicine.

For those of you who have either forgotten or just circumvented your high school physics course, entropy is a concept of physics which tells us that in any closed system (excepting the intake of sunlight from 93 million miles away, and the miniscule influence of various celestial bodies, planet Earth is a fairly closed system), the amount of energy available to do work (be it in the form of oil, coal, timber, etc.) is finite, and so without the infusion of additional, usable energy from outside the system, deterioriation results. Within the system, you see orderliness (high energy state) become disorderliness (low energy state); organization become chaos; action become inaction; efficiency become inefficiency; life (again, high energy state) become death (low energy state), etc. Most of what you and I call "progress" (negative entropy) – or what we might think of as a defiance of entropy – is nothing more than an acceleration of it through an increased rate of energy resource usage. We create increasing order, wealth, opulence, high society – the good life – by creating disorderliness somewhere else. Entropy can be minimized by living in harmony with the environment – what ecologists call "sustainability," but you never completely escape it.

Entropy is an immutable law of the universe.

This concept is derived from the laws of thermodynamics, which Rifkin summarizes with: "The total energy content of the universe is constant, and the total entropy is continually increasing."[3]

The relationship that exists between low entropy (greater energy and orderliness, lower rate of consumption in the use of surrounding energy) and higher entropy (less energy, more disorderliness, higher rate of consumption in the use of surrounding energy) has a direct correlation between what I call endosomatic-dominant and exosomatic-dominant systems of work. For example, if I walk down the block to buy some orange juice at the convenience store (endosomatic), I use a tiny fraction of the energy, measurable in ergs, that I would use if I got into my car (exosomatic) and made the same round trip.

"Man has 'wants' which he likes to regard as 'needs.' He has basic physiological needs for food and drink. He has other elementary wants for clothing and heating. Finally he has, as it were, 'high standard' wants, like reading, listening to music, travelling, amusing himself. Human wants have no upper limit, but they have a lower limit – the minimum food necessary to maintain life."

Carlo M. Cipolla[4]

Modern civilization, as we know it, has been made possible by a movement away from endosomatic solutions for life – to those that are exosomatic. We are tool users on steroids, and at our present rate of resource consumption to create, use, service,

[3] The classical definitions of the two classical laws of thermodynamics are: (1) "Energy can be changed from one form to another, but it cannot be created or destroyed. The total amount of energy and matter in the Universe remains constant, merely changing from one form to another. The First Law of Thermodynamics (Conservation) states that energy is always conserved, it cannot be created or destroyed. In essence, energy can be converted from one form into another." When my father was in school, this was also referred to as Humboldt's Law (1848); and (2) what is often called "The Entropy Law," namely, "that in all energy exchanges, if no energy enters or leaves the system, the potential energy of the state will always be less than that of the initial state."

[4] See: Carlo M. Cipolla, The Economic History of World Population, (1974). p. 35.

and replace our beloved tools, we are bringing civilization to a roadblock unlike the world has ever seen – a conclusion that can be readily drawn just on the basis of our dependence on non-renewable oil, the lack of any reasonable technology on the drawing board that will cost effectively replace it – in TIME, its ubiquitous use in personal transportation, commercial shipping, energy production, manufacturing (steel, plastics, chemical, etc.), agriculture – well, just about every facet of our lives – and then there's the irrefutability of Hubbert's Peak,[5 6 7 8 9] the greatest implication of which is, we will begin to run out of food relative to our world population "load," concurrent with running out of oil . . .

But never mind all that . . . 'tis a trifling matter.

Let's get back to medicine.

In a society with a cultural infrastructure devoted to a highly specialized, highly entropic, highly exosomatic orientation, the one area that most rebels against "the machine" is people, the person, the human body, us!

A human being is not a car, a house, a television, or a cellphone. All those things are exosomatic. So you can improve upon them by using exosomatic methods. But the human body is not one of our exosomatic tools. It is us. It is a well-crafted creation of Nature, not an artificial construct we created in a laboratory or manufacturing plant. In no other area has modern

[5] See: Richard Heinberg, The Party's Over: Oil, War and the Fate of Industrial Societies, (2003). I could list 50 more references I have on this subject – all of them good – but since this is tangential and not terribly relevant to our current focus, I'll just list this one reference, plus the next four – since they approach the issue from slightly different angles.

[6] See: Kenneth S. Deffeyes, Hubbert's Peak: The Impending World Oil Shortage, (2001).

[7] See: C.J. Campbell, The Coming Oil Crisis, (1997).

[8] See: Justin Lahart, "Oil-Price Forecasts Seem to Miss Upward Trend," WSJ, p. C-3, May 19, 2004. In case you think the oil shortage issue is a far-fetched doom and gloom issue, this Wall Street Journal article is an intellectual dose of ephedra. Deffeyes, a former Princeton geology professor, who has spent more than 30 years studying Hubbert's Peak, believes that world oil production "is set to peak on Thanksgiving Day, 2005, give or take a few weeks." His colleague, Tom Petri, head of Petrie Parkman, a Denver investment bank specializing in energy, says, "I spent the first 12 years of my career thinking Hubbert was wrong . . . and I spent the next 20 realizing how right he was." This doesn't spell "doom" in 2005. But it does signal that the era of cheap oil is over. We're now down to "resource wars." Want to know why we really went to Afghanistan and Iraq? Read Michael T. Klare's \ Resource Wars: The New Landscape of Global Conflict, Henry Holt & Company, 2001.

[9] See: Thom Hartmann, The Last Hours of Ancient Sunlight, (1998)

civilization failed us more than in the area of medicine – and the power elite have used all its powers of advertising, persuasion, regulation, education, and obfuscation to try and convince us that exosomatic methods employed on Nature's most perfect endosomatic specimen are the only right way.

Upon what scientific, or moral, or ethical, or legal . . . meat doth this, our Medical Establishment, feed that it is so corrupt? The answer is, it feeds on the supremely misguided notion that you can achieve perfection by forcing exosomatic methods on an endosomatic system.

And for all the modern medical apologists who would attempt to argue that increased longevity, or decreased infant mortality, or falling rates of infectious disease, are a sign of unqualified success, there is an even more powerful argument that modern medicine and its brethren in the industrial community have brought us lives of untold ecological destruction, financial servitude, marginally functioning immune systems, limited vision, and a disconnectedness from our natural roots and the wisdom, as a people, that we could only obtain and sustain through a communion with the Earth and her natural bounty.

You will not understand what this means unless you can grasp the nature of the continuum, the Axis – as I call it –through which we pass from the endosomatic to the exosomatic, and the inherent trade-offs that result.

In the table below, you will find four categories that mark changes in properties, attitudes, approach as you proceed from Pure Endosomatic to Pure Exosomatic. As you read through the Table, if you have any intuitive sensibilities at all, you will get the "gist" of this reality to the point where you could well add categories of your own. It is only important to get the basic concept, because, together with the material on Occam's Razor, this material forms core building blocks that are needed to understand the material in later chapters.

Conventional medical thinkers will find portions of the Table quite offensive.

Tough.

If you "get" the concepts, it doesn't matter if you agree or disagree with any one or more particular positions or attributes I ascribe to any part of the table. You will only internalize and accept what your consciousness allows you to anyway.

Caton's Exosomatic Chart begins on the next page.

Caton's Exosomatic Axis

Axial Progression	Pure Endosomatic	Endosomatic dominant / Exosomatic subordinate	Exosomatic dominant / Endosomatic subordinate	Pure Exosomatic
Definitional Overview & Basic Properties				
Seed Concept	Me. My body, mind & spirit -- and my connections to the non-physical world. The greatest, most valuable tools I use are those that are within myself -- and in my relationship with the non-physical, be that identified as God, an unmanifest Supreme Good, etc.	The emphasis is on my person. The "tools" in my environment are utilized in a sustainable way, because consciousness at this level respects the interconnectedness between "me" and the environment that is "not me."	The emphasis is on the objectified outer world -- but there is a still a knowingness of the value of the subjective.	Man is defined by his ability to maximize the utility of his "tools." The Inner Man, the subjective value of humanity, is most suppressed at this stage.
General Orientation	The answer is within us. Whatever problem that can arise from within, can be solved from within. A failure to recognize this emanates from ignorance and a lower state of consciousness.	The answer to our problems starts from within. The solutions outside of us must take the "inner" into consideration.	The solution resides outside of us, but it is helpful not to forget that the inner component is a contributing factor.	Man defines his very intelligence -- indeed, his superiority over apes -- by his ability to use tools. Our solutions clearly reside in objective reality. Science and technology, regardless of discipline, theoretical or applied, dictate that we find solutions by mastering Nature, which is clearly external to whatever we define as "ourselves."
Consciousness	Highest level of consciousness or "self-actualization." Highest level of spiritual development. Spirit -- rarified.	Lower level of consciousness. More density in physical matter.	Still lower level of consciousness. Man's absorption in the physical world is high, and his consciousness of non-physical worlds is lower still.	The lowest level of consciousness. This level of consciousness has given way to our current mechanistic worldview, as well as our twisted systems of legal, moral, and ethical relativism.
Complexity	Tend to be simple.	More complex.	And still more complex.	Most complex.
Cooperation versus Competition	Cooperative. At this end of the axis, the fabric of unity that ties all humanity together is self-evident. Competition is seen as selfish and unnecessary.	Less cooperative with some competition, but cooperation is dominant.	More competitive with some cooperation, but competition is dominant.	Most competition. Even "apparent" cooperation has competitive overtones.

Caton's Exosomatic Axis				
Axial Progression	Pure Endosomatic	Endosomatic dominant / Exosomatic subordinate	Exosomatic dominant / Endosomatic subordinate	Pure Exosomatic
Definitional Overview & Basic Properties				
Specialization	Least specialized. Most generalized. Comfortable operating in the abstract. Mimics an Indian proverb about the process of becoming 'enlightened': "A man who controls a fortress automatically controls all the paths leading up to the fortress. Focus on controlling the fortress and not the paths!"	More specialized. Not quite as generalized. Slightly more concrete. Here there is still the understanding that great healing draws from the wellspring of the great generalist. Another Indian proverb: "Water the root to enjoy the fruit."	Still more speciliza-tion. Even less generalized. Still more concrete.	Maximum tendency towards specialization. Least generalized. Everything is concrete and there is discomfort operating in the abstract. In a highly mechanistic environment, everything must appear in great detail, every 't' crossed, every 'i' dotted. A generalist is a specialist wannabe.
Thermo-dynamic Effect	Low entropy. Takes the least energy away from its environment, and puts the most back in.	More entropic.	And still more entropic.	Most entropy. Exosomatic systems of healing steal the most from their environment and put the least back in.
Ultimate Source of Healing: Inner to outer; subjective to objective; mind to matter.	Man is, above all things, a spiritual being. The ultimate source of all healing resides INSIDE him. Whatever healing tools are employed, they are extensions of what is within us.	The spirit and mind of man must be taken into primary consideration. Healing cannot take place if the mind of the patient is not properly predisposed -- without observing this principle, a doctor is only addressing gross physical symptoms.	The mind of man is a concern -- after all, do not many illnesses have a psychosomatic component? Nonetheless, the tools of healing largely stand on their own merit, independent of what the patient does or does not think.	Everything that is necessary to heal man's ills resides OUTSIDE him. Science tells us that we can only know reality by adhering to the truth of objectivity -- for subjectivity can only fail us.
Modalities: Systems of healing, methods, products, and protocols as they reside along the Exosomatic Axis.	Faith and 'psychic' healing practices, power of positive thinking, Reiki, therapeutic massage, chiropractic and osteopathic subluxation manipulations, 'psychic surgery'; exercise, hatha yoga, and related practices.	Nutrition and diet; natural vitamin / mineral supplementation; herbology (phytopharmacology / ethnobotanical medicine), iatrochemistry (involving naturally occurring minerals and compounds), balneology, bio-oxidative therapy, etc.	Artificial diet supplementation (or compound not as readily assimilated as from natural sources); minor surgery, pharmacologicals involving compounds that are close to those of natural sources (i.e. phytopharmacology, etc.)	Those farthest from man's natural origins: this would include most of the drugs now on the market in the West; chemotherapy with chemical compounds not found in nature, radiation treatment, radical surgery, etc. Those in this group tend to be immunosuppressive in some way; not immunosupportive -- a propensity to work one's will ON nature instead of work WITH nature.

Caton's Exosomatic Axis				
Axial Progression	Pure Endosomatic	Endosomatic dominant / Exosomatic subordinate	Exosomatic dominant / Endosomatic subordinate	Pure Exosomatic
Between Unmanifest & Manifest				
Relationship Between Spiritual & Material Describe using set theory.	The spiritual (God) is the master set. All things in the material world are a subset of this reality -- for all things in the material are given birth by the Divine. 'As above -- so below.' All members of the material set are contained in the spiritual set.	The material world is subordinate to the spiritual. But the material is its own reality. I try to work in the 'intersection' set.	All things spiritual are a subset of a much larger Universe where the laws of nature are both material in nature and paramount. There is no intersection set.	The laws of science are the "master set." Things that appear to be spiritual can all be explained in strictly scientific terms. The mechanistic view of the Universe reigns supreme. Not only is there no intersection set; there is no spiritual set.
Role of Spirituality: On the part of patient or practitioner, what role belief in the Divine or Higher Power or Spirituality contributes to the healing process.	Central to the healing process. Heavy reliance on the 'innate intelligence of the body' by practitioner, and usually patient. 'Man does not live by bread alone, but by every Word that comes from the mouth of God . . .' 'If you but had the Faith of a mustard seed . . .' 'By Faith you are healed . . .'	Still a primary component of the healing process, followed closely by the right material means outside the body and observance of the scientific method.	May or may not have some influence. But our true faith must exist in science and the discovery of the helpful, mechanistic forces that exist outside the body. For science, by definition, we know -- and our spiritual beliefs are only conjecture.	Exists for those who believe in quack medicine. God is dead. Religion is the opium of the masses. Only gullible people believe in such things. Nutrition is unimportant or over-emphasized by quacks. Science will cure all our ills. A Higher Power exerts influence over my medical outcome? Oh please!
Human In Relationship With the Divine	We're spiritual beings having a human experience. [Deepak Chopra]	We're human beings, where the spiritual should matter more than the material.	We're human beings -- material (the seen) by nature. The spiritual (the unseen) is a secondary part of our nature.	We're material beings. Spirituality, at its best, is mere unprovable conjecture.

Caton's Exosomatic Axis				
Axial Progression	Pure Endosomatic	Endosomatic dominant / Exosomatic subordinate	Exosomatic dominant / Endosomatic subordinate	Pure Exosomatic
Between Unmanifest & Manifest				
Role of God In Healing Process: Our 'relationship" with that role.	"GOD is my partner in the healing process. There is nothing I do that does not come from the spiritual. I carry this view if I am a practitioner ... or I am a patient."	"GOD is important in my life, and my attention on the spiritual component of the healing process works closely with the material."	"GOD or the spiritual element plays a part, but science is the most critical component in the process."	"GOD has nothing to do with healing. Healing is a science, pure and simple. I'll go this far and no farther. If the patient 'thinks' that his or her outlook, or spirituality, or some other non-scientific mumbo-jumbo is helping them, it's fine with me."
Good Vs. Evil	Pure Goodness.	Goodness has the upper hand over Evil.	Evil has the upper hand over Goodness.	At its extreme, Evil reigns supreme. After all, can we even say that goodness exists? Isn't goodness an artificial, subjective value? [Moral relativism].
Mind Vs. Matter	Mind (spirit) over Matter. The physical universe follows causatively from the Word (thought).	Mind can influence Matter.	Mind and matter can influence each other. The role of Mind is just one among many.	The laws of science are immutable. Matter over mind.
Light Vs. Darkness	"I work from the Light. I see Darkness as an absence of Light."	"I draw from the Light. But I am adept at working in the many shades of Grey."	"I work in the Dark, because the Earth resides in Darkness, with occasional help from the Light."	"There is only Darkness. It is the Light that is an illusion."
Form Vs. Substance	Substance follows Form. Form is acknowledged as the all-powerful causative factor.	More attention on Form -- and Substance follows.	More attention on Substance -- and Form follows.	Substance is all that matters. Form is an illusion used to control our objectives.

Caton's Exosomatic Axis				
Axial Progression	Pure Endosomatic	Endosomatic dominant / Exosomatic subordinate	Exosomatic dominant / Endosomatic subordinate	Pure Exosomatic
The Medical Intermediary				
Physician's Subjective View of His Role	"I am at my best when I am in tune with the Divine Healer within me." "I am but an Instrument, a Facilitator of Spirit." . . . "Not my will, but Thine be done."	"I draw inspiration from intuition and other subjective components of Mind that aren't taught in medical school."	"Adherence to proven medical principles is paramount, though I admit that some 'help from above' doesn't hurt."	"I am God."
Physician's Attitude To Compensation	"Helping my patients is paramount. If I devote all my attention to the wellness of those under my care, God will take care of my needs. I am uncompromising in doing what is best for my patient -- for my aid to my fellow man is part and parcel of my relationship with the Divine" . . . "As ye do to the least of my Brethren, so you do unto Me . . ." My best work DOES make me wealthy -- but with a wealth that cannot be measured merely in bank deposits.	"Helping my patients is what is uppermost on my mind. The products, services, and protocols I employ must benefit the patient or I will not use them. I charge my patient a fair rate for what I do. I need to be properly compensated for my talents and abilities, but I put the welfare of my patients over my desire to make money. In fact, I would give up my practice before I would allow a regulatory or other authorative body to force me to use methods that I suspected were not beneficial to my patients."	"Getting paid comes first. I do whatever I can to help my patient, but regardless of the outcome, practicing medicine is a business -- and those who foolishly forget this will not have a successful practice. Nevertheless (and secondarily), I will not use a product or protocol if I have any reason to believe it will harm the patient."	"Medicine is a business. You are in it to make money. The diagnostic techniques we use, drugs we prescribe, services we render, must earn a profit. If I make a referral, I expect a fee. There are recommenda-tions I make that I know will not help some of my patients, but as long as 'it's legal' and I've covered myself to the letter of the Law, I'm fine with it. I use techniques on my patients that I wouldn't think of using on members of my own family. I would never take the risk of saving a patient's life if it meant that I would lose money ... or risk my license."

Caton's Exosomatic Axis				
Axial Progression	Pure Endosomatic	Endosomatic dominant / Exosomatic subordinate	Exosomatic dominant / Endosomatic subordinate	Pure Exosomatic
The Medical Intermediary				
Medicine & The Role of Profitability	Marginally profitable compared to exosomatic approaches -- simply because money is not where the focus is . . . "I put the mission before the commission . . . " Again, the wealth that a practitioner obtains through adhering to endosomatic practices cannot be measured in money alone.	Always self-supporting -- because money still makes the world go round. But the best rewards, for both practitioner and patient, are still well outside the domain of money.	Probably quite profitable, because earning a profit is a primary concern. But the welfare of the patient is still important.	Very profitable. After all -- you don't support a medical product unless it has the potential to make money. Good medicine and good business go hand in hand. And good business, by definition, means you're earning good money. The relationship is linear: you make MORE MONEY because good business becomes better business. And better business means better medicine -- a kind of monetary biofeedback.

Caton's Exosomatic Axis				
Axial Progression	Pure Endosomatic	Endosomatic dominant / Exosomatic subordinate	Exosomatic dominant / Endosomatic subordinate	Pure Exosomatic
Law, Politics & Other Artificial Constructs				
The Source Of Authority Centralized vs. Localized	The ultimate source of authority is the individual, the endosomatic wellspring. So authority is localized -- what is closest and most empowering to the individual. All endosomatic, low entropy cultures share a decentralized political system.	Movement towards more centralization. As we move along the exosomatic axis, the specialization of tools brings the opportunity to create 'power cells,' and these can only be consolidated through progressive centralization. Localized, dominant; centralized, subordinate.	Some authority is localized, but the emphasis is on centralization. Centralized, dominant; localized, subordinate.	Centralization rules -- in political structure, standards, laws, etc. Localized authority exists but is dwarfed by the power and dominance of centralized authoritative entities.
The Role Of Law In Healing	Natural Law is the foundation of healing in its purest form. We can only degrade healing when we depart from Natural Law.	Doing what's right takes precedent over the 'letter of the law.'	The 'letter of the law,' unfortunately, is still the law. You have to follow the Law even if you know it isn't right. Life is about compromises.	Medicine is business. Business needs protection. Law provides protection. What is "right" is not the issue, because rightness is subjective.
Patents & Proprietary Claims	Endosomatic methods of healing, by their nature, are not patentable. No one, but God, can claim ownership. When healers do their best work they are still just borrowing something they know belongs to no mere man. True healers know that real medical knowledge rests in a realm that is beyond money, patents, proprietary claims, monopolies, and, indeed, all manner of commerce. Such things belong to artificial, economic and political constructs that WE create. They are foreign to Nature and to Natural Law.	Various medical practitioners or groups may have their 'formulary secrets,' or elements of their work not in the 'public domain,' fleeting and temporary though these claims may be. Nonetheless, every conscientious practitioner knows that the source of their best work resides in a field of life and thought that is beyond the gross material plane. It resides in the "collective unconscious" for all to see, if they merely develop their Inner Vision.	Good medicine is rooted in progress and you promote progress by providing incentives to protect proprietary invention. That goes for every area of technology, not just medicine. That the source of such inventiveness may come from areas of life that reside outside commerce and the more practical areas of human endeavor doesn't marginalize the need to enforce effective, proprietary systems that make progress possible.	Again, medicine is business. You cannot have good business without respect for intellectual property rights. Great medical inventions come from people -- not God, angels, fairies, or other unseen forces. Strictly enforced patent law makes medical progress possible. If a medical product or procedure isn't patentable, it is, no doubt, inferior. Medical progress -- the forward march of scientific achievement through time -- moves us forward, not backward. And the incentive to make money by providing proprietary protection cannot be divorced from good medicine.

Caton's Exosomatic Axis				
Axial Progression	Pure Endosomatic	Endosomatic dominant / Exosomatic subordinate	Exosomatic dominant / Endosomatic subordinate	Pure Exosomatic
Law, Politics & Other Artificial Constructs				
Imputations To Time	Natural Law exists outside linear time, as we know it. As the old proverb states: "There is nothing new under the sun" -- capturing the limitations of a linear view of time, discovery, and evolution that a less expansive view can only truncate. A highly evolved healer knows that by tapping into the collective unconscious, the akashic records, call it what you will, he operates outside of time. He draws from the same inspirational sources that healers did 3,000 years ago, assuming they had the same level of awareness. Discovery, advancement, evolution, or well-being cannot be measured in time; they are rooted in pure consciousness which knows no time.	Although medical advances have appeared to accrue over time, we still adhere to those practices that work. Our allegiance is to what helps the patient. Just because something is old, doesn't mean it isn't effective; just because it's proprietary doesn't make it better. Just because it makes more money, doesn't mean we should employ it. Conversely, just because a medical technique is new, doesn't mean it is superior to a tried and true method that is over 1,000 years old.	Emphasis should be placed on using the newest and best. Medical progress IS linear. We get better at what we do all the time. We are better healers today than our brethren one hundred years ago. They were better than those one hundred years before them, and so on. History clearly reflects that the advancement of medicine has occurred over time. Nonetheless, a real healer is still an empiricist: he doesn't ignore older healing techniques if a newer one fails to benefit the patient.	Since medicine is business and good business demands progress, it only stands to reason that all regulatory and legal forces should be deployed at protecting the latest medical developments. These developments occur over time. Time is the ubiquitous foundation for how we measure our work, evaluate our advances, and determine quantitatively our profitability. All good things come from a strict adherence to linear time. The absence of this adherence brings chaos.

Appendix B

Below are notes related to the "C_Ervana" YouTube posting mentioned in Chapter 8. As I stated previously, it is astonishing that men who lived in the 1700s and 1800s would come to a collective agreement as to an "end time" – the time we currently live in – exactly when everything appears to be becoming unhinged.

THE END in 2016:

(or roughly the 2015-2020 time frame)

The SHOCKING Predictions of 12 Mysterious Men[1]

Published on May 7, 2016

This video covers 12 men who made predictions about a time period from 2015-2016. These men come from diverse backgrounds, nationalities, and time periods, and yet, they all seem to arrive at the same time frame for the unfolding of prophetic events. Some of these men predicted the destruction of the Vatican, others predicted the beginning of the millennial kingdom, others predicted the coming of the Antichrist, some predicted the coming of the Messiah, and still others believed that the window of the church would close after a 2000 year ministry of the Holy Spirit.

Without a doubt, 2016 was the year to watch among these scholars. Many of them appear to be influenced by the predictions of Isaac Newton, and they cited him in connection with 2016. These men held to a historicist interpretation of scripture, which meant that prophecy was gradually unfolding throughout history. Most believers now are futurists, meaning that they believe prophecy will be accomplished in a short span of time set in the future. Despite this, it is unusual that so many theologians across several centuries seemed to agree with each other on the time frame, and that this pointed to 2015-2016 for the accom-

[1] See: https://www.youtube.com/watch?v=AkHpdMhn29Q

plishment of major biblical events.

Please note: None of this video is my own prophecy or predictions. I am NOT A PROPHET nor have I ever claimed to be one. I am a researcher interested in historical texts that point us to the end of days.

1. Patrick Nesbitt

"An Abridgement of Ecclesiastical History" (1776)

Gave thanks to Isaac Newton for coming up with an end date of 2016. The papacy would be destroyed. Starts September, 2016. Cites Isaac Newton. Cites numerological code. 90 A.D. (when the Book of Revelation was written), add 666 years to get 756 A.D., then add 1260 years.

2. Simon Patrick

"A Critical Commentary and Paraphase on the Old and New Testament and the Apocrypha." (1822)

His timeline ends in 2016. In fact "2016" is the last year of the Roman empire. Most unusual of the group.

Last pope takes over in 2016, but his reign would be short because he would end up being totally destroyed.

3. Moses Lowman

"Notes on the Revelation of St. John" (1773)

From 2000 to 2016 – there would be plagues.

"2016 is the end of it all." The end of Babylon.

Written 244 years ago (from 2017).

All three world wars are all within the time period that he cites. End of mystical Babylon.

4. William J. Reid

"Lectures on the Revelation" (1878)

The end of the papacy in 2012.

By 2016 the papacy would be subsumed into the New World Order. 3.5 year period of tribulation ensues, when the Church would transition.

5. Rev. C. Van Rensselaer, D.D.

Presbyterian Magazine – (October, 1858)

Felt that 2016 is the first year of the beginning of a new epoch . . . that epoch being the Millennial kingdom.

He also felt that 2016 was the latest date that this epoch could commence.

6. Joseph F. Berg

"Lectures on Romanism" – (1840)

Millennial kingdom begins in 2016 and the papacy would end. He identified the Jesuits as being part of the final kingdom. Coincidental with Francis being the first Jesuit Pontiff.

7. Panoplyst Missionary Magazine – 1809

Discusses 6,000 year timeline of Creation.

Pope took on temporal powers in 756 A.D.

And so 1260 years after this date (2016) would usher in the final year of the Vatican.

8. Adam Clark (Methodist)

Penned a 6000 page commentary on the whole Bible.

One of Britain's great biblical scholars.

Felt that people COULD know the dates of prophecy with sufficient knowledge of the Scripture, but NOT by using the Roman calendar. You have to use the Hebrew calendar. Said 2015 is the beginning of the downfall of papacy.

9. William Mackray

"The Character and Prospects of The Church of Rome: In Two Discourses." In 2016 the Church would be exposed to the wrath of God for having opposed the Lord. That a great jubilee would happen to the church. Believers would be protected from harm for 1,000 years. We started jubilee year beginning Sept. 23, 2016.

10. Robert Clayton.

"A Dictionary of Writers of the Prophecies, with the titles

and occasional description of their works."

Made these predictions in the 18th century (around 1750). Cleaton was a contemporary of Isaac Newton.

Beginning in 2015, saw end of the Jewish diaspora, end of the papacy, the coming of the Messiah, and the restoration of the Jews. End of the 2000 reign of the Church. Did not use the Julian calendar. He used the Hebrew calendar.

11. John Brown

"A Dictionary of the Holy Bible."

All Jews would undergo a mass conversion, accepting Jesus, starting in 2016. Turkey and its allies will come against Israel. This force will be completely destroyed.

12. Phillip Doddridge

"A Course of Lectures on the principal subjects in pneumatology, ethics, and divinity: with reference to the most considerable authors on each subject."

Also begins 756 A.D. is the year the papacy became a temporary power. Again, add 1260 years (from Daniel's 1260 days) and you get 2016. Antichrist system completely ushered in by 2016.

13. Isaac Newton

Influenced all the other Bible scholars.

Dedicated 10% of his time to science, the 90% to Bible study, particularly Daniel and Revelation.

The end of 2015 through 2016.

Bibliography

The list below contains the complete list of published books referenced in this work. Since the newer book cataloging software programs often make searching easier using ISBN numbers, either the 10 or 13 ISBN number is provided for the books listed below.

Alford, C. Fred, Whistleblowers: Broken Lives and Organizational Power, Cornell University Press; Ithaca, NY, (2001), ISBN: #0801487803

Allen, Gary and Larry Abraham, None Dare Call It Conspiracy, Buccaneer Books, Inc., Cutchogue, NY. (https://www.jacketflap.com/buccaneer-books-inc-publisher-633) (1976) ISBN: #0899666612.

Backster, Cleve, Primary Perceptions: Biocommunication with Plants, Living Foods, and Human Cells, White Rose Millennium Press, Anza, CA. (2003). ISBN: #0966435435.

Bigelsen, Harvey, M.D., Doctors Are More Harmful Than Germs, North Atlantic Books, Berkeley, CA (https://www.northatlanticbooks.com/) (2011). ISBN: #9781556439582.

Borjesson, Kristina (ed.), Into the Buzzsaw: Leading Journalists Expose the Myth of a Free Press, Prometheus Books, NY (https://www.prometheusbooks.com/). (2004). ISBN: #1591022304.

Bucke, Richard Maurice (M.D.), Cosmic Consciousness: A Study in the Evolution of the Human Mind, (1901, Innes & Sons). This is a classic in the field of human consciousness. I own several copies, with one of them going back to my late teens – one that has travelled with me all over the world: E.P. Dutton & Co., Inc. (1969), ISBN: #0525472452.

Budziszewski, J., Written on the Heart: The Case for Natural Law, InterVarsity Press, Downers Grove, IL. (https://www.ivpress.com/) (2009). ISBN: #9780830877805.

Butler, Smedley D., War is a Racket: The Antiwar Classic by America's Most Decorated Soldier, Feral House, L.A. (http://feralhouse.com) (2003). ISBN: #0922915865.

Campbell, C.J., The Coming Oil Crisis, Multi-Science Publishing Company & Petroconsultants, S.A., Brentwood, Essex, England. (1997). ISBN: #0906522110

Cashill, Jack, TWA 800: The Crash, the Cover-up, and the Conspiracy, Regnery Publishing (http://www.regnery.com/) (2016). ISBN #1621574717.

Caton, G.J., Lumen: Food for a New Age, Calcasieu Graphics, Lake Charles, LA. (Second edition, 1988). ISBN: #9780939955015.

Caton, Greg, The Gospel of 2012 According to Ayahuasca: The End of Faith and the Beginning of Knowingness. (self-published). ISBN: #9780939955091.

Catton, William R., Jr., Overshoot: The Ecological Basis of Revolutionary Change, University of Illinois Press, Urbana, IL, (1980). ISBN: #0252009886

Cheney, Margaret, Tesla: Man Out of Time, Touchstone Books (www.simonandschusterpublishing.com/touchstone/), 1st edition (October 9, 2001). ISBN: #9780743215367.

Cipolla, Carlo M., The Economic History of World Population, Penguin Books, Inc., Baltimore, Maryland; sixth edition, (1974). ISBN: #0140205373

Cleckley, Hervey, The Mask of Sanity: An Attempt to Reinterpret the So-Called Psychopathic Personality, 1st ed., C.V. Mosby Company, now an imprint of Elsevier (https://www.elsevier.com/) (1941). ASIN: #B000WU-0F4Y.

Collier, Christopher and Kenneth F. Collier, Votescam: The Stealing of America, Victoria House Press, USA. (http://wesavedemocracy.org/) (1992) ISBN: #0963416308.

Collins, Phillip Darrell and Paul David Collins, The Ascendancy of the Scientific Dictatorship: An Examination of Epistemic Autocracy From the 19th to the 21st Century, BookSurge (http://www.booksurge.com), (2006). ASIN: #B01K0RJSVY.

Coogan, Gertrude M., Money Creators, Noontide Press (http://noontidepress.com/) (1986). This is a republishing of the original (1935). ISBN: #0317532995.

Corsi, Jerome, Who Really Killed Kennedy?: 50 Years Later: Stunning New Revelations About the JFK Assassination, WND Books (http://wndbooks.wnd.com) (2013) ISBN: #193806710X.

Cremo, Michael and Richard L. Thompson, Forbidden Archeology:

The Hidden History of the Human Race, Bhaktivedanta Book Trust (http://www.bbti.org/), revised edition, (January, 1998). ISBN: #9780892132942.

De Las Casas, Bartolome, A Short Account of the Destruction of the Indies, Penguin Classics, an imprint of the Penguin Group (http://www.penguin.com/). Written in 1542. Updated and released by Penguin Classics in 1999. ISBN: #0140445625.

Deffeyes, Kenneth S., Hubbert's Peak: The Impending World Oil Shortage, Princeton University Press, Princeton, NJ. 2001. ISBN: #0691090866

Dermer, Gerald B., The Immortal Cell: Why Cancer Research Fails, Avery Publishing Group, Garden City Park, NY, an imprint of the Penguin Group (http://www.penguin.com/) (1994) ISBN: #0895295822.

Dudley, William (ed.), Biological Warfare: Opposing Views, Greenhaven Press, Farmington Hills, MI. (https://greenhavenpublishing.com) (2004). ISBN: #9780737716726.

Duesberg, Peter and John Yiamouyiannis, AIDS: The good news is that HIV doesn't cause it – the bad news is that 'recreational drugs' and medical treatments like AZT do, Health Action Press (http://www.duesberg.com/books/) (1995). ISBN: #0913571059.

Duesberg, Peter, Inventing the AIDS Virus, Regnery Publishing (http://www.regnery.com/) (1998). ISBN: #0895263998.

Emoto, Masaru, The Hidden Messages in Water, Beyond Worlds Publishing, Inc., Hillsboro, OR. (https://beyondword.com/) (2004). ISBN: #1582701148.

Emry, Sheldon, Billions for the Bankers, Debts for the People, Lord's Convenent Church, America's Promise Broadcast, (1982). ASIN: #B00071JQHA.

Farrell, Joseph, LBJ and the Conspiracy to Kill Kennedy: A Coalescence of Interests, Adventures Unlimited Press (https://www.adventuresunlimitedpress.com/) (2011). ISBN: #1935487183

Frazier, Vidya, Awakening to the Fifth Dimension – A Guide for Navigating the Global Shift, First Edition Design Publishing (http://www.firsteditiondesignpublishing.com/) (2014). ISBN: #9781622876297.

Frazier, Vidya, Ascension – Embracing the Transformation, First

Edition Design Publishing (http://www.firsteditiondesignpublishing.com/) (2014). ISBN: #9781506900605.

Gatto, John Taylor, Weapons of Mass Instruction: A Schoolteacher's Journey Through the Dark World of Compulsory Schooling, New Society Publishers (https://www.newsociety.com/) Reprint edition. (April 1, 2010). ISBN: #9780865716698.

Griffin, David, Debunking 9/11: An Answer to Popular Mechanics and Other Defenders of the Official Conspiracy Theory, Olive Branch Press (http://www.ink-shop.org/olive-branch-press) (2017). ISBN: #9781566568685.

Griffin, David, 9/11 Ten Years Later, Interlink Books (http://www.interlinkbooks.com/) (2011). ISBN: #9781566568685.

Hamilton, Alexander; James Madison; and John Jay, The Federalist Papers, (1788). Read online at: http://www.gutenberg.org/files/1404/1404-h/1404-h.htm

Hartmann, Thom, The Last Hours of Ancient Sunlight, Harmony Books, New York, 1998. ISBN: #1400051576

Heinberg, Richard, The Party's Over: Oil, War and the Fate of Industrial Societies, New Society Publishers, Gabriola Island, BC, Canada; (2003). ISBN: #0865715297

Hitchcock, Andrew Carrington, The Synagogue of Satan, (self-published). (2012) ISBN: #9781471034848.

Hodgkinson, Nevill, AIDS: The Failure of Contemporary Science: How a virus that never was deceived the world, (self-published) (1996). ISBN: #1857023374.

Horn, Thomas and Putnam, Cris, Petrus Romanus, Defender (Publishing), Crane, MO (2012) ISBN: #9780984825615.

Hounam, Peter, Operation Cyanide: How the Bombing of the USS Liberty Nearly Caused World War Three, Vision Books (2003). ISBN: #1904132197.

Huang, Alfred (Taoist Master), The Complete I Ching, Inner Traditions International, Rochester, VT (http://www.innertraditions.com) (1998). ISBN: #0892816562.

Icke, David, The Biggest Secret, Bridge of Love Publications USA, Wildwood, MO, (2001). ISBN: #0952614766

Iserbyt, Charlotte Thomson, The Deliberate Dumbing Down of America, Conscience Press, P.O. Box 449, Ravenna, Ohio 44266–0449. Revised edition (2011). ISBN: #9780966707113 / 0966707109 See: http://www.lovethetruth.com/books/deliberate_dumbing_down.pdf

Jacke, Dave, Edible Forest Gardens – Volume 1: Ecological Vision, Theory for Temperate Climate Permaculture. Chelsea Green Publishing, White River Ju3nction, VT (http://chelseagreen.com) (August 30, 2005), p. 126-127. ISBN: #9781931498791.

Jenkins, John Major, Maya Cosmogenesis 2012: The True Meaning of the Maya Calendar End-Date, Bear & Company, Rochester, VT (https://www.innertraditions.com/) (1998), ISBN: #1879181487.

Jensen, Derrick, The Culture of Make Believe, Chelsea Green Publishing, White River Junction, VT (http://chelseagreen.com), (2004). ISBN: #1931498571.

Jensen, Derrick and Aric McBay, Deep Green Resistance: Strategy to Save the Planet, Seven Stories Press (https://www.sevenstories.com/), (2011). ISBN: #1583229299.

Jensen, Derrick, A Language Older Than Words, Chelsea Green Publishing, White River Junction, VT (http://chelseagreen.com), (2004). ISBN: #9781931498555.

Johnson, Chalmers, Nemesis: The Last Days of the American Republic, Metropolitan Books (https://us.macmillan.com/henryholt/), Reprint edition (2008). ISBN: #9780805087284.

Joyce, Elizabeth, Ascension – Accessing the Fifth Dimension, Visions of Reality (https://www.visions-of-reality.com/) (2013), ISBN: #9780989802949.

Kolbert, Elizabeth, The Sixth Extinction: An Unnatural History, Picador Publishing, (2015). ISBN: #1250062187

Kuhn, Thomas, The Structure of Scientific Revolutions, University of Chicago Press (http://www.press.uchicago.edu/index.html) (1962). ISBN: #9780226458113.

Lauritsen, John, The AIDS War: Propaganda, Profiteering and Genocide from the Medical Industrial Complex, Asklepios (1993). ISBN: #0943742080.

Levitt, Stephen D. and Stephen J. Dubner, Freakonomics: A Rogue Economist Explores the Hidden Side of Everything, William Morrow, a div. of HarperCollins (https://www.harpercollins.com/) (2009), ISBN: #0060731338.

Lobaczewski, Andrew M., Political Ponerology, Red Pill Press, Grande Prairie, Canada (https://www.redpillpress.com/), 2nd ed. (April 4, 2007). ISBN: #9781897244258.

Maharishi Mahesh Yogi, Science of Being and Art of Living, Plume Publishing, an imprint of Penguin Group (http://www.penguin.com/publishers/plume/). Reissue edition (2001). ISBN: #0452282667.

Maharishi, Mahesh Yogi, The Scientific Age Rising to be the Age of Enlightenment, Maharishi European Research University Press (http://www.merupress.org/) (1977). ASIN: #B004V9XJSQ.

Mander, Jerry, Four Arguments for the Elimination of Television, William Morrow, a div. of HarperCollins (https://www.harpercollins.com/) Reprint edition (1978). ISBN: #9780688082741.

Marrs, Jim, Crossfire: The Plot That Killed Kennedy, Carroll & Graf, now an imprint of Perseus Books (1989). ISBN: #0881846481.

Marrs, Jim, The Terror Conspiracy: Deception, 9/11, and the Loss of Liberty, The Disinformation Company Publisher, NY (2006). ISBN: #1932857435.

Marsden, Victor E. (trans.), Protocols of the Learned Elders of Zion. (1934) The version that I have and used in connection with this book lists no publisher or other identifying information. This was a common practice by publishers of older copies of The Protocols, due to the risks involved in being associated with its publication and distribution.

Melley, Tim, Empire of Conspiracy: The Culture of Paranoia in Postwar America, Cornell University Press (http://www.cornellpress.cornell.edu/) (2000). ISBN: #0801486068.

Meyer, Marvin (ed.), The Nag Hammadi Scriptures, The International Edition, HarperOne, an imprint of HarperCollins Publishers (http://harperone.hc.com/), 1st ed., (May 29, 2007), ISBN: #9780060523787.

Meyer, Stephen C., Signature in the Cell: DNA and the Evidence for Intelligent Design, HarperOne, an imprint of HarperCollins, NY (http://harperone.hc.com/) (2010). ISBN: #9780061472794.

Miller, G. Tyler, Jr., Energetics, Kinetics and Life: Ecological approach, Wadsworth Publishing, CA, 1971. ISBN #053400136X

Miller, Neil Z., Vaccines: Are They Really Safe & Effective?, New Atlantean Press (http://thinkchoice.com/), first edition, (September 15, 2015), ISBN: #9781881217305.

Montaigne, David, Antichrist 2016-2019, Mystery Babylon, Barack Obama & The Islamic Caliphate (self-published), p. 1-2, ISBN: #1501025392

Montaigne, David, End Times and 2019: The End of the Mayan Calendar and the Countdown to Judgement Day, Adventures Unlimited Press, Kempton, IL. P. 280. ISBN: #9781935487920

Narby, Jeremy, The Cosmic Serpent: DNA and the Origins of Knowledge, Jeremy P. Tarcher/Putnam Publisher, NY (http://www.tarcherbooks.com/) (1998). ISBN: #0874779642.

Newman, Craig, The Assassination of JFK – Who Really Did It and Why, (independently published) (2017). ISBN: # 1521251592.

Parkinson, C(yril) Northcote, Parkinson: The Law Complete, Random House Publishing Group, NY (http://www.randomhousebooks.com/), (1983). ISBN: #0345300645.

Parkinson, C(yril) Northcote, Parkinson's Law: And Other Studies in Administration, Buccaneer Books, Inc. (https://www.jacketflap.com/buccaneer-books-inc-publisher-633) (1957). ISBN: #1568490151.

Parkinson, C(yril) Northcote, Parkinson's Law: The Pursuit of Progress, Penguin Books, NY (http://www.penguin.com/) (5 Sept. 2002), ISBN: #9780141186856.

Pepper, Dr. William F. (Esq.), The Plot to Kill King: The Truth Behind the Assassination of Martin Luther King, Jr., Skyhorse Publishing (http://www.skyhorsepublishing.com/) (2016). ISBN: #1510702172.

Perkins, John, Confessions of an Economic Hit Man, Berrett-Koehler Publishers, Inc., San Francisco, CA. (https://www.bkconnection.com/) (2004). ISBN: #1576753018.

Perkins, John, The Secret History of the American Empire, Penguin Group (USA), Inc., NY. (http://www.penguin.com/) (2007) ISBN: #9780525950158.

Postman, Neil, Technopoly: The Surrender of Culture to Technology, Vintage Books, NY. (http://knopfdoubleday.com/imprint/vintage/) (1993). ISBN: #9780679745402.

Rappoport, Jon, AIDS Inc.: Scandal of the Century, Namaste Publishing (http://www.namastepublishing.com/) (2003). ISBN: #0954659015.

Rifkin, Jeremy, Entropy: A New World View, Bantam Books, a div. of Random House, NY (http://www.randomhousebooks.com/) (1981). ISBN: #0553202154.

Robinson, John, Proofs of a Conspiracy Against all Religions and Governments of Europe, Carried on in the Secret Meetings of Freemasons, Illuminati, and Reading Societies, (1797). Republished by Forgotten Books (https://www.forgottenbooks.com/en) (2008). ISBN: #9781606201015.

Roth, Rebekah, Methodical Illusion, KTYS Media (http://www.ktysmedia.com/) (2014). ISBN: # 9780982757130.

Russell, Walter, Atomic Suicide?, Univ. of Science & Philosophy (http://www.philosophy.org/) (June, 1981). ISBN: #9781879605114.`

Sahlins, Marshall, Stone Age Economics, Taylor & Francis Group (http://taylorandfrancis.com/) (1972). ISBN: #9780415513975.

Sanders, James, The Downing of TWA Flight 800: The Shocking Truth Behind the Worst Airplane Disaster in U.S. History, Pinnacle Books, an imprint of Kensington Books (http://www.kensingtonbooks.com/) (1997) ISBN: #0821758292.

Schweizer, Peter, Clinton Cash, Harper Paperbacks, an imprint of HarperCollins (https://www.harpercollins.com/) (2009), reprint edition (July 26, 2016). ISBN: #9780062369291.

Sennholz, Hans F., Inflation is Theft, The Foundation for Economic Education, Inc. (publisher), Irvington-on-Hudson, NY (https://fee.org/) (1994). ISBN: #0910614997.

Sheridan, Thomas, Puzzling People: The Labyrinth of the Psychopath, Velluminous Press, (March 1, 2011). ISBN: #9781905605286.

Skousen, W. Cleon, The Naked Communist, Ensign Publishing Co. (https://www.manta.com/c/mm8lk47/ensign-publishing), 8th ed. (1961). ASIN: #B00G58SEXQ. There are numerous editions of this popular book available, spread out over more than a half century of publishing.

Stich, Rodney, David vs. Goliath: 9/11 & Other Tragedies, Silverpeak Enterprises (https://www.linkedin.com/in/rodney-stich-907b9b9) (2005). ISBN: #0932438253.

Stich, Rodney, Defrauding America, Diablo Western Press, expanded edition. (January, 1994). ISBN: #9780932438089.

Stich, Rodney, Unfriendly Skies: Saga of Corruption, Diablo Western Press, 3rd edition (July 1990). ISBN: #9780932438027.

Sutton, Antony Cyril, Wall Street and the Rise of Hitler: The Astonishing True Story of the Financiers Who Bankrolled the Nazis, Clairview Books (http://www.clairviewbooks.com/). (2010) ASIN: B00HTJMHE2.

Tainter, Joseph A., The Collapse of Complex Societies, Cambridge University Press, (http://www.cambridge.org/) (1990) ISBN: #052138673X.

Tarpley, Webster, 9/11 Synthetic Terror, Progressive Press, Joshua Tree, CA. (http://www.progressivepress.com/) (2011). ISBN: #0930852311.

Tarpley, Webster, George Bush: The Unauthorized Biography, Progressive Press, Joshua Tree, CA. (http://progressivepress.com/), ISBN: #9780930852924.

Taylor, John (of Caroline), Tyranny Unmasked (1821). Republished by Cosimo, Inc., NY (http://www.cosimobooks.com/) (2005). ISBN: #1596052511.

Taylor, Steve, The Fall, IFF Books (http://www.iff-books.com/), (2005). ISBN: #1905047207 or 9781905047208.

Tocqueville, Alexis de, Democracy in America, Penguin Group, London, UK. (http://www.penguinrandomhouse.com/) (2003). Republication of the work first published in 1835. Hackett Publishing Company, Inc., originally published in 1835. ISBN: #0140447601.

Tompkins, Peter and Christopher Bird, The Secret Life of Plants, Harper & Row, an imprint of HarperCollins (https://www.harpercollins.com/) NY (1973), ISBN: #0060143266.

Turner, William and John Christian, The Assassination of Robert F. Kennedy: The Conspiracy and Coverup, Basic Books (http://www.basicbooks.com/) (1993). ISBN: #0786719796.

Tytler, Alexander Fraser, Elements of General History: Ancient and Modern, University of Michigan Library, (1837), ASIN: #B002JTVRHU.

Vassilatos, Gerry, Lost Science, Adventures Unlimited Press (https://www.adventuresunlimitedpress.com/), (March 1, 2000). ISBN: #9780932813756.

Ventura, Jesse, American Conspiracies, Skyhorse Publishing (http://www.skyhorsepublishing.com/) (2010). ISBN: #9781602398023.

Vidal, Gore, Perpetual War for Perpetual Peace: How We Got to Be So Hated, Nation Books (http://www.nationinstitute.org/), (April 10, 2002), ISBN: #9781560254058.

Vonnegut, Kurt, A Man Without a Country, Random House, Inc., NY (http://www.randomhousebooks.com/) (2007). ISBN: #9780812977363.

Waldron, Lamar, The Hidden History of the JFK Assassination, Group West (http://www.pgw.com/home/) (2013). ISBN: #1521251592.

Washburn, Katharine and John Thorton, Dumbing Down: Essays on the Strip Mining of American Culture, W.W. Norton & Company, NY. (http://books.wwnorton.com/books/index.aspx), (1997). ISBN: #9780393317237.

Webre, Alfred Lambremont, The Omniverse, Bear & Company, Rochester, VT. (https://www.innertraditions.com/) (2015). ISBN: #9781591432159.

Williams, William Appleman, The Contours of American History, W.W. Norton, NY. (http://books.wwnorton.com/books/index.aspx) (1988). ISBN: #0393305619.

Zerzan, John, Running on Emptiness: The Pathology of Civilization, Feral House, L.A. (http://feralhouse.com), (2002), ISBN: #092291575X.

Zinn, Howard; Paul Buhle, and Mike Konopacki, A People's History of American Empire, Metropolitan Books, a div. of Henry Holt, NY. (https://

us.macmillan.com/henryholt/) (2008). ISBN: #0805087443.

Index

Note on Indexing: I choose to index this work by hand. As an avid reader myself I find most indices today to be cluttered by words, often common nouns not important to the author's message, that no one would ever reference. The introduction of indexing software, with or without subsequent thorough editing, has only added to the clutter. This is predictable because no indexing software can discriminate with a sense of reference value as can the work's creator.

I also don't reference words of high frequency, except for words with important introductions, definitions, or varied uses attached to them. Additionally, I left in all bibliographed authors (the primary authors), but not their book titles. That's what the bibliography is for. I did, however, allow for a handful of notable exceptions.

Attention was placed on words and phrases that were most likely to be referenced by the book's readers. Page numbers set in **bold** have added importance. Other words and phrases are in bold, italics, underlined, presented parenthetically ( ), or otherwise altered as to help visually navigate through the Index. Where you see "bb" following a page number, this indicates reference to a published work that appears in the Bibliography. G.C.

0-9

A

D

E

F

G

H

I

J

K

L

M

N

O

P

Q

R

S

T

U

V

W

X / Y

Z

About the Author

Greg Caton is an American herbalist, inventor and manufacturer. His journey through the U.S. criminal justice system, which was the inspiration for Joys of Psychopathocracy, is documented in a free on-line work, Meditopia (meditopia.org, -- 2004 to present).

He is the co-founder of Alpha Omega Labs (altcancer.com) and lives outside the city of Cuenca, Ecuador, with his wife, Cathryn.

More complete information on his work can be found at: **greg-caton.com**.

About the Illustrator

David Dees is an American commercial artist with a background in magazine, billboard, advertising design and illustration, video covers, toy packaging, movie store displays, and children's illustrations. For 13 years he was a monthly featured artist in Sesame Street magazine.

In 2003, Dees woke up to the scam of 9/11. Lifelong patriotism shaken, he began researching secret societies and Government corruption. In 2006 Dees designed his first political illustration, unleashing a tirade of blistering commentary that appeared on the Internet 9/11 Truth scene. Dees' art is now seen in countless alternative news documentaries, blogs, and websites, circulating virally through the Internet and today has gained a wide international audience.

Dees has released three coffee table quality art books designed to wake up your friends and family to the matrix, books that together showcase 280 full page activist illustrations. As one fan wrote, "Your books are excellent at breaking the egg shell brains of a lot of people here in Australia. They look at the pictures and it allows them to ask questions about some of their surroundings a bit more. Just telling people doesn't work that well. I've had people sit down and actually look very hard – sometimes going through your books page per page – and you can see the cogs clicking."

You can purchase Dees' books and see his latest art at **DDees.com.**

Made in the USA
Columbia, SC
03 March 2018